Jean-Marc Heimerdinger is a lecturer in Hebrew and Judaism at London Bible College (Associated College of Brunel University), Northwood, Middlesex.

JOURNAL FOR THE STUDY OF THE OLD TESTAMENT SUPPLEMENT SERIES

295

Editors
David J.A. Clines
Philip R. Davies

Executive Editor
John Jarick

Editorial Board
Robert P. Carroll, Richard J. Coggins, Alan Cooper, J. Cheryl Exum,
John Goldingay, Robert P. Gordon, Norman K. Gottwald,
Andrew D.H. Mayes, Carol Meyers, Patrick D. Miller

Sheffield Academic Press

Topic, Focus and Foreground in Ancient Hebrew Narratives

Jean-Marc Heimerdinger

Journal for the Study of the Old Testament
Supplement Series 295

BS
521.7
.H440
1999

Copyright © 1999 Sheffield Academic Press

Published by Sheffield Academic Press Ltd
Mansion House
19 Kingfield Road
Sheffield S11 9AS
England

Printed on acid-free paper in Great Britain
by Biddles
Guildford, Surrey

British Library Cataloguing in Publication Data

A catalogue record for this book is available
from the British Library

ISBN 1-84127-014-8

JESUIT - KRAUSS - McCORMICK - LIBRARY
1100 EAST 55th STREET
CHICAGO, ILLINOIS 60615

CONTENTS

PREFACE

This study has its origin in my PhD dissertation at Reading University, Department of Linguistic Science. The research has been intertwined with so many other events and occupations that there are inevitaby many people who, knowingly or unknowingly, have played a part in its formation. I would like to make particular mention of the following.

I would first of all like to gratefully acknowledge the understanding and support of my colleagues at the London Bible College. For the first three years of study, I received financial assistance from the College for which I am thankful.

I have had the good fortune throughout the time of my research of being able to be in contact with the Summer Institute of Linguistics at their headquarters in England. In particular, I should like to thank Dr Ivan Lowe and Dr John Callow whose prompting and encouragement have been of the highest value.

I am most thankful to Dr I. Philippaki-Warburton of Reading University for her help, comprehension and encouragment in her role as supervisor and also to Professor D.A. Wilkins for acting as supervisor for one year in her absence.

On a personal level, special thanks are due to my wife Jenny whose advice and perception have so often helped to clarify and formulate ideas.

Finally, I owe a debt of gratitude to two groups of people. First to the many students who have followed my Hebrew courses over the years at London Bible College. It is while reading and studying the Hebrew Bible with them that many of the data were discovered and that a clearer picture of the means of prominence in narratives emerged. Their interest, curiosity and valuable comments have been a constant encouragement. Secondly, my gratitude goes to the still too small group of pioneering scholars who have sought to break the bonds of grammatical tradition and have sought to integrate Hebrew grammar with insights from discourse analysis. Their names and works appear in the bibliography.

ABBREVIATIONS

Linguistic Terms

A	Adverbial
ADVP	Adverbial Phrase
C	Complement
DFE	Dominant Focal Element
DO	Direct Object
IO	Indirect Object
N	Noun
NP	Noun Phrase
O	Object
P	Predicate
PRO[1]	Pronoun
S	Subject
V	Verb
VP	Verb Phrase

Other Terms

BHS	*Biblia hebraica stuttgartensia*
GKC	*Gesenius' Hebrew Grammar* (ed. E. Kautzsch, revised and trans. A.E. Cowley; Oxford: Clarendon Press, 1910).

Other Nomenclature

Fronted	An element is fronted when it has been moved to the right without altering the clause initial position of the V.
Forefronted	An element is forefronted when it has been moved in preverbal position and so has become clause initial.

1. In this study the abbreviation is not used with the meaning it has in government-binding theory (i.e. a base-generated S of certain infinitives). It refers to the closed set of items which can be used to substitute for a noun phrase or a noun.

INTRODUCTION

1. *Background to Research*

In the study of Old Hebrew,[1] there have been two important developments over the last 30 years. These form the background and the motivation for the research presented in this work.

The first development is that, since the 1960s or so, the study of Old Hebrew has begun to take account of methods of description and investigation which are those used in modern linguistics. Up to that time descriptive techniques had been fairly unsophisticated and the explanations for grammatical or morphological facts were dominated by historical explanations or by analogies drawn from other Semitic languages. A change took place as Hebraists became dissatisfied with explanations which came exclusively from outside the language itself and sought instead to understand specific linguistic features through a consideration of Old Hebrew as forming a system in its own right, within which there were rules for choosing among different possible units or forms. This new perspective also led progressively to increased attention being directed to the systematic analysis of Old Hebrew linguistic features beyond the limits of the sentence, ranging from the paragraph to the study of a whole discourse. In the field of discourse analysis of Old Hebrew texts, one can perhaps loosely speak of one group of Hebraists working within the context of a developed tagmemic theory, which includes Andersen, Longacre and Dawson. Another group of mainly

1. It is more appropriate to use this designation to refer to the Hebrew found in the Hebrew Bible than the traditional term Biblical Hebrew, or the term Classical Hebrew. This form of Hebrew was used not only for recording the religious writings of the Hebrew scriptures but was more generally the language which the Israelites and Judaeans used in speaking and writing, as the discovery of epigraphical material demonstrates (see, for example, Davies 1991 and Lemaire 1977). One can identify three stratifications of Old Hebrew reflected in the Hebrew Bible and corresponding to the diachronic development of Old Hebrew: Archaic Hebrew (twelfth–tenth century BCE), Classical Hebrew (tenth–sixth century BCE) and Late Hebrew (late sixth–third century BCE).

German biblical scholars such as Richter, Gross and Schneider have developed their own concepts of structural linguistics in their analytical methods. Today, however, it seems correct to say that Longacre's model, fully exploited in his book, *Joseph: A Story of Divine Providence. A Text Theoretical and Textlinguistic Analysis of Genesis 37 and 39–48* (Longacre 1989) has come to dominate the world of Old Hebrew discourse analysis and his conclusions are often accepted without reservations. A book recently published by one of Longacre's followers, David A. Dawson, demonstrates this well. Its aim is to make Longacre's method understandable to the non-specialist, to show why Longacre's approach is better than some others and to apply it to specific texts. Dawson's unreserved acceptance of Longacre's method and conclusions is reflected in his eulogistic tone. In his opinion, Longacre's book containing a discourse analysis of the Joseph's story 'represents the most significant advancement in Hebrew textlinguistics seen to date. It contains much of near-revolutionary value to the student of Classical Hebrew syntax' (Dawson 1994: 56).

The analyses which are set out in the present work contrast radically with Dawson's assessment of Longacre. In fact, they have arisen from a profound disagreement with both Longacre's method and his conclusions. This divergence was prompted by reflection arising from the second significant development in Old Hebrew studies: the so-called 'literary approach' to the texts of the Hebrew Bible.

Indeed, just like the study of the language of the Hebrew Bible, so also the study of biblical narrative has undergone a considerable change over the past thirty years. It has shifted its focus away from a critical study of the texts seen as historical documents, to a study of the narratives as literature. The advent of modern literary criticism (in fiction particularly) led biblical scholars to an ever-increasing appreciation of biblical narratives as literary artefacts which could be understood by precise and expert analyses whose aim was to elucidate the actual literary techniques and devices used by the authors. Numerous literary analyses of Old Hebrew stories have been offered in specialised journals or books.[2] All these various literary approaches have led to the elaboration of a poetics of biblical narratives, that is, a description of the basic devices and components of Old Hebrew stories and the rule

2. A historical survey of the literary approach to the Bible is found in D. Norton (1993: 262-300; 357-88). Among well-known studies are those written by Alter, Bar-Efrat, Gunn and Fewell, Berlin and Sternberg.

governing their use.[3] The features receiving attention are matters such as repeated words or patterns, structuring techniques, anticipatory information, resumptive repetitions, symmetries, stylistic techniques, modes of narration, characterization techniques, the question of point of view and so forth. Working together, these features are clues given to the reader or hearer, which act as prompts in the determination of meaning. They represent nothing less than communicative techniques.

When one turns from the findings of the literary approach to Longacre's analysis and its results, the question which inevitably arises is how it is that none of the devices identified by literary critics are captured by Longacre's text-linguistic analysis. A consultation of Longacre's *Joseph* shows that his conclusions, in spite of their technicalities, are frustratingly rudimentary, explaining very few of the numerous patterns or devices identified by his literary colleagues. One could surmise that this refusal to examine all aspects of language is a deliberate choice: the 'literary' devices could be regarded as belonging to the domain of stylistics and not linguistics. Such a dichotomy, however, has proven not to be valid. Linguists have found that even everyday stories told in conversation display much of the sophistication attributed to artistic prose and that the so-called 'literary' devices are not merely aesthetic or ornamental but perform very distinctive linguistic or pragmatic functions. The very specificity of literary language is being re-examined. Deborah Tannen, for example, bases her book, *Talking Voices*, on the central idea 'that ordinary conversation is made up of linguistic strategies that have been thought quintessentially literary' (1989: 1). Even if one accepts that literary discourse has specific features, from a discourse point of view, stylistic or rhetorical evidence is no different from any other kind of linguistic evidence. As a result, it is to be expected that a discourse approach should be able to account at least for some of these features.

An explanation which can be offered for the absence of any linguistic account of the literary devices is that it is the method of analysis itself which is inadequate. This is the conclusion one is forced towards when, starting with a thorough familiarity with the biblical stories and an appreciation of the richness of its technique, one reads Longacres'

3. A. Berlin defines poetics as 'an inductive science that seeks to abstract the general principles of literature from many different manifestations of those principles as they occur in actual literary texts ... Poetics strive to write a grammar, as it were, of literature' (1983: 15).

building-block analysis of the Joseph story (1989: 209-310) or tries to reconcile his information-based view of foreground–background with the whole range of saliency devices available for story-telling.

It will be shown in the course of this study that it is, in fact, the overall notion of foreground–background, based as it is on the nature of information contained in clauses, which poses a problem. An artistic and visual metaphor will help to identify the problem better. Grounding by level of information as proposed by Longacre may be compared to the drawing of a picture in black and white. Foreground clauses provide the contour shape of the object, and the pragmatic weighting of information from background to foreground is similar to the light and shade applied to the sketch. Through contrast and the casting of clear-cut shadows, this weighting throws the texture and contours of the object into sharp relief and makes it stand out from the background. In contrast, the view of foregrounding which is derived from literary studies is not one of a picture in which things are made to stand out, but rather one which has the function of creating centres of interest. A picture depicting a scene which lacks a centre of interest remains dull. Through selective illumination, the artist, as a manipulator of light, must succeed in concentrating the viewer's attention on one or more specific areas of the picture. Metaphorically, this is what happens in Old Hebrew stories. Foregrounding, or the assignment of saliency, may be broadly compared to a paintbrush operation resulting in some of the narrative material being brought to the attention of the reader.

One of the concerns of this study has been the identification of some of the main linguistic mechanisms which contribute to this kind of foregrounding. For this purpose, it was thought that the best way to proceed was first to understand better the pragmatic articulations (topic-comment; presupposition-focus) in the clause and secondly to find out the role these articulations may have in foregrounding. As Longacre's theory is centered upon the narrative verbal clause, which he sees as having a foregrounding function, the research was circumscribed to an analysis of the two main types of third person verbal clauses (vayyiqtol clause and NP + qatal clause) which function in close cooperation in narratives. In the last chapter of the the work other analytical categories, sociolinguistic and cognitive in particular, are applied.

An additional incentive for this research, this one more peripheral, must be mentioned. It has to do with the methods used and conclusions reached in many of the modern linguistic analyses of Old Hebrew texts.

Overall, these studies might be characterized as abundant in formal analyses but somewhat skimpy on meaning.[4] A good justification for describing Old Hebrew through the analyses of forms and their distributions might be found in the fact that such methods provide an objective entry point into the understanding of a language of which there are no native speakers. However, one of their major drawbacks is that, in the end, what is drawn out of the inventory of the forms is a 'formal meaning', that is meaning described in terms of relationship between items in a complex of relations. Other kinds of meanings (for example pragmatic meanings), of which there is so much in narrative texts, are left out. The descriptive studies of forms and constructions are of value since they represent systematic and rigorous inventories of specific linguistic phenomena. They sort out items and classify them, giving a clearer picture of the linguistic material at hand in Old Hebrew. But one has to remember that it is not syntactic forms and construction types on their own which produce meaning in natural language understanding.

A re-examination of the notion of foregrounding and its mechanisms, together with a concern for meaning, necessitated that new analytical tools should be used and tested to study Old Hebrew texts. These tools are not used only to highlight the problems arising from Longacre's view of foregrounding applied to Old Hebrew texts, but also, more positively, to offer new perspectives and show new directions of research, using notions not employed so far in Old Hebrew studies and exploring areas not yet investigated (such as the role of the pragmatic presupposition/non-presupposition distinction on elements of the clause, or cognitive activation). To this end, an inductive method of investigation has been chosen intentionally and the approach deliberately leans towards the discussion of specific examples. It is hoped that this will serve to demonstrate how these new analytical notions can be successfully applied.

2. *Procedure*

In order to examine the notion of prominence accurately, it will be necessary to analyse the clause from a pragmatic point of view. It has already been indicated that this study would take as its point of

4. I have in mind the distributional analyses of Schneider (1985), Talstra (1983), Richter (1980) and Niccacci (1990), and also the functionally-oriented studies of Gross (1987).

departure the two pragmatic articulations of topic–comment and presupposition–focus. These two articulations belong to four interrelated sets of categories that are present in what has been called the information structure of a sentence (Halliday 1967). The latter concept can be explained in the following way. Information structure is the component of a language in which propositions as conceptual representations of state of affairs undergo pragmatic organization according to the utterance contexts in which these states of affairs are to be communicated. In particular, the structure of a clause reflects a speaker's assumptions about the hearer's state of knowledge and consciousness at the time of an utterance. The connection between speaker assumptions and the formal organization of the sentence is governed by rules of grammar, in a grammatical component called information structure. As information structure deals with the way a speaker tailors an utterance to meet the particular needs of the intended hearer or receiver, it reflects the speaker's hypothesis about the hearer's assumptions and beliefs and it is concerned with the form and structure of utterances in relation to the assumed mental states of speakers and hearers.

Four interconnected categories can be identified in the information structure of a clause.

The first set of categories comprises the presupposition and pragmatic assertion which have to do with the speaker's assumptions about the hearer's state of knowledge and awareness at the time of an utterance. The presupposition is a set of propositions that the speaker assumes the hearer already knows and takes for granted. The assertion, on the other hand, is the proposition expressed by a sentence, that the hearer is expected to know as a result of hearing the sentence uttered.

The second set of categories is identifiability and activation. A referent is identifiable when a shared representation already exists in the speaker's and hearer's minds at the time of the utterance. Activation has to do with the changes the representation of a given referent undergoes in the development of discourse.

The third category is the topic of a clause. The topic is the discourse referent which the proposition expressed in the sentence is about.

The fourth category is the focus of a clause. The focus is the element of information whereby the assertion differs from the presupposition. It is the element that cannot be taken for granted at the time of speech, the element that permits shared and not yet shared knowledge to be differentiated from each other.

The analyses which follow examine the relationship between the structure of narrative clauses and the linguistic and extra-linguistic contexts in which these sentences are used as units of propositional information. It assesses the range of options that the grammar allows for expressing propositional contents in a variety of grammatical forms and under varying discourse circumstances.

In the last chapter, yet another type of assumptions is examined. These have to do with the general knowledge of life shared by speakers and hearers and with their common expectations expressed linguistically in specific knowledge structures. Speakers can exploit these structures in order to highlight some specific information.

All theses devices have been left insufficiently explored in Old Hebrew studies. A few studies, however, can be found which are concerned with the question of prominence understood in terms of foreground–background. Before launching into the analyses, it will be useful to briefly outline some of the explanations and theories that have been offered by Hebraists, particularly explanations of verbal forms that are rooted in discourse considerations. Additionally, discussions on the way the Hebrew verbal clause should be defined need to be considered as well.

3. *Previous Relevant Discourse Research*

The main peculiarity of the verbal system, in the Old Hebrew classical period especially, is that the two forms qatal and yiqtol can be used preceded by the proclitic waw ('and') when the verb occurs in a clause initial position. The prefix form yiqtol with proclitic waw has the form vayyiqtol, the suffix form qatal with proclitic waw has the form veqatal. As a result, four verbal forms, qatal, vayyiqtol, yiqtol, veqatal, are central to the verbal system.[5] Scholars, however, do not agree on the meaning these forms express.[6] Opinions range from a description of Old Hebrew as a typical example of a tenseless language[7] to the other extreme claim that 'the verbal system of biblical Hebrew does not mark

5. For a recent study, see Revell (1989a: 1-13).

6. Leslie McFall (1982) wrote a thorough survey of the various explanatory theories offered until the 1950s. Waltke and O'Connor (1990: 455-75) provide a good account of more contemporary explanations.

7. Siedl (1971: 7) asserts that every analysis of a tense system in Semitic languages must start from the fact that the Semitic tense is simply not a tense.

aspect' and that 'the ascription of aspect without tense to Hebrew must be considered as having had its day'.[8] These explanations fall into three categories: tense, aspect and mixed theory. Whichever theory is advocated, the claims are always asserted unequivocally and with a striking confidence, as if no disagreement or doubt existed.[9] However, it is not so much the temporal or aspectual meanings of the verbal forms which of relevance here, but rather other types of explanations which are discourse-based.[10] Among studies made, Longacre's work must be singled out as a more thorough attempt at providing coherent explanations of the Hebrew verb using a well-defined methodology. His approach will be examined in detail separately in Chapter 2. Here other studies will be summarized.

Kustár's study (1972) may be described as providing the first pragmatic insights, however crude, into the use of the verbal forms in discourse. Kustár seeks primarily to explain the use of qatal and yiqtol. He rejects the temporal explanations of Bauer, the action categories of S.R. Driver and the aspectual categories of Rundgren. Explanations must combine aspect and action together. Qatal and yiqtol have an aspectual meaning inasmuch as they represent the way the speaker envisages the action. An action may be viewed by a speaker as 'determining' that is as being the starting point, the motive, the purpose, the consequence or outcome of another action. Then it is encoded in a qatal verbal form. Alternatively, an action may be seen as 'determined' (1972: 55). It depends exclusively on the view and the judgment of the speaker, which actions he views as determining and which as determined.

Kustár does not expand his analysis of the notions of 'determining' and 'determined', but his description reminds one of the foreground–background distinction, although the terminology is not used. Qatal clauses would describe facts or events disengaged from the flow of

8. Zevit 1988: 26.

9. A more systematic examination of the counter-examples would cause the numer of peremptory statements made by scholars to be reduced. McFall (1982) lists a number of exceptions to the tense theory in Appendix 1, p. 187-89; counter-examples for the aspectual theory are given in his critical analysis of Ewald's theory (1982: 35, 50-56).

10. It will become clear when we consider Longacre's theory that discourse explanations of the verbal forms lead almost inevitably to a primarily temporal understanding of the Old Hebrew verbal system. Longacre writes of the vayyiqtol form: '... this form is historically descended from an archaic preterite' (1992a: 179).

action and expressing presuppositions, causes, purposes, recapitulations and evaluations. Yiqtol expresses actions resulting from these facts. As for the vayyiqtol and veqatal forms, Kustár rejects the idea that the forms with waw represent a mere grammatical extension by which a new meaning is produced (1972: 32). The difference between yiqtol and vayyiqtol is not semantic but syntactic. The waw in vayyiqtol and veqatal indicates a connection between clauses and has no temporal value. The verbal forms with waw are used when the speaker wishes to underline the close connection of sentences and to construct series of thoughts and actions (1972: 29, 40).

Kustár's hypothesis was a novel one; unfortunately it was not further investigated by scholars. But we have here in an embryonic form an interesting reflection on the pragmatic role of the waw as a clause connector and on the grammatical coding of pragmatic choices made by the speaker.

F.I. Andersen (1974) has been a pioneer in using discourse analytical principles in the study of the Old Hebrew sentence.[11] Examining the formal features of the prose of the Pentateuch, he notes that clause types and verbal forms have a discourse function. The chains of vayyiqtol clauses constitute the main building blocks of the discourse. Other clause types (subject-predicate clauses, for example) are most of the time situated at the margins of vayyiqtol clause clusters: their function is to indicate the boundaries of these clusters. Thus, clearly delinated episodes or paragraphs can be identified. The non-vayyiqtol clauses mark either episode onset, interruption or close out; they are circumstancial clauses.

Givón (1977) associates discourse phenomena with types of clauses and word order in the clauses. Verbal clauses have distinct discourse functions. Those using the imperfect verbal form,[12] have a continuity

11. This study was preceded by an analysis of the royal inscription on the Moabite stele from a discourse perspective (1966). The study is relevant to Old Hebrew as the language of the inscription is a closely related dialect of Canaanite. Andersen discovered that sentences describing the actions of King Omri use the waw consecutive, whereas his other various achievements, such as building operations, are reported in general with different verbal forms. The clause patterns create distinct groupings of clauses which can be called 'paragraphs'.

12. Givón uses 'imperfect' in an unusual way. The term designates a combination of three different forms: the Imperfect proper used mainly with future meaning, the Jussive (imperative of the third person) and the vayyiqtol form. Although the three forms are identical for many verbs, they do differ in a number of cases.

function: they express the continuity of the same subject. In realis clauses they present in-sequence, punctual events, and advance the storyline. They have a characteristic VS order. Anteriority clauses interrupt the chronological flow of events and so do not advance the storyline. These 'out-of-sequence' clauses use the perfect form of the verb. They describe events which, in real time, took place earlier than the time reached at that point by the storyline. Anterior clauses have a SV order, having an element (subject, object, prepositional phrase) placed before the verb. As for non-verbal clauses, copular clauses represent states, do not advance the action and so are SV most of the time. In participial clauses the 'verb' is used as a noun in the majority of cases and so the clauses do not normally advance the storyline. It has usually a SV order.

Finally, in his study of the verbal system, Niccacci (1990) makes a meticuluous use of the theoretical model created by the German linguist Harald Weinreich (1977).[13] It had been previously applied to Old Hebrew by Wolfgang Schneider (1974, 1982: sixth edn). Niccacci makes an initial distinction between narrative and discourse[14] and identifies primary and secondary verbal forms in each group. The primary verbal forms are vayyiqtol in narrative and yiqtol in discourse.[15] The secondary forms are qatal in narrative and qatal as well as veqatal in discourse. Niccacci then carefully studies the distribution of forms

13. Viewing language as a means of communication, Weinreich considers that to give an account of the syntax of a language is first to distinguish between language items which belong directly to the communication situation (hearer-speaker) and those which are not directly related to the communication. Thus for example, verbal forms can be classifed as either referring directly to the communication situation (present, perfect and future) or referring to what lies outside this situation (simple past, pluperfect, conditional). Weinrich calls this distinction 'linguistic attitude'. The two other distinctions are: (A) Linguistic perspective, with its three levels: 1. retrieved information (flashback); 2. degree zero (level of the story); 3. anticipated information (disclosure); (B) Emphasis, with two levels: 1. foreground; 2. background.

14. In narrative, the third person is used as it deals with persons or events which are not present or current in the relationship involving writer–reader. Discourse in which the speaker addresses the listener directly is subdivided into 'discourse' and 'comment'. Comment occurs 'when the writer holds up the story in order to relate his reflection on the events narrated or to define them in some way' (1990: 33-34).

15. Schneider (1985: 48) had reached the same conclusion: 'Imperfekt und Imperfekt consecutivum sind die Haupt-Tempora.'

and of their positioning in texts. I shall focus here only on what Niccacci has to say about narrative texts.Vayyiqtol is used to narrate an event and chains of vayyiqtol verb clauses constitute the foreground of a narrative. Niccacci observes that in narrative a qatal verb is never clause initial and so the qatal clause has always a [x-qatal] order; x may be a conjunction or a particle in the case of a retrospective qatal or it can be a nominal or an adverbial element. Niccacci examines particularly the [waw-x-qatal] clause and how it functions within a chunk of text (1990: 36-41). The kind of information conveyed by the [waw-x-qatal] clause depends on its place in the narrative and on the types of clause which either precede of follow it. When it occurs at the very beginning, it reports retrospective information, recalling information given earlier. The sequence of clauses is: (1) [waw-x-qatal] + (2) [vayyiqtol], and their functions are: (1) antecedent information + (2) beginning of narrative. When the [waw-x-qatal] clause is non-initial, it interrups the narrative flow to communicate various kinds of backgound or peripheral information such as antecedent circumstance (flashback), a simultaneous event, contrast, or circumstance of following vayyiqtol (1990: 64-66).

Another kind of qatal clause has the order [ve-qatal]; it interrupts the vayyiqtol chains in order to also impart background information, namely a repeated action, when used together with a [waw-x-yiqtol] clause type. A last type of clause, [x-qatal], expresses emphasis (1990: 69-71).[16] Finally a nominal clause (verbless clause) provides the background information of a simultaneous event (1990: 65).

Niccacci's study seems to demonstrate that, with a limited number of forms, the verbal system creates meaning through (a) the disposition of formal elements in clauses; (b) the combination of clause types in the text; (c) the particular positions of these clauses in the text.This highly formal description of the verbal sytem provides an initial classification of the material which is useful. It is arguable, however, whether this kind of formal classification can also lead to entirely satisfactory explanations. Niccacci identifies patterns, combinations of clause patterns and position of patterns in a narrative, but the semantic or pragmatic explanations of these formal arrangements are reduced to a few

16. Niccacci is inconsistent here as he classifies this clause later (p. 71) in the group [waw-x-qatal).

functions. Such a classification may provide a starting point for pragmatic functions, but it needs also to be developed and refined. Some new explanatory parameters need also to be added.

4. *The Verbal Clause: Syntactic Aspects*

Two kinds of clauses use a subject-predicate construction: the verbal and the verbless clause. In a verbless or nominal[17] clause the predicate has no overt verb form.[18] A verbal clause has a predicate containing an overt verb form. But the presence of a verb is not always seen by Old Hebrew grammarians as indicative of the nature of the clause.

a. *Defining the Verbal Clause*

There is still a difference of opinion as to which criteria should be selected to classify a clause as verbal. Some consider that the decisive criterion is the nature of the initial element in the clause.[19] In using this rule, they follow the approach of Arab grammarians who traditionally have called 'nominal clause' any clause which begins with the subject (noun or pronoun) and verbal clause a clause which begins with a verb. Niccacci writes: 'The following definition, which follows the model of Arabic grammarians, is better suited to Hebrew syntax than the generally accepted definition: a verbal clause begins with a verb, a noun clause begins with a noun' (1990: 23). He complicates the classification by calling a noun followed by a verb a 'complex noun clause'. Similarly, Schneider considers that not only the clause without a verb, but also the clause which begins with a noun (even when a finite verb

17. Most Hebraists use the designation nominal clause to refer to the verbless clause. For GKC (par. 140e), any sentence which has a noun or its equivalent (a participle) as subject or predicate is a nominal sentence. Joüon and Muraoka (1991: 562 n. 2) would prefer the term 'non-verbal clause' but decide to use the conventional nomenclature, which, they claim, accommodate more readily the participle as predicate. See also Blau (1976: 85; par 58.2). The traditional term 'nominal clause' will be used here too, but it is important to note that the predicate of a nominal clause is not necessarily a noun.

18. The nominal clause is a construction consisting of the juxtaposition of a subject with a noun or a pronoun, an adjective, an adverb, a prepositional phrase, a participle used as noun or an infinitive used as noun.

19. R. Meyer (1966: 72), D. Michel (1960: 182-84), Schneider (1985) and Niccacci (1990) hold this view.

follows) belong to the group of nominal clause (1985: 160, par. 44.1.2.3).

One important consequence of this perspective, which is also a significant drawback, is that the word orders S-V (S-P in a verbless clause) and V-S are each respectively and exclusively bound to one particular kind of clause. The order S-V will always be found in a nominal clause. This prohibits an adequate account of the use and function of word order at discourse level in the verbal clause. The correlation created between word order and clause type leads to explanations based on clause types only and excludes a proper study of the pragmatics of word order.

The choice of the positional criterion of an element to determine the nature of a clause comes from the Arabic grammatical tradition and may reflect justifiable linguistic intuition in Arabic.[20] But Arab grammarians never took the notion of grammatical Subject as a starting point for their analyses. Rather they were primarily interested in the semantic notion of Agent and the position of agent is understood as the starting point of a predication. If such a view were to be applied to Old Hebrew a precise study of case roles would need to be done first, but as it stands, this theory leaves the question of basic word order in the clause unexamined.

The definition of a verbal clause chosen here is based on the nature of the clause predicate. In order for a clause to be verbal its predicate must have as its head word a verb.[21] Usually the verb will be finite.

b. *Word Order in the Verbal Clause*

The SVO word order appears only with a qatal verb. The following example illustrates word order in qatal transitive clauses:

20. David Cohen's article (1970: 224-28) seeks to bring out the linguistic validity of such an approach. He says: 'Il n'est peut-être pas inutile d'essayer de discerner la part d'intuition linguistique qui peut motiver dans une certaine mesure une telle conception' (p. 225). Cf. also *GKC*, p. 451, par. 140f: 'this more complicated view of the Arab grammarians may be regarded as at least relatively correct, namely, in classifying verbal clauses according as the subject precedes or follows the verb, a distinction which is often of great importance in Hebrew also.'

21. This definition agrees with most definitions found in grammars. For example, *GKC*, p.450, par. 140b: 'Every sentence, the subject of which is a noun (or pronoun included in a verbal clause) and its predicate a finite verb, is called a *verbal-clause*.' Similarly, Joüon and Muraoka (1991: 579).

Gen. 36.2:

עשׂו לקח את־נשׁיו מבנות כנען

Esau took his wives from the Canaanites.

Clause sequence in narrative is characterized by the clause initial connective waw. However, when waw and qatal are combined in a past narrative environment, the resulting veqatal form may take on various specific aspectual meanings such as iterative, durative or habitual as in 1 Sam. 16.23.[22]

ולקח דוד את־הכנור ונגן בידו

[And whenever the evil spirit from God came upon Saul] David took the lyre and played.

As a result, whereas the VSO word order in a qatal clause is commonly found in direct speech, in narrative sequence where it is preceded by waw, its occurrence is rarer because of the specific meanings veqatal may have.

When S is not clause initial, a NP in the function of O or A may be fronted as in Exod. 14.6:

ואת־עמו לקח עמו

And his army he took with him.

By contrast with qatal, the VSO order is found only with a vayyiqtol verbal form. The reason is that vayyiqtol prohibits the occurrence of any preverbal element, such as S or O between the connective waw and the verb itself. This normal word order is found when constituents are NPs, as in Num. 20.14:

וישׁלח משׁה מלאכים מקדשׁ אל־מלך אדום

And Moses sent messengers from Qaddesh to the king of Edom.

When the O or A is a pronoun it is usually found immediately after the verb, as in 2 Sam. 13.27:

וישׁלח אתו את־אמנון

And he sent Amnon with him.

With verbs which have full NPs as DO and IO, the word order is: V-(S)-DO-IO, as in Exod. 20.1:

וידבר אלהים את כל־הדברים האלה לאמר

And God spoke all these words, saying …

22. In non-past contexts veqatal is used with a future meaning as in Lev. 14.12: ולקח הכהן את־הכבשׂ האחד, 'and the priest shall take one of the lambs.'

Negation is typically formed by the adjunction of the negative particle לא before the main verb, or the nominal predicate. As vayyiqtol is prevented from having any preverbal element, לא cannot be used before the form vayyiqtol. When a verb is used with the negation it is the qatal verb which must be used, as in Gen. 31.33:

ולא מצא

And he did not find.

To summarize, the following word orders, with full NPs, are the most common in the qatal and vayyiqtol narrative clauses:

ve-S + qatal + O	vayyiqtol + S + O + A
ve-O + qatal + S	
ve-A + qatal + S + O	

The sequence S + qatal is possible as well, but rare.

c. *The Participial and Infinitive Clauses*

The problem of the grammatical status of the quasi-nominal categories of uninflected forms such as the participles both active and passive and the infinitives construct and absolute has been solved in various ways. In this study, the participial clauses will be categorized as a special type of verbal clause. The unusual feature of the verb is that it is non-finite, as it agrees with the head noun S in number and gender, but not in person.[23] The unmarked word order in a declarative participial clauses is S-Predicate, whether the S is a N or PRO, as exemplified in Gen. 25.27 and Gen. 14.12.

Gen. 25.28:

רבקה אהבת את־יעקב

Rebekah loved Jacob.

23. A participle may function as either a noun or a verb. Andersen (1970) includes the clauses with predicate participles in the group of verbless clauses. In the same way *GKC*, p. 450, par. 140a says: 'Every sentence, the subject and predicate of which are nouns or their equivalents (esp. participles) is called a *noun-clause*.' Blau (1976: 95, par. 58.2) distinguishes between clause types and grammatical functions: a sentence having a participle as its predicate behaves as a nominal clause but participles often govern as verbs. Waltke and O'Connor acknowledge that the participle has a 'verbal character' (1990: 624, par. 37.6b) but add that a participle is often used as the predicate of a verbless clause (1990: 623, par. 37.6a) on grounds which are not very clear. They say that the usual syntactic structure for a participial predicate is a verbless clause (1990: 624, par. 37.6b).

Gen. 14.12:

והוא ישב בסדם

And he was dwelling in Sodom.

Old Hebrew has two infinitive types: the infinitive absolute and construct. Both are non-finite verb forms and both may be used as nouns (with functions of S, O, C, etc.) or verbs.[24] When used as a noun, the infinitive construct is a nuclear constituent of a clause functioning, for example, as S or C of a verb. But most characteristic is its use as an extra-nuclear constituent, in a gerundive phrase which functions in a clause-modifying adverbial capacity. Commonly, the infinitive construct forms a prepositional phrase expressing time, purpose or result, with often overt S, as in Gen. 4.8:

ויהי בהיותם בשדה ויקם קין

And when they were in the field, Cain rose up …

5. *Word Order in Old Hebrew*

Research on word order in Old Hebrew has been following two paths. Most studies consider that there is only one homogeneous group of verb initial clauses. They do not pay attention to the fact that the determinants of word order in vayyiqtol clauses are different from those of other verbal clauses. In other studies, the atypical features of vayyiqtol clauses is noted but, as a result, vayyiqtol clauses are excluded altogether from the discussion on word order.

Waltke and O'Connor represent the first approach:

> For verbal clauses the basic Hebrew word order is *verb* + *subject* (VS). This verb-first word order usually obtains where a clause has no introductory material, where a clause begins with a *waw*-relative (i.e. *waw* consecutive) construction, or where a clause begins with adverbial materials.[25]

Lambdin maintains that in the verbal sentence the verb usually stands first, then the subject, object, and various adverbial elements (1973: 39). Similarly, Mayer writes that the normal word order in a verbal clause is verb-subject-object (and adverbial) (1972: 437).[26] Jongeling affirms:

24. However, the infinitive absolute as finite verb occurs in direct speech only.
25. Waltke and O'Connor 1990: 12.
26. The accompanying explanation (par. 1277, note 3) is linguistically doubtful:

'The VSO order is best considered to be the basic order of classical Hebrew' (1991: 106). GKC maintains the same view on the basis of a correlation betweeen clause type and word order. It is argued that in the verbal clause the emphasis rests upon the action which proceeds from (or is experienced by) the subject, and accordingly the verb naturally comes first (1910: 455, par. 142a).[27]

Muraoka is representative of the second approach. Starting from the premise that V-S is the unmarked word order in Hebrew (1985.30),[28] he examines the relative order of V and S in the verbal clause. He notes that in vayyiqtol clauses the word order is automatically V-S and so draws the conclusion that such clauses are of little value for the purpose of examining neutral word order and emphatic order in verbal clauses. As a result, he takes the methodological decision of excluding the waw consecutive forms altogether from his investigation (1985: 28-30). Although Muraoka identifies eight grounds for the fronting of S, some of them semantic, others pragmatic,[29] his decision not to consider vayyiqtol forms certainly results in an impoverished analysis of word order and particularly of the emphasizing system at work in the narrative clause.

Mention must also be made of views which do not agree with the traditional description of Old Hebrew as a V-S language. Joüon maintains that the word order of the unmarked verbal clause is S-V (1965: par. 155k).[30] Hadas-Lebel makes the observation that word order in the

'Cet ordre prouve que, d'habitude, en hébreu, on insiste sur l'acte; c'est pourquoi le verbe précède le sujet.'

27. More recently Williams (1976: 96, par. 572). However, Muraoka (1985: 4) points out that this view is in no way universally accepted. He stresses that it is important to remember that there is disagreement among hebraists as to the validity of the assumption that there is a word-order polarity discernible in the two main sentence types (i.e. the nominal clause shows the order S-P and the verbal clause the order V-S).

28. This means that in this arrangement neither S nor V receives special emphasis. It is important to note that Muraoka reaches this conclusion on the basis of statistics. This view is reiterated in Joüon and Muraoka (1991: 579, par. 155k).

29. They are (1985: 33-37): emphasis or contrast; circumstancial clause; avoidance of waw consecutive; the subject is 'a man' or 'God'; special groups of verbs denoting movement or knowledge; chiastic construction; reply to question.

30. For Joüon, the order S-V is the normal order both in the verbal and the nominal clause.

clause is remarkably flexible, given that Old Hebrew has no case-inflections. The normal word order, she adds, is S-V, but word order inversion is extemely frequent (1977: 93). Revell opts for what seems to be a free word order:

> The constituents of a verbal clause are commonly said to appear in standard order, but this order is 'standard' only in the sense of being the most common. In principle any constituent may stand in any position. Their order is conditioned by semantic considerations, not by syntax (1989b: 2).

Although, unfortunately, these authors do not provide detailed clarifications, one gets the impression that such differing views on word order can only be arrived at by isolating the numerous cases of vayyiqtol clauses and treating them as special cases of V initial clauses.

Vayyiqtol clauses are the main object of Givón's analysis (1977). In his examination of the drift from VSO to SVO in Old Hebrew, Givón combines statistical results with pragmatic explanations. Statistics confirm that there is a basic word order which is syntactically controlled but also affected by various pragmatic reordering processes. Givón takes the view that Old Hebrew is 'a rigid VO language with flexible subject position' (1989: 230).[31] The S position is examined through a statistical study of Genesis (1977: 189) which shows that there is a dominant V-S order in the realis clauses. This order is explained pragmatically: V comes first because it is new information and there is a general tendency in VO languages to put new information in the initial position.

The view arrived at in the course of this research and adopted in it, is that Old Hebrew is a VSO language.

6. *The Text Analysed*

This study is based on the standard academic Hebrew text *Biblia hebraica stuttgartensia* (Stuttgart: Deutsche Bibelstiftung, 1977), the Stuttgart Hebrew Bible, which reproduces the handwritten Leningrad Codex B 19a dating from about 1008 CE. Inevitably, the Hebrew text in this manuscript has not reached us in exactly the same form in which it left the hands of the writers. Ancient texts are affected by the process of

31. Similarly, Givón writes elsewhere (1983: 28): 'This ancient Semitic language (i.e. Biblical Hebrew) is rigidly VO but shows a pragmatically controlled VS/SV variation.'

constant copying, making mistakes, omitting or repeating words or lines for instance, and the Masoretic text of the Leningrad codex B 19a is not perfect or free of errors. At the same time, it is very important that a linguistic study which seeks to examine and analyse facts should be based on an existing and actual text rather than depend on a reconstructed text or reconstructed passages which never existed in reality. Reconstructed readings might solve certain difficulties, but are too speculative and hazardous when we are looking for factual and not conjectural explanations. The choice then of the Masoretic Text of *BHS*, and the decision to adhere to it, are based on methodological principles.

The data for the analysis is found in the following texts of the Hebrew Bible: Genesis, Exodus 1–12, Numbers 20–25, Joshua, Judges, 1 and 2 Samuel, 1 and 2 Kings. The analysis is based on an exhaustive study of these texts. Passages cited in the course of the study are given as examples and are not intended to be all the possible passages that could have been cited. Rather, they are intended to be representative.

A necessary starting point for this type of pursuit is that the stories should be considered from a synchronic viewpoint: the approach employed will concentrate on one stage of the text, in this case the final form of the text. This is in contrast with a diachronic view of the texts that examines the historical development of the literature. The concentration on the final form of the text helps to explore the role of devices in giving a story its shape and to identify clues to its major emphases expressed through word order, arrangement of phrases or larger linguistic units.

7. *Organization of the Work*

The study which follows is organized in the following way. Chapter 1 describes the approach to the grammatical description used in the analysis, the functional view, and the particular emphasis laid on the communicative aspect of language. Literary narration is viewed as a type of communication between a writer and a reader. A special section describes the particular features of narratives and shows how such texts may legitimately be studied from a pragmatic angle. The purpose of the chapter is not to provide a theory, but rather to describe the mechanisms of communication which underly some of the phenomena later investigated in the thesis.

Chapter 2 is a detailed examination and criticism of Longacre's text-linguistic analysis of Old Hebrew narrative texts. An evaluation is made of the method as a whole, as well as the theory of foregrounding it contains, and the conclusions drawn by him when applied to Old Hebrew texts.

Chapter 3 studies the grammatical encoding of topical entities in a specific story (Genesis 22) using a method devised by Tomlin, and with special reference to the encoding of topical importance in clauses.

Chapter 4 explore further the grammatical aspects of the encoding of referents as topic. It discusses specifically the correlation between the use of the two types of verbal clause in narration and the activation state of the referents which occur as topics.

Chapter 5 pays attention to the two main narrative clauses from the angle of the presupposition-focus articulation. Having looked at types of focus in the direct speech clauses first, it then examines the role of focus assignment in the throwing into relief of constituents in their clauses.

Chapter 6, finally, studies another two more methods of foregrounding. The first one is extra-clausal and relies upon stereotyped and fixed knowledge structures. The second one is linked to the direct involvement of the narrator or speaker in the story.

Chapter 1

LANGUAGE, DISCOURSE AND NARRATIVE: AN ANALYTICAL FRAMEWORK

The purpose of this chapter is to describe the general theoretical framework and to introduce some of the analytical tools that will inform the following studies. Descriptive notions and analytical tools are borrowed from various disciplines. The justification for this eclectic stance[1] is that what is intended here is neither the creation of a unified discourse theory comparable to Longacre's discourse grammar, nor the development of a model, but rather the explanations of specific problems.

1. *Views of Language and Aspects of Discourse*

The notion of discourse has been defined in numerous ways. The variety of definitions arises partly from the fact that different analytical paradigms are used to describe discourse. As the object analysed is defined by the method of analysis, it is necessary first to explain the paradigm chosen to study language.

At the risk of oversimplification, one can say that two main general paradigms are currently used in linguistics: the formalist and the functional. While accepting that language has social functions, the formalist approach affirms that the grammar of a language forms an autonomous

1. Linguists have now commonly accepted the 'vastness' of discourse analysis as a field of study, as Deborah Schiffrin (1994: 5) describes it. They recognize that by its very nature discourse analysis is an interdisciplinary field. To give a proper account of this vastness any reductionist procedure must be avoided. A comment made by Schiffrin applies well to some Old Hebrew discourse analyses: 'I believe that at relatively early stages of an endeavour, reduction just for the sake of simplification can too drastically limit the range of interesting questions that can and should be asked' (1994: 5).

system and as a result, grammatical forms should be analysed oblivious of what speakers do with them, and of the time, place and circumstances of the utterance. In so far as this view is applied to discourse analysis, a text is spoken of rather than discourse, where there is a collection of well-formed clauses constituting some kind of super-sentence. Text-grammar is seen as an extension of the grammar of the clause. The super-sentence can be described as a hierarchical structure made out of units of various sizes.[2] With respect to method, the grammatical approach operates deductively. The lower-level units are identified (clause types or propositions), as well as, sometimes, formal higher constituents (paragraphs, episodes etc.) and in the light of these 'discourse categories' a text-grammar is established. The limitations of this approach are readily identifiable. Mey, for example, is sceptical of any analysis which views a text first as a 'sentence-like object' and then tries to match it to spoken or written texts.[3] In order to go beyond the notion of text as an isolated artefact and to see it instead as human language in use it is more productive to adopt a functional view of language.

a. *The Functional Orientation*

The basic assumption of functionalism[4] is that language serves functions external to the language system itself and that factors outside language affect the internal organization of language. Form cannot be understood independently of function and so the aim of functionalim is to discover and describe what linguistic structures are used for—the functions they serve—and the factors which determine the selection of one structure over against another.[5]

2. Longacre (1989: 17) uses the notion of macrostructure to describe this discourse level.

3. Mey (1993: 184) writes: 'Pursuing any extensional conception of text grammar, we find ourselves in a kind of double-bind: on the one hand, we think of a text as an (infinitely expandable) sentence or sentence-like object; on the other, such an abstract, theoretical construct will never match the concrete, finite reality of spoken or written texts ... Text ... is not a particularly helpful or interesting concept in understanding human speech behaviour.'

4. A good overall view is provided by Siewierska (1991) or Dik (1981).

5. This assumption shapes the way functional linguists understand the connections between syntactic forms and semantic or pragmatic functions. Syntactic features are explained by semantic and pragmatic facts. Semantics deals with the

The unifying theme of functionalist approaches is that language is primarily a system of human communication. As a result, grammatical units and constructions must be studied in terms of their functional communicative role. Human beings communicate interactively and in well-defined sociocultural contexts with specific social roles. Interactive functions and sociocultural factors are seen as playing a central role in determining the grammar of a language.

The functional view of language implies that a speaker must possess various kinds of knowledge in order to achieve successful communication. Among other things, a speaker's knowledge of language must include knowledge of social conventions and social constraints. Moreover, the speaker's linguistic knowledge must go beyond the level of the sentence: they must, that is, possess a textual competence which serves to construct discourse.

The functional view has become increasingly more interested in the possibility of more internal factors playing a role in the shaping of language structure. The basic hypothesis is that many of the properties crucial to the structure and functions of language in discourse reflect properties of human cognition and perception. In other words, language takes a certain form because of the way human beings perceive and conceptualize subject matter and entities in the world. Typical psychological explanations are based on the notion of the limitations of human memory and have been used to explain various language universals. Prominence and highlighting structures are seen as based on perceptual and attentional principles. Particular cognitive categories have been posited explaining foreground and background (Hopper and Thompson 1980). Recency of mention has been analysed as correlating negatively with the cognitive notion of importance (Givón 1988). All these studies show that it is important that cognitive categories be tied to objective linguistic phenomena, and that they also indicate what kinds of connection might be established between language structures and more abstract cognitive categories.

The approach taken in this work will be broadly functional, but at the same time a critical awareness towards functional explanations will be exercised. As the brief survey above indicates, there are different kinds

relation between forms and the use made of these forms by the speaker in communication, at the propositional or illocutionary level. Pragmatics deals with the two previous levels of linguistic form and the communicative functions these forms fulfil within the larger framework of the context in which the forms occur.

of functionalisms. Assumptions, methodologies and categories of functions vary from one model to another. Functionalists differ particularly from each other in the degree of openness to external factors they assign to the linguistic system. Radical functionalism sees language as an open system whose internal organization is entirely moulded by external factors. Moderate functionalism accepts a basic formal organization of language and sees external factors as influencing various aspects of it. A weaker version still of functionalism adds a diachronic dimension to the question and limits in time the influence of external factors upon the internal organization. Labov's warnings on the 'overestimation' of functional explanations will be taken seriously here and it is a weak version of functionalism which will guide this research.[6]

b. *Discourse and Text*

As consistent with a functional view, Brown and Yule's definition of discourse provides a useful starting point:

> The analysis of discourse is necessarily the analysis of language in use. As such, it cannot be restricted to the description of linguistic forms independent of the purposes or functions which these forms are designed to serve in human affairs (1983: 1).

It is necessary to add a few specifications to this definition. Discourse is a sized unit of language use. It is a stretch of language use with a beginning, a middle and an end. It is also characterized by sequentiality and connectivity: sequences of utterances have a non-random character and are connected syntactically, semantically and pragmatically.

Face-to-face conversation helps us pinpoint some more characteristics. First, discourse is dynamic: it unfolds as it progresses and moves from one point to another. Participants are aware of what has been said but not of what is yet to be said. As a result, when an element of a discourse is analysed, its point of occurrence in the discourse must be taken into account and the analysis will be conditioned by the stretch of discourse preceding it. Sinclair offers the important principle: 'each

6. The words of caution towards some functional explanations of language changes given by William Labov in his article 'The Overestimation of Functionalism' (1987) and more recently in his book *Principles of Linguistic Changes* (1994) can be validly applied to some functional explanations of sentence forms in Old Hebrew based on the verbal context. Not all properties of a language have to be functionally explained, as moderate functionalists recognize.

utterance sets the scene for the next. No matter what it is, the way it will be interpreted is determined by the previous utterance, and in particular by the immediately previous one.'[7] Secondly, conversation is a human activity which is purposeful. This is closely related to the view of H. Clark who studies discourse from the perspective of language as 'action'.[8] The purposefulness of discourse means that it should have an outcome[9] which, usually, is registered linguistically. In the particular case of conversational narrative the purpose may be described as the eliciting of an evaluative interpretation from the hearer. Such an evaluative element should likewise be expected in literary narrative.

The analysis of literary narrative deals with a text. Text is the specific artefact produced during the process of discourse creation. Brown and Yule write: 'a text is the verbal record of a communicative event' (1983: 6). In other words, a discourse is performed in an actual situation and in real time, and a text could be described as its symbolic (lexical and grammatical) representation.

c. *Communicative Processing*

Leech identifies the problems faced by speaker and hearer in discourse processing in the following way:

> A speaker, *qua* communicator, has to solve the problem: 'Given that I want to bring about such-and-such a result in the hearer's consciousness, what is the best way to accomplish this aim by using language? ' For the hearer there is another kind of the problem to solve: 'Given that the speaker said-such-and-such, what did the speaker mean me to understand by that?' (Leech 1983: x).

Discourse processing, then, has a double dimension: production and comprehension. Moreover, discourse processing is both a cognitive and a social event. It is the product of a set of various active processes originating on the one hand, from the cognitive and psycholinguistic make-up of the discourse participants, and on the other hand, from

7. Sinclair 1985: 15.

8. The 'action' view of language is opposed, according to Clark (1992: xi-xv), to the 'product' tradition interested in the formal description of discourse. Thus it is also in harmony with a functional analytical approach.

9. Martin Warren (1987: 198) writes: 'discourse always has an *outcome* which he [i.e. Sinclair] defines as an irreversible change, however small, that takes place in relation to the outside world.'

the sociolinguistic (contextual) conventions according to which they interact.

i. *A Basic Model of Discourse Production*

The cognitive aspects of discourse processing are summarized in the following diagram:

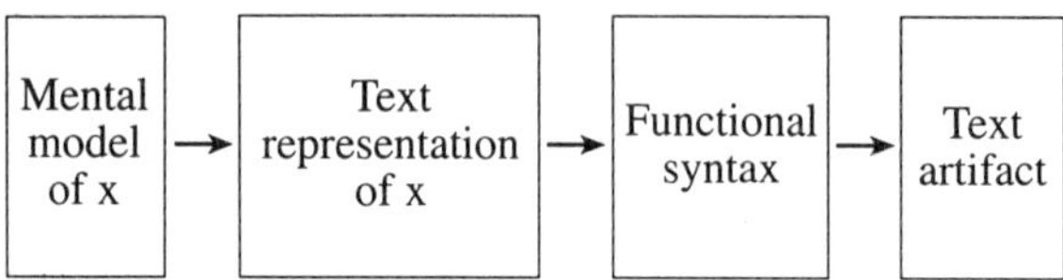

The main goal is the construction of a text artifact. The speaker has initially a mental representation of a subject matter which they want the hearer to construct during discourse comprehension.[10] The formulation and processing of the text representation takes place during discourse. The speaker takes into account the estimated hearer's familiarity with the subject (given and new articulation) and helps the hearer recognize particular features of the subject matter (topic-comment and prominence marking).

The text representation undergoes syntactical encoding and results in the production of the text. Syntactic arrangements at local level are conditioned by specific pragmatic factors which, in turn, depend on global discourse pragmatics.

ii. *Communication and Comprehension Process*

Discourse comprehension is similar to the interpretation of the other actions of human beings: it uses the interpretive human ability to build hypotheses about goals and intentions underlying an action. The guiding principles of discourse comprehension are the following.

(1) What is meant by the speaker is primary.

(2) What is meant by the speaker is represented by the intended meaning of the utterance.

(3) To capture the intended meaning is the main concern of the hearer in linguistic communication, as Georgia Green's statement reminds us:

10. Van Dijk and Kintsch (1983: 6) write: 'Discourse processing is a strategic process in which a mental representation is constructed of the discourse in memory, using both external and internal types of information, with the goal of interpreting (understanding) the discourse.'

> Communication is... the successful interpretation by an addressee of a speaker's intention in performing a linguistic act (1989: 1).

Comprehension is thus conceived as the process by which people arrive at the interpretation the speaker intended them to grasp for a particular utterance in a given context. Consider for example the advertisement:

> *You get a better kitchen if you grill people.*[11]

In an informal way, it could be said that such an utterance makes no sense. A more thoughtful approach would focus on 'grill' and suggest that its meaning is 'to subject to insistent questioning', rather than 'to cook on fire'. The meaning would be: *You get a better kitchen if beforehand you keep on asking people (about kitchens).* This would be a step in the right direction. But communication through the advertisement will be considered successful only if the readers understand that they are invited to order a catalogue offering a wide range of fitted kitchens, created as a result of consulting many people.

(4) The speaker-intended meaning is different from word and sentence meaning (or propositional meaning). Syntax, semantics, the lexicon have a conventional meaning. It is not in constructing meaning in accordance with it that an utterance will be understood as intended, because what a speaker means is not exhausted by sentence meaning. The hearer is usually expected to derive other meanings from the words uttered which function only as a guide in the recovery of the intended meaning.

(5) In order for the intended meaning to be derived, it is necessary that the 'context' be taken into account. Meaning results from two different types of information: a semantic or propositional meaning which is conveyed through the linguistic material, and contextual information which is provided by extra-linguistic information. Consider the utterance:

> *The light is on in the sitting room.*

It can have different meanings depending on who says it, to whom, and in what situation. Said by a husband to his wife as they come back from the restaurant at 11.30 at night, its meaning might be an expression of worry. Told by a father to his son, it might function as a rebuke and as an order. Made as a remark by Hercule Poirot at the scene of a burglary,

11. An advertisement by a furniture chain which appeared in a newspaper.

it might be part of an explanation of the crime. The meaning of a sentence used as an utterance varies with context. The sentence has a time-free and place-free meaning which is its semantic meaning. But it is language use, that is actual communication, which determines the meaning conveyed by the speaker. In other words, it is the combination of context and lexico-grammatical elements which is the real communication signal. The goal of the hearer is to recover the meaning intended by the speaker, that is the meaning the sentence takes in a particular context. This is the only meaning the hearer usually considers worth recovering. A closer look will now be taken at the interpretative tools and steps necessary to get at meaning in discourse.

iii. *Constructed Meaning in Discourse*

In order to recover the intended meaning, a number of intepretative moves have to take place in discourse processing. The speaker provides input data in the form of text to the hearer. The data comprise the text surface (lexical features and syntactic choices) and contextual information. Meaning is the result of interpretations of the propositions, the illocutionary force and the inferences, which take place in context, and it also depends on the cognitive and conceptual systems of the speaker and hearer. But also, importantly, meaning is constructed in and by the speaker–hearer relationship. Speakers and hearers are in a situation known to both of them with an amount of shared knowledge and experience. The speakers select the words and constructions to express what they want to say, and they use them as signals of their meaning. The lexical and syntactic choices assist the hearers with differentiation among possible meanings. The hearers incorporate the language of the speakers into their knowledge and cognitive resources, in order to understand these signals in the way in which they were meant.

Processing the propositional content of a communication is the first step in establishing the meaning of an utterance. Propositional meaning is obtained through the interpretation of lexical meanings and syntactic structures. The proposition is the smallest unit of communication; it has referential elements, concepts representing things, events, attributes and relations. These relations connect the concepts within a proposition with each other (case roles: agent, undergoer, etc.). Propositions cluster together through various relations and configurations representing larger units of communication.

The next step for the hearer is to understand how the propositional meaning is functioning in the context of communication. The propositional content of an utterance is sometimes called its locutionary meaning. It gives an utterance its determinate sense and reference. But in real life, propositional contents are often used in 'speech acts' or as actions happening in the world, for utterances have various aspects or forces which may bring about an effect on the hearer.[12] This effect is not part of the meaning of the utterance. 'Go away' has a locutionary force because it makes a reference to an action. It has the illocutionary force of an order, if it is said by the right person in the right place. 'I'm putting you in detention' has a perlocutionary force. A language user must have a knowledge of the particular conditions and rules under which these effects will be produced. This level of meaning shows that language users must know more than grammatical rules and lexical meanings to handle language competently. They must know when, how and to whom to speak, as well as in what situation and for what desired effect. This adds a pragmatic dimension to the propositional level. The pragmatic dimension raises the question of the role of the context in communication.

The Context. Clark proposes to redefine what he calls the 'intrinsic context'[13] of communication in the following way:

> The intrinsic context for a listener trying to understand what a speaker means on a particular occasion is the common ground that the listener believes holds at that moment between the speaker and the listener he or she is speaking to (1992: 67)

The common ground (or mutual knowledge, beliefs, suppositions) is the information speaker and hearer share. It comes from three main sources: (1) Cultural (shared knowledge, beliefs and assumptions about the world, taken for granted in the cultural community[14]); (2) Perceptual (physical co-presence; immediate physical environment); (3) Linguistic

12. An utterance has an illocutionary force when it does something: state, promise, declare, announce, command, request, propose etc. It has a perlocutionary force when it brings about an effect on the hearer when it is uttered.

13. Clark (1992: 65-66) distinguishes between intrinsic and incidental context. The intrinsic context is a context which is necessary for the comprehension of the intended meaning to be successful. Incidental context is the context which is never consulted. It does not belong to the process of linguistic communication.

14. Such as religious beliefs, cultural assumptions, knowledge of scientific laws, etc.

(prior linguistic context; semantic, syntactic context). Misunderstanding comes about when the listener makes a wrong assessment of common ground.

Inferencing. Inference is a cognitive process by which a hearer, taking the context of the discourse into account, obtains new information from explicit verbal information. Given that verbal information and context represent evidence in the comprehension process, it may be said that the purpose of inferencing is the recognition of the speaker's intended meaning by a hearer.[15]

The role played by inferencing means that discourse comprehension cannot legitimately be reduced to the description proposed in what is known as the 'code-model' of communication. This uses three basic elements: a message (a 'proposition' or a 'thought') which is unobservable; observable signals which in verbal communication are phonetic or graphemic, and a code (words and grammar) which is shared between speaker and hearer. In the code-model the speaker encodes the message that cannot travel into a signal that can travel. The signals are transmitted and the hearer decodes and understands those signals in the way they were meant. There is a double weakness in such a model. First, it assumes that the decoder will be able to understand the message by relying exclusively upon the medium of transmission, the linguistic code. The construction of the meaning of the message results exclusively from the processing of lexico-grammatical information and contextual information is excluded. Secondly, it sees the linguistic sign as having an exclusively symbolic meaning. Comprehension of a sentence is viewed as the recovery of the semantic representation of the sentence. This position prevents the understanding of language in use, in which the sign does not function as a symbol but rather as an index: it directs

15. Clark and Clark (1977: 72-132) distinguish between the 'construction' process in which the listener figures out what a sentence is meant to express and the 'utilization' process in which the listener uses the sentence in the way the speaker intended. Inference belongs to the construction process of creating meaning at the propositional meaning. However, they note that this is an approximate division: 'The line between the construction processes and the utilization processes is not a sharp one. Formally, it is not easy to say when listeners are building a representation and when they are using it. And psychologically it is often not possible to infer the propositions underlying a sentence without simultaneously registering the speaker's purpose' (1977: 87).

away the attention from language to the context of discourse. The token meaning of the sign is realized in association with the context of discourse.

The inferential model corrects these deficiencies by allowing the context to play its full role. The message of a sender comprises a set of propositions: one is expressed through the meaning of words and the grammar, the other is conveyed indirectly by making use of information available in the context. The process of comprehension is described by Sperber and Wilson in the following way:

> The speaker's intentions are not decoded but non-demonstratively inferred, by a process of hypothesis formation and confirmation which, like scientific theorizing and unlike grammatical analysis, has free access to contextual information. The hearer's aim is to arrive at the most plausible hypothesis about the speaker's intentions; but the most plausible hypothesis, in pragmatic interpretation as in science, may still be wrong (1991: 585).

This is not to say that coding and decoding should not be taken into account in verbal communication. Rather the decoding component and inference should work together.[16]

Our understanding of inferences in comprehension is as yet inadequate[17] and discussion of conceptual and theoretical aspects can be done only in a rather incomplete way. However, the propositional meaning of an utterance is only one factor in establishing its full intended meaning. Utterances have potentially multiple meanings and

16. Wilson and Sperber 1986: 27 write: 'Verbal communication is a complex form of communication. Linguistic coding and decoding is involved, but the linguistic meaning of an uttered sentence falls short of encoding what the speaker means: it merely helps the audience infer what she means ... In other words, a coding-decoding process is subservient to a Gricean inferential process.' The nature of the relationship between speech signals and the message they convey is a complicated one, and it is important to distinguish between the message being conveyed, and the words used as the vehicle for conveying it. The meaning of any utterance cannot be reduced to the meaning of words and the grammatical constructions used to link them together. Rather, it is dependent on the cognitive and conceptual systems of the speaker and hearer and the context in which they are communicating.

17. To witness is the recent debate on mutual knowledge for example, or the disagreement between Stephen Levinson and proponents of the 'Relevance approach'; cf. Sperber and Wilson 1986b.

the use of inference with contextual information reduces the choice among possible alternative meanings.

d. *Communication and Knowledge of the World*

The above sketch shows that language users must possess a variety of 'knowledges' in order to process language adequately. One particular kind of knowledge, 'world knowedge', which is related to the proposition-meaning level, has been a focus of interest in recent discourse studies and needs to be explained in more detail.

Humans have a large amount of general knowledge collected in long-term memory. During discourse, incoming language information is processed while relevant parts of this general background knowledge available to participants are activated and applied. This internalized information consists of common-sense knowledge of how people think or behave in common situations of standardized routine. The cognitive aspect of this knowledge has occupied the interest of artificial intelligence specialists who believe that it is organized as packages of stereotypical descriptions easily storable in long-term memory. A central characteristic of these information packages, often referred to through the generic term of 'schemas', is that they store information in an economical way. Schemas are simplified descriptions of an object, a situation, an event, a sequence of events. The typical properties of an object, or what usually happens in a situation need not be mentioned as they are implicitly expected and potentially expressed through the mental presence of the schema. A schema thus contains an implicit body of related knowledge to be used in reasoning. Minsky (1980) describes an 'object' schema which he calls a frame. Schank and Abelson (1977) have developed the notions of scripts, plans and goals. These structures of knowledge are employed in the production and understanding of discourse. A process of pattern recognition takes place, the hearer assuming that the discourse is made up of instances of known discourse and reasoning pattern. The comprehension process is oriented towards trying to identify the presence of such patterns.

As a storehouse of stereotypical information a pattern such as a schema, for example, has a tremendous in-built predictive power. Through schema, expectations are created about how events should develop or how things or events should relate to one another, or about what things or events will be present. If information from the linguistic output is flawed or missing the hearer can fill in or repair what is necessary on the basis of a schema. This expectation-creating hallmark of schema may be manipulated by speakers for specific purposes as will be considered in the last chapter.

e. *Conclusion*

The construction and production of discourse are not very different from other types of behaviour. Behaviour results from the interaction of information available from the environment (stimulus information) and information stored in the mind or 'knowledge'. By taking into account and applying some of the principles presented above, it will be possible to describe how meaning and specific language patterns are constructed by a writer and interpreted by a reader.

2. *Narrative Discourse: Basic Characteristics and Pragmatic Features*

For a long time the study of narrative texts has been the exclusive domain of literary research done by narratologists of different schools.[18] Recent discourse-based analyses of narratives make great use of the notions found in these studies. Although controlled by various theories of interpretation and using arcane terminologies, literary approaches reveal great areas of consensus on the nature of narratives. The purpose of this section is to provide a brief description of the key features of narrative texts and to identify the pragmatic aspects of these texts justifying their discourse-oriented study.

a. *The Specificity of Narrative*

For the purpose of this study, a narrative is defined as the verbal representation of a number of events in a time sequence. A narrative recounts a series of facts or events, either real or imaginary and establishes a temporal connection between them. The temporal sequence tends to be predominantly iconic: the order of the clauses matches the chronological unfolding of events in the world described by the narrative. Narrative clauses are arranged in the following order and have the following propositional content:

18. See for example Mieke Bal (1985), Seymour Chatman (1978), Gérard Genette (1972), Gerald Prince (1982), Boris Uspensky (1973), W.C. Booth (1983), Shlomit Rimmon-Kenan (1983).

1. A (actor) is X at time t 1.
2. Event Y happens to A (or A does Y) at time t 2.
3. A is X' at time t 3.

This outline shows that three elements are necessary to make up a narrative: (1) Temporal markers indicating the temporal succession (t1, t2, t3) of events; (2) Some development made visible by an opposition between predicate: X and X'; (3) A participant (Actor) which remains identical throughout the chronological development. Although propositions 1 or 3 may be left unexpressed and may have to be reconstructed by the hearer or reader, a basic narrative scheme can be represented as follows:

/t 1/	/t 2/	/t 3/
A is X	Y happens to A (A does Y)	A is X'

The important feature is the continuous presence of A, and the relation between the initial predicate X and the final predicate X'.

b. *The Narrative Genre: Account of Events and Story*

The terms 'narrative' and 'story' are often used interchangeably. The definition of narrative given above is of a generic type. Narrative refers to a general group of narrated genres. It designates an inclusive category comprising various specific forms such as story or account of events.

When a narrative is concerned with simply reporting a temporal sequence of events, we are dealing with an 'account of events'. The connection established between events is purely chronological in character. A diary, a travel journal, a daily record, a biography, a description of incidents, a relation of an experience, memoirs are examples of accounts of events, or 'reportage'.[19] Events are normally arranged in the time sequence of their occurrence, that is chronologically. An account of events may read like a listing of fortuitous events. But, in fact, a

19. In the Hebrew Bible, accounts of events may be classify according to their contents. There are historical reports (Gen. 21.22-34: the treaty between Abimelech and Abraham; Josh. 5.2-12: the institution of circumcision); etiological reports (Josh. 4.1-9 explains the presence of a heap of stones in the Jordan); anecdotes (1 Kgs 9.10-14 is about the gift-cities given by Solomon to Hiram of Tyre); annals (1 Kgs 9.15-23); memoirs (Ezra and Nehemiah); lists (genealogies, itineraries; lists of victories or defeats).

sense of unity or some kind of meaningful connection between the events always eliminate randomness. All types of unifying factors may be used: description of a theatre of war, military campaign, and so on.

As for the story, it is intrinsically more complicated in its shape than an account of events. In a story the temporal sequence of events is overshadowed by a sense of causality often made apparent through causal linkage between propositions. For example, 'the king died and then the queen died' is an account of events, a chronicle. But 'the king died and then the queen died of grief' is a story.

Many definitions of story, however, emphasize the particular role of plot. By plot is meant a particular pattern which presents a flow of action from one state of balance (beginning) to another state of balance (resolution) through an intervening process of disequilibrium or imbalance (middle). A plot progresses from an activating starting point through the stage of complication, to a peak or point of climax. From there, the plot line descends to a resolved ending, or denouement, and a closure.

Undoubtedly the plot-pattern appears in numerous stories and this is why it is seen as the canonical format of story. But the position taken in this study is that it would be wrong to consider plot as a defining feature of story. Rather, plot is a rhetorical highlighting of causality. It could be described as dramatizing causality in seeing events as going in a particular direction, culminating in crisis and continuing to fulfilment in the form of a resolution. The design is used because it is exciting, creating mystery and causing surprise. It offers tension and release and as such is a powerful rhetorical device. Significantly, Labov and Waletzky have identified this pattern in oral versions of personal experience (1967). It should also be remembered that plot was borrowed from drama, performed on stage, a context requiring a vivid presentation of events. In written stories, rhetorical requirements are of a different kind and so the degree of emplotment may vary, from the tightly structured and highly dramatic plot pattern to the loosely structured plot with some episodes of the story not fully integrated.

If causality is indispensable to a story, plot is dispensable. The sense of continuation through tension and fulfilment through resolution is not a *sine qua non* of story. The various stages of plot (exposition, conflict, evaluation, resolution) are not necessarily found in all stories. Stories may have ends which offer no clear resolutions, or no sense of a neat ending.[20] Movement, progression and fulfilment may be realized through mere temporal continuity, the sequence of events being not particularly designed to create suspense and tension.

c. *Pragmatic Aspects of Narratives*

Studying written narratives does not mean that it is not possible heuristically to envisage written communication from the double perspective of oral verbalization and interaction. Fillmore writes that the basic principles of pragmatics are found in the language of face-to-face conversation, and he believes that 'other types of discourse can be usefully described in terms of their deviation from such a base' (1981: 165). Such an approach to written texts is used increasingly by linguists who recognize that literary storytelling is simply an elaboration of conversational storytelling (Tannen 1989: 27), and that all the strategies and devices of conversational discourse are found in written literary discourse in an adapted form. Three brief points need to be made regarding literary storytelling.

First, interaction in written discourse is of a special type. Texts are written by someone, for someone and for something. But communication through a written text is complicated by the fact that the production and reception of language do not take place within a single context of time and space. A written story is produced in one place by an author and is received by a reader in another place. The writer and the reader of a story are not in a face-to-face situation. Reading is not a direct interchange between author and reader. In spite of this, interaction does take place in written communication: it happens in the reading of the text by a person. In the reading process, writer and reader may be said to indirectly interact with each other.[21] If the features of this interaction are considered more closely, it is possible to add that it is a layered interaction which involve not only an author and a reader, but also a narrator and a narratee.

20. Earl Miner (1990: 139-142) mentions Asian narratives which often are characterized by deferred completion. In the Hebrew Bible, the last historical book, 2 Kings, finishes abruptly with the deportation of the population of Jerusalem.

21. It is important to note that, by contrast with modern literary communication, in the case of biblical texts the reader is perhaps better described as a collective reader, in the sense of a community.

i. *Layered Interaction: Author and Reader*

In written interaction, at the encoding end, the author[22] does not interact with a real reader, but with a provisionally represented reader. Similarly, at the decoding end, the author is only provisionally represented to the reader. Authors construct for themselves a target reader, a model of the possible reader (Eco 1979: 7), whom they may explicitly or implicitly address. The model reader is a reader that is anticipated by the author and any given text is organized to take account of this 'possible' reader. Only the written text can tell us what kind of reader its author postulates. The model reader is moulded by the text in the form of instructions given to and presuppositions shared by the anticipated reader of the text.[23] The real reader, in the process of reading, looks for the implied author, as the real author is not present. The implied author is the real reader's construct, derived from the text read. It is a 'text-guided image of the author' (Lategan and Vorster 1985: 70) built up by a dense network of numerous literary devices and strategies. The situation can be represented in the the following way:

Real Author ——— constructs ———→ Implied Reader

Implied Author ←——— constructs ——— Real Reader

The real author does not interact directly with the real reader, nor does the implied author interact with the implied reader as they are both constructs of different people.[24] The text is something like an arena in which reader and author participate in a game of the imagination. In

22. It is assumed here that the author is the creator of the message, and not a mere copier or transmitter of a message

23. In literary theory, the target reader has been called the 'mock reader' or 'implied reader' (Iser 1974) or else 'the reader in the text', or 'the encoded reader', or 'the textually defined reader'.

24. I disagree here with Leech and Short's description (1981: 262-64) which claims that the reader (Addressee I) interacts with the real author (Addresser I) and that the Implied Author (Addresser 2) interacts with the Implied Reader (Addressee 2). Implied author and implied reader are constructs of the different participants in the interaction and so the four entities cannot be situated at the same level. Lategan (1989: 10) describes the interaction in the following way: 'The real author, when writing, is reaching out for the implied reader (as no other reader is present at this moment). The real reader, when reading, is reaching out for the implied author (as no other author is present).'

this game author and reader stand in a chiastic relationship to one another. The real author relies upon his construct of an implied reader and the real reader relies upon his construct of an implied author. The first construct serves to prepare the expected response to the text, the latter is a text-guided image which helps the reader to capture this intended response.

ii. *Layered Interaction: Narrator and Narratee*

In story-telling, the real author creates a narrator who has the role of the storyteller.[25] This creates an additional layer of interaction, represented by the relation narrator–narratee: the persons who are supposedly telling and listening to the story. The situation narrator–narratee can be described as verbally mirroring what happens in oral story-telling where narrator and audience (narratee) are immediately identifiable, being physically present to each other. This is not the case in a written story. The narratee is not a physically given participant, but is the author's construct and, as a result, it belongs to the text of the story.

The real author has a number of options when they come to construct a narrator. In a third-person narrative, the narrator is detached from the events, omniscient, and providing a comprehensive account of all the aspects of the story. Alternatively, in first-person narratives, narrators may be overtly portrayed as characters in the story when they participate in the action which is described. Finally, the narrator may choose to adopt the point of view of the reader (or of a character in the story). By adopting this vantage point, the narrator's omniscience disappears. The real author may switch from one mode of narration to another or use them in combination.

iii. *Pragmatic Strategies in Written Stories*

A written text being disconnected from immediate interaction, the author is obliged to create what can be called 'a secondary language system'. A written text can be seen as the theatre of a special kind of activity involving the creation of a network of patterned instructions which enable speaker and reader to construct meaning. These patterns have been seen by some scholars as constituting the 'literary features' of a text.[26] In reality, this activity is not unlike that which occurs in oral

25. Even though sometimes narrators may not be easily distinguished from authors, they constitute an entity distinct from authors.

26. Widdowson (1975: 54) explains that it is because a literary work is

face-to-face communication and it operates by similar processes.

Deborah Tannen's findings (1982) have led her to review the traditional dichotomy between spoken versus written language. By analysing samples of written and oral texts, she discovered that linguistic strategies expected to occur in spontaneous conversation were in fact also used in written language. When she compared the spoken and written versions of the same story, she found that when speakers were asked to write down a story they had told earlier in an oral form, two types of story forms were produced. Most speakers tended to condense their long-winded oral stories into concise, expository prose. However, one female speaker combined in her written story features of expository prose with various techniques characteristic of oral storytelling, thus producing a short story.

Tannen (1989: 1, 15) also observed that ordinary conversation and literary discourse have more in common than has been commonly thought. The characteristic techniques used in oral story-telling are to be understood in the linguistic sense, that is they are a systematic way of using language. Tannen describes them as 'involvement' strategies in the sense that they are particular ways in which coordinated interaction, active participation of speaker and hearer, and a sense of identification of speaker and hearer with features of the message are manifested at the linguistic level.[27] In conversational interaction, typical involvement strategies include rhythm, repetitions of phonemes, morphemes, words, or longer chunks of discourse, ellipsis, figures of speech, constructed dialogue, imagery and storytelling.[28] Tannen suggests that the basic phenomenon underlying all these techniques is repetition. Moreover, whereas they are widespread, unplanned and unsophisticated in conversation, they become well constructed, intricate and enhanced in literary discourse (1989: 9). This explains why reading a novel or a story is a

dissociated from other social interaction that the writer is required to work the language into patterns.

27. In face-to-face conversation, participants are not merely satisfied with transmitting or decoding representational contents. They seek to make impressions on each other, to project an image, they are involved in the conversation. Signalling involvement may be done directly through words or indirectly through non-verbal signals such as gestures.

28. Telling a story is a particular way of showing one is involved in the conversation. High-involvement speakers tell more stories in a conversation than more reserved participants. However, storytelling is an involvement strategy of a different order because it employs all the other strategies as well (Tannen 1989: 28).

different kind of experience from reading other texts. A good story gets the reader involved in a particular use of words which calls for a special kind of attention, similar to that required for oral discourse.

3. *The Temporal Dimension of Story Content*

A last aspect of narrative needs to be considered: the relation between the chunk of experience communicated and its verbal representation in language or, in other words, the relation between narrative as text and the real world. One main process is of interest here, namely the temporal ordering of events.

The process of constructing a story comprises a cognitive operation and a linguistic operation. The cognitive operation consists in establishing a mental representation of the experience by carving out the flow of experience into identifiable cognitive items of information which are called events. In the course of the second operation which is linguistic, these items of information must be encoded in verbal form. This encoding follows a linear order because linearity is an essential property of the linguistic sign, and the operation is known as linearization. In narrative, linearization corresponds also to temporal iconicity. The clauses relating the events are arranged sequentially so that the linear presentation of events imitates the purported chronological sequence of events in the real world.

Narratologists make a similar distinction between the ordering of real experience and its linguistic representation by using the two notions of *fabula* and *syuzhet*.[29] The *fabula* is the deep structure or content of a narrative. It is a non-textual and objective given which corresponds to the actual, real-life experience, independently of its manifestation in discourse. It consists of an abstracted set of events in their chronological order as well as the various actors and (sometimes but not necessarily) a spatial location. The *fabula* is a series of chronologically related events which are caused or experienced by actors (Bal 1985: 18). But the *syuzhet* [30] is the sequence of events as actually narrated. It is the *fabula* told and presented in a certain way, with its shifts, digressions, flashbacks, anticipations and all the other narrative techniques. When

29. These were introduced into the theory of narrative by the Russian narratologists of the Formalist school in the 1920s.

30. Called *discours*, that is discourse, by Todorov, 'story' by Mieke Baal, *récit* by Genette. In French structuralism the term used is *histoire*.

the order of events in the *fabula* matches the order of the *syuzhet* the sequence is iconic.

Genette (1972: 77-182) has identified three central aspects of temporal relations holding between the order of events presented in the story (*syuzhet*) and the sequence of events in the *fabula*: order, duration and frequency. Order concerns the relations between the sequence of events in the *fabula* and the order of their occurrence in the presentation of the story in the text. Duration refers to the relation between the amount of time events are supposed to have taken up and the amount of textual encoding given to them in the presentation. Frequency compares how often a particular event occurs in the *fabula* and the number of times it is represented in the text. These distinctions which may combine in the actual presentation of events are important to pinpoint pragmatic features of narrative. Only the question of the ordering of events will be developed here.

Events may be in sequence or not in sequence in the real world. Two events are in sequence when they come one after another in a fixed order. Two events are not in sequence when they take place at the same time, or when the second event is not related in time (or space) to the first. Text time is inescapably linear: it can describe changes or progresses from one stage to another only one at a time. This constitutes the foundation for a sequential organization of events in narration. The fact that there is a correspondence between sequentiality of events in the real world (*fabula*) and sequentiality in the text through linearity is exploited in narration. The unmarked natural ordering of events is iconic sequence: the sequential order of the clauses reporting the events follows the chronology of events as we would expect them to occur in the real world.[31] In other words, the sequence of events of the *syuzhet* mirrors the sequence of events of the *fabula*. However, in the *syuzhet*, we find the author's (or narrator's) created order of events. The author may choose to change and disrupt the default iconical order of events by introducing what Genette has called anachronies (1972: 78-89). An

31. Ong (1982: 147) comments: 'We find ourselves today delighted by exact correspondence between the linear order of elements in discourse and the referential order, the chronological order in the world to which the discourse refers. We like sequence in verbal reports to parallel exactly what we experience or can arrrange to experience.'

anachrony is a departure from the natural and chronological order of events.

Two main types of such dischronologizations are known as 'flashback' or 'retrospection' or 'prolepsis' on the one hand, or 'foreshadowing', 'flashforward', 'anticipation' or 'analepsis' on the other.[32] Flashback and foreshadowing can be combined with the frequency factor. In this case an event can be represented two times in the following ways:

(1) Flashback + repetition: an event (B1) is reported in the normal chronological way; later the event is reported a second time (as B2).
(2) Flashforward + repetition: an event (C1) is reported out of sequence and before its time. Later it is reported in its expected chronological order (C2).

The following diagram summarizes the various temporal possibilities:

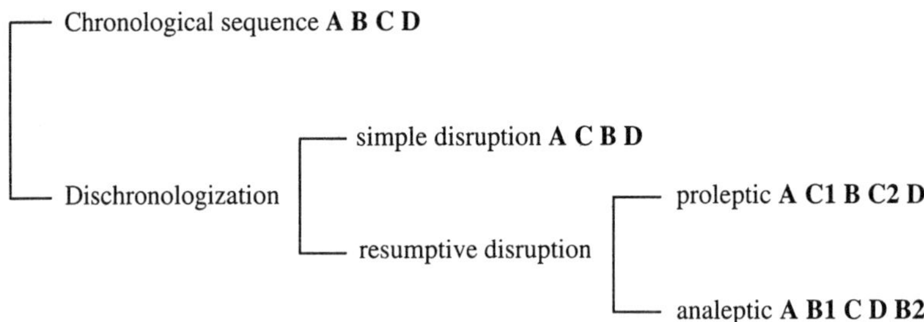

The temporal ordering of events is constrained by the linearity of language. This constraint results in a sequential ordering of events which is iconic and non-problematic as it parallels the order of events in real life. However, a problem arises when the linear constraint has to be applied to that which is inherently non-linear in the real world. States which accompany the actions have to be encoded at a particular point of the linear sequence. Two events may have to be reported as occurring simultaneously.

32. A flashback is a break in the chronology of the narration in which one goes back to an earlier point in time than the point currently reported. A flashforward is a break in the chronology of the narration in which one goes forward in time so that a future event is related 'before its time', that is before the recounting of chronologically intermediate events.

four broad types of prose discourse: narrative, expository, hortatory and procedural. Narrative is distinguished from other genres by its characteristic use of the first or third person, its actor-orientation, its encoding of accomplished time and chronological linkage, and the presence of 'plot'.

Derived from this apparatus, three major analytical tools are used: (1) constituency structure, based on the paragraph; (2) discourse profile which uses the notion of plot; (3) storyline scheme based on clause forms.[2]

a. *Constituency Structure*

The clauses of a text form local groupings which, in turn, constitute larger groups which eventually comprise the major division of the text. Apart from the clause unit, Longacre propounds that any text can be analysed by positing no more units than the discourse ('story' in narrative genre) and the paragraph. Paragraphs are of various types and determined first by the types of discourse in which they are used: a paragraph can be narrative, predictive, hortatory, procedural, expository. The main categories can be further subdivided into various types determined by positing a system of logical relations or notional categories which underline such paragraphs. The notional categories are established on the basis of interclausal relations (1989: 77-149). In the analysis of the Joseph story, Longacre offers a subdivision of the narrative paragraph into nine types: (1) sequence, (2) simple, (3) reason, (4) result, (5) comment, (6) amplification, (7) paraphrase, (8) coordinate, (9) antithetical. A paragraph can be ascribed a degree of ranking according to the relative importance of its clauses measured in terms of the scale described below in (c.).

b. *Discourse Profile*

Discourse profile is a blueprint of the overall structure of a text. For a text to make sense it must be 'going somewhere'. Since Aristotle's study of *mythos* in his *Poetics*, Western rhetoricians have tended to hold to the view that in a story there must be unity of action associated with a particular type of progression. A story develops out of an initial

2. In his analysis of the Joseph story, Longacre also examines in a more traditional way the question of participant reference (1989: 141-57) and the role of dialogue in the story (1989: 158-84).

situation in a chain of actions toward a central event, which is the prime cause of change in the situation. Then, out of a succession of events, the story moves toward a final state of affairs. Such a design, called plot, constitutes for Longacre the discourse profile of a narrative. Plot can be studied at two levels: (1) the deep (semantic) or underlying notional structure which is of a universal type; (2) the surface (grammatical, lexical, phonological) structure manifested by a given text in a given language, more specific in nature.

i. *Discourse Profile: Deep Structure*

On this analysis, the deep structure of narrative has the shape of a plot. Plot development may be traced in narrative discourses at all levels of complexity, from a simple description of one event to a whole story or novel. The specific shape of plot adopted by Longacre is climactic: it goes up from an activating starting point through the stages of complication to the climax of conflict and tension. From there, it rapidly goes to the point of resolution or denouement and its closure. Seven elements of plot structure are identified.

1. EXPOSITION provides a certain amount of essential information about the place, the time and the participants.
2. INCITING MOMENT (or EXPOSITION 2): in this section the problem or the conflict is identified.
3. DEVELOPING CONFLICT: the action is rising with a situation which intensifies or gets worse.

3a. FURTHER COMPLICATION: it delays the climax and so increases the tension.)

4. CLIMAX is the place where everything is coming to a head; the tension reaches a maximum.
5. DENOUEMENT is the critical turning point with the unravelling of the crisis.
6. FINAL SUSPENSE wraps up the loose ends and works out the details of the resolution.
7. CONCLUSION brings the story to an end.

ii. *Discourse Profile: Surface Structure*

The seven stages of plot development constitute slots called episodes. Episode-slots are deep structure elements which may be filled by two of the structural units (constituents) posited by Longacre: the discourse or the paragraph. In a simple story the paragraph is the normal filler (or expounder) of the episode. However, both the discourse and the paragraph are recursive units. An episode slot may be filled by an embedded discourse (a story), that is a story within a story. Or, several layers of paragraphs (embedded paragraphs) might occur within a paragraph. It is also possible that some of the seven elements of the line of development may not be realized by overt features in the surface structure.

An episode can be classified according to its function in the narrative. Three episodes in particular contain marked linguistic features as they are found at places in the development of the plot where they introduce a higher level of tension. They are: (1) the inciting incident, (2) the climax of tension and confrontation, (3) the denouement or resolution. To these moments correspond the following episodes:

1. The stage setting episode is found at the beginning of the narrative. It helps to identify the problem, the conflict or the question. It is effected by staging it, that is presenting it in some appropriate form.
2. The climax of tension (e.g. problem, conflict), often with special surface marking, is found in the episode called peak.
3. The episode which contains the resolution or release of tension is called peak-denouement (abbreviated peak 1). Peak and peak 1 are sometimes followed by an explanatory or confirmatory post-peak episode.

These three elements are the principal constituents of a story. Usually an end episode called closure provides the story with a conclusion. Moreover, Longacre also recognizes the presence of other elements which together with the main episodes make up a narrative discourse:

1. The title is a formula which introduces or identifies genre.
2. The aperture which is often a formulaic phrase or sentence. However, aperture is strictly a feature of surface structure.
3. The pre-peak episodes. A narrative can move directly from the staging of the issue to its resolution. But usually, intermediate episodes are used to clarify the issue, to highlight its significance. These pre-peak episodes may be inserted to delay the resolution and so to increase tension. Among the pre-peak episodes, the inciting incident episode gets the action going.
4. Finis or terminus is a formulaic phrase or sentence closing the story. Like aperture this is also strictly a feature of surface structure.

iii. *Discourse Profile and Morpho-Syntactic Marking*

Particular linguistic devices are used in the surface structure actualization to signal the crucial deep level elements.[3] The Peak-Episode particularly is described as a 'zone of turbulence'. Its surface structure is an actualization of the Climax or the Denouement, the two points of highest tension in a narrative. As a result, Peaking is always marked so as to draw special attention to the high point of the story. This is effected by various means, but particularly by changes in the grammar or by characteristic participant references. Among the devices most commonly used in the world's languages to highlight the climax of a story, Longacre lists the following (1983: 25-38; 1990: 8-9):

1. Augmented sequence: the storyline which consists of sequential and punctiliar events/actions undergoes some kind of rhetorical underlining such as restatement of information in parallelisms, paraphrases or tautologies. A series of fast-moving actions may be mentioned or detailed actions may be reported which would not normally be described.

2. Maximum interlacing of participant reference. Usually the handling of participants takes two forms: the assembling of all the characters or the removing of all the participants so as to leave the stage to the main characters only. If more participants are on stage this results in an increased use of explicit methods of participant tracking such as nouns and the use of specific personal pronouns (first person). There also might be a change of vantage point, for example a change in the focal person in the story. These elements produce a sense of heightened vividness.

3. Immediacy: the author transports their audience more directly into the world of the story through the use of various devices such as a shift in person (from third person singular to first person plural), a sudden move from narrative to pseudo-dialogue, to dialogue or to drama. Asyndetic coordination is a preferred way of connecting peak-marking clauses. Other devices include a shift to the historical present, the addition of extra background material and the use of onomatopeia, words which sound like their referents.

3. This claim is based on Longacre's examination of a large number of narratives in different languages. His most recent study (1990) covers languages spoken in Ethiopia, Sudan, and Niger-Congo.

c. *Storyline Scheme*

For Longacre, Classical Hebrew is a language which, in narratives, has storyline forms and non-storyline forms.[4] The description of the imperfect with waw consecutive (vayyiqtol) as a narrative tense, which is found in the GKC grammar (1910: 326) serves as a point of departure for the analysis (Longacre 1989: 64). The storyline or backbone of a narrative is marked grammatically by clauses using a vayyiqtol verb This means that the typical word order of main line clauses is VSO. Other non-storyline forms occur which encode various degrees of departure from the storyline (1989: 80-82). These forms can be arranged in a diagram in their order of progressive degree of departure from the storyline. A verb ranking system of five bands in which the levels are arranged on a cline from the most dynamic (event-line) verbal/clausal forms to the most static ones is thus created.[5]

Band 1:
Story line * vayyiqtol (preterite)
Band 2:
Backgrounded * perfect
Actions * noun + perfect
Band 3:
Backgrounded * hinneh + participle
Activities * participle
* noun + participle
Band 4
Setting * preterite of *hāyā*
* perfect *hāyā*
* nominal clause
* existential clause with *yēš*
Band 5 * negation of verb clause: irrealis

A narrative discourse is thus constituted of a cluster of clause types characterized by diverse tense/aspect/mood verb forms. The vayyiqtol form of the verb predominates with its storytelling function. It is called

4. Longacre (1976: 239) writes: 'The backbone of this narrative is carried here as in Hebrew prose narrative in general by waw plus prefixal verb—which is increasingly recognized as a special narrative tense for Hebrew.' Similarly in Longacre 1983: 17.

5. According to Longacre (1992a: 179) 'these various forms do not constitute a haphazard conglomeration, but rather a structured scheme in which ever lower positions in the scheme reflect progressive degrees of departure from the story line preterites.'

the preterite. Clauses with a verb in the perfect have a secondary function: they mark backgrounded actions. As for clauses with a participle, they mark backgrounded activities. Other forms, such as nominal, equational and existential clauses, further flesh out the story and are assigned in varying degrees to the background.

Vayyiqtol verbs are 'punctiliar' and 'sequential'[6] and have the important property of advancing the progress of a narrative. Narrative clauses in which such verbs are found report events[7] in the same order as their succession in the real world. Storyline clauses with their preterite vayyiqtol verbs also serve to build various kinds of narrative paragraphs.

d. *Discourse Typology*

The three components described—constituency structure, discourse profile and storyline form—are discourse-specific and so require that a typology of discourse be established before the analysis can start.

Main lines of development differ from discourse type to discourse type. It must be expected that a narrative storyline will show different verbal forms and clausal forms than the forms used in the line of procedure of a procedural discourse or in the line of exhortation in a hortatory discourse. A given temporal form can have a quite different function according to the type of discourse in which it is used.

Similarly, the notion of discourse profile, based on the fact that a text is 'going somewhere', will vary from one type of discourse to another. The characteristic profile of narrative is the plot structure with its climax and denouement; another kind of discourse, such as expository, will have a different profile, with different components making up the profile, and a distinctive marking of these components.

e. *Observations*

The theoretical framework offered by Longacre is certainly impressive in its scope. By using various constructs Longacre hopes to account for

6. Longacre 1989: 59 explains: 'Here the waw-consecutive imperfect is seen to be mainline in that it is punctiliar and sequential in function.' Elsewhere in his study, discussing the narrative paragraph, Longacre writes: 'the essence of a narrative paragraph is reporting events in temporal order' (1989: 90).

7. It is to be noticed that these 'Preterite' verbal forms represent happenings of all types: motions, actions, cognitive events, speech acts, and even events which have no voluntary agent (of the type *Sam had a flat tyre*).

most linguistic aspects of narrative. Moreover, these constructs seem to be firmly established through reference to other languages.[8] However, in spite of the framework's comprehensiveness, it will be shown that the validity of some of its components is questionable. Moreover, when they are applied to Old Hebrew stories, these components fail to provide a correct account of some linguistic features of these texts. Some language forms are forced into the straitjacket of the constructs, or counter-examples are simply ignored. The next sections will be devoted to a critical appraisal of Longacre's theoretical framework with a focus on its two central structures: plot and storyline. Elements missing from Longacre's analyses will also be examined.

2. *Plot as an Analytical Construct*

Longacre claims that a plot-like discourse profile explains some grammatical constructions and other linguistic features in stories. In so doing, he makes several assumptions which must be examined:

(1) Story profile (deep structure) has a climactic shape and is a universal configuration to which all narrative stretches of texts conform.
(2) Climactic plot is an organizational device which is objectively identifiable.
(3) Climactic plot is a structure in the sense that predictive statements can be made about it.

a. *Story Profile and Climactic Plot*

Longacre uses the classical view of plot derived from the description of Greek tragedy presented by Aristotle (*Poetics* 1451b-1452b). Aristotle identified three essential elements: *peripeteia,* a reversal of the hero's fortune from good to bad, *anagnorisis*, the recognition of a change such as the coming to light of a secret, and *catastrophe*, the final downfall of the hero. Emplotment (*muthos*) has thus a double aspect: (a) it is an organization of events which has a recognized beginning, middle and end; (b) it is an organization centering on conflict.

8. The volume edited by Longacre (1990) contains analyses of various African languages, which make use of Longacre's constructs. The scholarly journal *Optat* 4 (1990) offers analyses of various Indo-Arian and Dravidian languages from the same perspective.

A theory of plot which has had a great influence on literary studies over the last hundred years is the 'pyramidal description' proposed, for example, by the German critic Gustav Freitag.[9] A five-act play has to have a pyramidal shape with action arising from the *introduction*, leading to *climax* and then falling away to *catastrophe.* Between the *introduction* (*exposition*) and *climax, complication* provides the highly dramatic moment of the exciting moment. Freitag's pyramid displays the following elements:

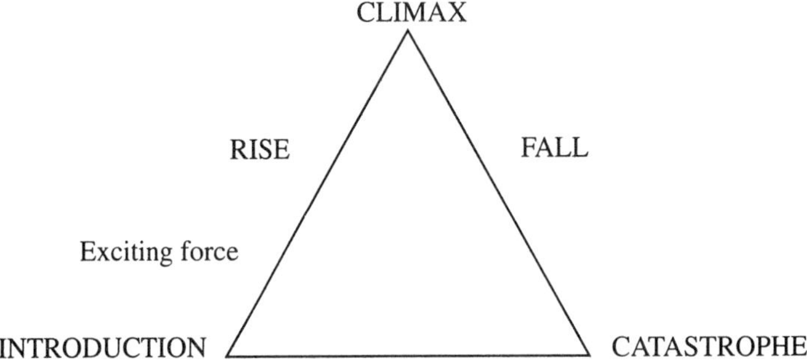

This tidy description of plot has been put to good use by literary critics and novelists. As an organizing principle, plot imposes a special movement to narrative which is progression through tension. Plot hints at a complication, an evolving conflict, an intrigue, a web of problems which requires a solution or a denouement. The denouement is characteristically dialectic: a shift takes place. There is a change in the pace of events from ambiguity or enigma to clarity or consciousness. As such, the denouement is a surprising and tension-filled moment. For many writers, this moment of crisis is the hub of every plot. It is, in fact, the real test of the quality of the work. The effect of emplotment is rhetorical in nature: it creates and maintains interest. Plot is a configuration which appeals to a wide general readership as the closely plotted traditional British detective story testifies. It can be described as a dramatic ordering of events.

b. *The Notion of Emplotment*

By choosing climactic plot as his analytical model, Longacre derives his deep structure from highly plotted stories. It is true that, according

9. Gustav Freitag (1816-1899) describes his diagrammatic representation of the structure of a tragedy in his *Technique of the Drama* (trans. Elias J. MacEwan; Chicago: Scott, 1894).

to some aesthetic standards of Western literature, what makes a 'good' story is the presence of a strong climactic plot. However, it would be a mistake to consider such a preference as a universal rule and to establish it as a model. First, not all stories are highly plotted. They display various degrees of emplotment, from the highly plotted modern detective story to the story with a tenuous plot. Certain authors have even questioned the notion of plot in narrative, suggesting that non-plotted stories do exist.[10] Similarly, the stories of the Hebrew Bible display various degrees of emplotment as several classification schemes offered by biblical scholars show. Coats (1985: 63-5), for example, divides Old Hebrew narratives into three groups:

(1) Narratives whose only goal is to report events in their proper sequence (anecdote, report).

(2) Narratives whose purpose is to recount events in an interesting way and which are controlled by a plot pattern, such as the tale and the novella. The tale has a limited number of characters, a single scene and a simple plot. It is found in abundance in Genesis: Gen. 2.4b–3.24; 4.1-16; 11.1-9; 16.1-16; 18.1-15; 21.1-21; 12.9–13.1; 19.1-29; 20.1-18; 21.22-34; 26.1-17; 26.34–28.9; 34.1-31. The novella is more complex and may use sub-plots: Gen. 13–14; 18–19; 38.1-30 (Coats 1983: 8, 319).

(3) Narratives which focus on the characterization of a central participant and not the events. In the legend the progression is not ensured by plot but by the highlighting of some particular characteristic of the hero. Thus the story in Genesis 22 spotlights the obedience of Abraham from various angles without resorting to tension and resolution. The important point here is that types 1 and 3 are not shaped by the plot pattern suggested by Longacre and, as a result, the deep structure in question would not apply to such texts.

c. *The Question of Subjectivity*

The second difficulty is the following: accepting that stories have a plot configuration, is such a configuration identifiable in the text with a

10. Earl Miner (1990: 148) comments: 'As someone who finds great satisfaction in plotted narratives, I think it has been slighted in discussions of narrative. But I cannot persuade myself that plot is necessary to narrative.'

degree of certainty high enough to produce a reliable analysis? The question of plot as a linguistic tool is linked to the possibility of identifiying the pattern in a text to produce precise predictive statements on the linguistic plane. In highly plotted stories, plot may be readily identifiable. The case is more complicated with Old Hebrew narratives.

First, there is the problem of determining story boundaries. The analytical use of plot presupposes that one can identify confidently the beginning, the middle and the end of a story. The boundaries of the story of Jonah, Esther or Ruth present no problem because they are self-contained stories. But in the books of Genesis or the historical books of Samuel and Kings, successive stories have often overlapping parts. For example, one episode might function as the end of a story but also as the beginning of another one.[11] Elsewhere, it often happens that one story is part of a larger narrative development.[12]

A second problem arises from the fact that even if a plot pattern is used, the exact shape of the pattern in the text is not always clearly identifiable. Often the plot is thin or even partial. Despite many studies of the story of Jonah, its plot has not been clearly elucidated. There is still debate as to where the peak of the story is and what constitutes its solution or resolution. Longacre identifies a plot in the Joseph story (Gen. 37–50) but what exactly is the plot of the Jacob cycle (Gen. 25.19–35.22) or the Abraham narrative (Gen. 12–25)? On the story of Ruth, which is short, Barbara Green comments: 'Though the story is judged fairly simple as biblical narrative goes, there is still no clear consensus on the plot even after a number of articles—some recent—dealing with this topic' (1982: 55). Similarly, Joel Rosenberg wonders whether one can speak of a story of Abraham.[13] Observations such as

11. Gunn and Fewell (1993: 112) mention the clear example of 1 Kgs 1–2 which might be seen as the end of David's story or the introduction to Solomon's story.

12. The story of how Abraham had a son by his wife's maidservant Hagar and of how Hagar fled into the desert from Sarah's wrath (Gen. 16.1-16) is in fact an episode in the story of God's promise of an heir to Abraham.

13. In his study 'Is There a Story of Abraham?' Rosenberg writes: 'Gen. 12–25 is not one but many kinds of literature. By this reckoning, there is not a single Abraham *story*, but *an anthology* of Abraham stories, redactionally doctored with great ingenuity to form roughly continuous chronology, but bearing little true continuity, and presuming no unified performance context' (1986: 70).

these plunge us in the current literary debate about narrative shape as perceived by the reader. Toolan comments:

> Perceiving non-random connectedness in a sequence of events is the prerogative of the addressee: it is idle for anyone else (e.g. a teller) to insist that there is a narrative if the addressee just doesn't see it as one. In this respect at least, the ultimate authority for ratifying a text as a narrative rests not with the teller but with the perceiver/addressee (1988: 8).

These observations apply to the question of plot in biblical stories.[14] The subjective character of plot analysis becomes apparent when one compares Longacre's description of the plot of the Joseph's story with the analysis of the plot provided by W. Lee Humphreys.[15] The following table makes plain the differences in the determination of the episodes of the story (the chapters refer to Genesis):

	Exposit.	Complic.	Interludes	Furth.cpl.	Resolut.	Denouement	Concl.
Humphreys	37.1-4	37.5-36	38–41	42–44	45.1-15	45.16–50.21	50.22-26
Longacre	37.2-36		41.1-57	42.1-38	43; 44; 45		
	Incit.incid.		Climax	Inter-peak	Denouem.		

Longacre's study of the Flood story (Gen. 6.9–9.17) produces the same uncertainties when the results are compared to another description of the discourse profile given by Allen Ross.[16] Whereas Longacre identifies the traditional plot pattern with an action peak (crisis), Ross views the account of the flood as arranged according to a pattern of antithetical paralleling (chiasmus) of thematic ideas. The symmetrical pattern of Ross (A-B-C-D-E-E'-D'-C'-B'-A') is compared to Longacre's plot profile in the following table.

14. As noticed by Gunn and Fewell (1993: 107): 'Repeated stories remind us that neither plot nor the reading of plot is always linear. Plots do not always move neatly from the problem to complication to resolution. They are not always oriented toward some final goal. Meaning is not always the product of cause and effect or of chronological ordering. Meaning sometimes emerges through association—and association is often in the eye of the beholder.'

15. Longacre (1989: 22-41, 210-310) and Humphreys (1988: 22-67) should be consulted for details.

16. See Longacre (1976: 235-61; 1985: 169-85) and Ross (1988: 190-91) for details.

Ross			*Longacre*		
			6.5-8	Preview	God's decision
Generations of Noah	Title	6.9a	6.9-12	Stage	Noah and world conditions
Description of Noah	Introd.	6.9-10			
God's decision	A	6.11-13			
Noah builds an ark	B	6.14-22	6.13-22	Episode P-1	The ark
Command to enter ark	C	7.1-9	7.1-10	Episode P-2	Noah enters ark
Flood begins	D	7.10-16	7.11-16	Episode P-3	Flood begins
Flood prevails	E	7.17-24	7.17-24	PEAK Crisis	Flood prevails
Flood recedes	E'	8.1b-5	8.1-5	Episode P+1	Receding waters
The earth dries	D'	8.6-14	8.6-12	Episode P+2	Noah sends birds
Noah leaves the ark	C'	8.15-19	8.13-19	Episode P+3	Leaving the ark
Noah builds altar	B'	8.20	8.20-22	Episode P+4	Sacrifice to God
God's decision	A'	8.21-22			
			9.1-17	Secondary peak: Final rise	Blessing+covenant

Among the many differences, a particularly significant one is that, for Ross, sections E and E' constitute the centre of the story, whereas for Longacre Ross's E section only represents the peak of the story. These examples confirm Gunn and Fewell's comment: 'Defining the boundary of a single narrative is as much a product of the reader's desire for reconstruction as it is the product of the narrator's art' (1993: 113).

One has to go further and say that subjectivity also affects the determination of the function of an episode in a story. Genesis 12.10-20 is the story of how Abram went to Egypt and what happened there to him and to his wife Sarai. Whereas Van Seters identifies the text as a typical unit of an oral tale,[17] Thompson writes: 'Without denying that Genesis 12 may have many characteristics similar to those found in oral tales, I hardly see this structure in the story of Genesis. The famine is not the

17. For Van Seters (1975: 167-191), the units are 'the basic structural requirements of Olrik's laws' (p. 169), that is (1) crisis: the famine; (2) plan: Sarai will pretend she is Abram's sister; (3) execution (+ complication): Sarah is taken into Pharaoh's harem; (4) outside intervention: God punishes Pharaoh; (5) consequences: Abram becomes rich.

crisis of the ensuing narrative plot' (1987: 53).[18]

d. *Story Patterns and Composition*

Climactic plot may be used as an effective rhetorical device designed to create interest in the reader or hearer, to 'hook them' as it were. It gives a story a greater degree of 'tellability ' or 'narrativity', as Prince says:

> A narrative depicting a conflict of some kind should function better narratively than one depicting no conflict at all ... 'The cat sat on the mat' is certainly not without interest but 'The cat sat on the dog's mat' may be the beginning of a good story (1982: 145).[19]

Plot is primarily a gripping pattern of action, but an author may choose to capture the attention of his readers by using other compositional patterns whose rhetorical purpose would be none the less effective. Advocating a literary approach to the Hebrew Bible, authors such as Alter (1981), Fokkelman (1975), Bar-Efrat (1989), Berlin (1983) and many others have identified various textual patterns in the extended stories as well as the shorter ones. In long stories, such as the 'family saga' of Genesis (the stories of Abraham, Isaac or Jacob) or the story of King David, which are made out of originally disparate material, one important role of the patterns is to hold together the otherwise heterogeneous mixes of stories, legends, chronicles, lists and so on[20] by inserting them into a unified structure. In addition, they also serve to present stories in a rhetorically effective way. As such, they have been

18. Thompson further explains (pp. 53-54): 'The plot function of the famine is initiatory only. The plot crisis is the danger which is involved in travelling as a *ger*. The plan and its execution follow, but there is no hint in the text that this is to forestalling suitors; *quite the contrary!* The plan has two aims: 'that it may go well with me because of you', and that Abram's life may be spared ... The story plot is not simple, but it is straightforward ... Van Seter's fifth element (i.e. consequences) has nothing to do with the conclusion of the tale as told in Genesis 12.'

19. Prince also comments (p. 147): 'There is a widespread agreement about the fact that different narratives have different degrees of narrativity, that some are more narrative than others, as it were, and "tell a better story".'

20. To give an illustration, Robert Cohn (1985: 24) analysing the story of King Jeroboam writes: 'The account of the rise and fall of king Jeroboam I (1 Kgs 11.26–14.20) offers a fine example of such composite artistry. Although the narrative is manifestly a compilation of several sources, it bears the marks of a talented author who, by ordering and editing, created a unified story.'

described as literary[21] devices. In the short self-contained stories, such as the story of the tower of Babel (Gen. 11.1-9), recognizable patterns are also present, which have primarily rhetorical functions such as focusing attention through repetition.

Many literary studies have shown that a common patterning device is correspondence between units. A unit (A) is mirrored in a unit (A'). The units might be formal units, such as words, phrases, sentences; literary components such as a scene (e.g. arrival of guests; sending of messengers; offering of sacrifice) or a motif [22] (e.g. unusual birth of the hero; strife between two wives), or more general elements such as a theme,[23] whether literary or religious (e.g. the wrath of God, death, deception, friendship). While the paired elements must have a relation to each other, that relation is not necessarily one of identity or similarity. Opposites can be paired too. The pairing of units does not take place with each unit following the other one in a linear way (A-A', B-B', C-C'). Rather, units are first gathered together in a panel (A-B-C-D) and then repeated in a second panel. This takes place in a normal or an inverted order (D-C-B-A). Exum has identified in the Samson story (Judges 13–16) an example of a panel of units repeated in normal order. The chart shows how ch. 14 balances ch. 15 (1981: 3-29).[24]

21. The proponents of the literary approach seek to show that the authors of the narratives were not mere chroniclers of catalogues of battles or genealogies, but skilled literary artists who used creatively deliberate and rather sophisticated artistic strategies such as wordplays, prosodic tricks or the manipulation of narrative formula. Their purpose was not merely aesthetic but also communicative. Thus tensions, inconsistencies, contradictions between the components of an extended story are viewed as deliberate artistic strategy on the part of the author. These literary strategies add a dimension in terms of the author's message. Textual patterns are only one aspect of narrative artistry.

22. A motif is a small and precise element in a story or tale which persists and is recurrent with its specific features in the literary or folkloric tradition of a particular group.

23. A theme is a more abstract and more general unit than a motif. As such a theme might comprise several motifs. A theme of the story of Jacob is deception. But 'stones' are a motif of the same story.

24. Exum writes (p. 9): 'In terms of their themes and the literary motifs which express them, chs. 14–15 and 16 are symmetrical. Coexistent and coterminous with this thematic symmetry between 14–15 and 16 is another pattern of organization in the saga according to which ch. 13 balances ch. 16 while ch. 14 corresponds to ch. 15.'

		Judges 14			*Judges 15*
1-4	a)	Conversation: Samson–his parents	1-3	a')	Conversation: Samson–wife's father
	b)	Parental objection		b')	Parental objection
	c)	To choose another woman.		c')	To choose another woman.
5-6		Samson refuses.	4-6		Samson refuses.
7-9 10-20	d)	Action involving an animal (lion) calling for prowess on Samson's part.	 6-8 9-17	d')	Action involving an animal (foxes) calling for prowess on Samson's part.
	e)	Action involving honey: generous act.		e')	Action involving retaliation: vicious act.
	f')	Conversations: Samson and Philistines; Samson–woman.		f')	Conversation: Men of Judah and Philistines.
	g)	Philistines threaten third party in order to gain advantage over Samson.		b)	Philistines threaten third party in order to gain advantage over Samson.
	h)	Spirit of Yahweh comes upon Samson; he defeats the Philistines.		c)	Spirit of Yahweh comes upon Samson; he defeats the Philistines.

Landes (1967: 16) points out a similar construction in the book of Jonah where one panel (Jon. 1.17–2.10) is parallel to another (Jon. 4.1-11). He also writes that chs. 1 and 2, as well as 3 and 4, exhibit several parallel motifs. When the second panel repeats the units in an inverted order the construction takes the form of a chiasmus. Conroy (1978: 89-90) argues that the account of Absalom's revolt (2 Sam. 15–20) is organized chiastically, as illustrated below:

A. Rebellion breaks out	15.1–12
B. The king's flight: meeting scenes	15.13–16.14
C. Clash of counsellors	16.15–17.23
C'. Clash of armies	17.24–19.9
B'. The king's return: meeting scenes	19.9-41
A'. The final stirrings of rebellion are crushed	19.42–20.22

To cite a few other examples, Gammie (1979: 121) writes that the Jacob cycle (Gen. 25–36) is arranged in a chiastic pattern according to its themes. Gooding (1982: 74) points out to the chiastic design of the Gideon story (Judg. 6–7) and Radday (1981: 64) to the chiastic arrangement of the twelve episodes of the life of Elijah (1 Kgs 17.1–2 Kgs 2.18).

A variant of chiasmus organizes the symmetry around an isolated central unit: A-B-C-*D*-C-B-A. Such a pattern may be labelled a concentric pattern. In Amit's description of the structure of the story of Ehud (Judg. 3.12-30), the basic units are scenes (1989: 100-103). They are arranged symmetrically around a center as shown in the diagram:

A. Exposition–the oppression: a continuing situation	vv. 12-15
B. The tricky dagger	v. 16
C. The tricky tribute offering	vv. 17-18
The murder	vv. 19-23
C'. The trick of fooling the servants	vv. 24-25
B'. The war trick	vv. 26-29
A'. End–eighty peaceful years: a continuing situation	v. 30

Savran (1987: 148) proposes that a concentric structure lies behind the two books of Kings.[25] The great themes are arranged as illustrated below:

A. Solomon/United Monarchy	1 Kgs 1.1–11.25
B. Jeroboam/Rehoboam; division of the kingdom	1 Kgs 11.26–14.31
C. Kings of Judah/Israel	1 Kgs 15.1–16.22
D. *Omride dynasty: rise and fall of Baal cult in of Judah/Israel*	1 Kgs 16.23–2 Kgs 12
C'. Kings of Judah/Israel	2 Kgs 13–16
B'. Fall of Northern Kingdom	2 Kgs 17
A'. Kingdom of Judah	2 Kgs 18–25

Many other studies of this kind show that it would be a mistake to restrict oneself to climactic plot to describe Old Hebrew story organization.[26]

Some scholars, particularly ethnologists and folklorists, view plot as an intrinsic element which belongs to some traditional stories and

25. Radday (1981: 62), on the other hand, prefers a concentric structure for the same two books, with 29 chapters ('the divided kingdom', 1 Kgs 12–2 Kgs 17) being the centrepiece.

26. As an illustrative sample, mention may be made of the following studies. Ridout (1974: 81) identifies a concentric structure in the the story of the rape of Tamar (2 Sam. 13.1-22); Kikawada (1974: 19) and Fishbane (1979: 36) in the story of the tower of Babel (Gen. 11.1-9); Radday (1981: 102) in the story of Joseph (Gen. 37–50); Cohn (1985: 24-25) in the story of King Jeroboam (1 Kgs 11.26–14.20); Long (1985: 405-16) in the story of the war betweeen King Ahab and King Ben-Hadad; Radday (1981: 62) and Frisch (1991: 10, 13) in the story of King Solomon (1 Kgs 1–12.24), with, significantly, the building of the temple as a focal point. For Gunn (1987: 110-11) a concentric structure unites two books (Joshua 23–24 and Judges 1–2.10), in the account of Judah and Benjamin.

which depends upon cultural scripts. Thus the tale of Little Riding Hood has an inbuilt plot. Other scholars see plot rather as a special arrangement and deployment of a story for rhetorical effects. It is seen more as a strategy developed in relation to a particular situation. On this view, climactic plot is a favourite compositional pattern because it offers with one mighty stroke the movement necessary for a gripping story. But what is common is not therefore necessary. Movement and the sense of completion can be provided through other arrangements. Longacre's mistake is to decide that a particular narrative configuration should serve as a universal analytical construct. Longacre's absolute reliance on one pattern excludes the possibility of other textual patterns being used in the composition of narrative texts.

It seems also important not to ignore the possible influence of orality on biblical stories. A number of biblical scholars would agree with Culley's description:

> I am not arguing that the Hebrew Bible, or any particular part of it, is folklore as such or stems directly from oral tradition, only that the Bible is *like* this kind of material in some important ways and may even have roots in it (1993: 20).

The question of the orality of biblical texts is admittedly an area fraught with uncertainties as we know little about how the material came into existence. But some scholars, using the results of the work of Lord (1960) on the oral narrative poetry of Serbo-Croatian singers, have identified oral features in the texts, such as compositional theme (journeys, feasts, mourning, etc.), traditional characters, repetition of sequences (type-scenes), basic story patterns (birth of the hero, triumph of the hero, etc.). Culley (1990, 1992) finds evidence of a traditional oral style in the repeated use of patterns of action or episodes which can be adapted or elaborated. Niditch (1987) has identified stock folktale characters such as underdogs and tricksters. Gunn (1974, 1976) hints at posssible links between compositional patterns and oral traditional composition.[27] Examining the oral characteristics of the story of the

27. He writes (1974: 286): 'A number of passages in the narrative of Judges and Samuel may be shown to exhibit an interesting measure of conventionality or stereotyping. This characteristic, it will be argued, is not only likely to reflect traditional composition but also quite possibly *oral* traditional composition.' In his 1976 article Gunn examines a number of other passages in the Succession Narrative (2 Sam. 9–20 and 1 Kgs 1–2) which are composed according to stereotypes. He classifies this material as traditional and thinks that it is 'quite likely' that it derives

Garden of Eden (Gen. 2.4b–3.24), Howard Wallace says that poetical elements such as chiasm, parallelism, euphony (repetition of words and letters) seem to point to the persistence of oral techniques of composition and oral style in the early written works.[28] Ronald Hendel (1987: 167) focuses on various episodes (birth story, revelation story, life of a hero) of the Jacob narrative (Genesis 27–36) in order to identify the oral substratum of this material. He concludes that the similarity between the stories forming the Jacob's cycle and other stories of the ancient Near East has its basis in 'the practice of storytelling that existed in the ancient world'.[29]

The influence of orality on the shaping of biblical stories seems then to be confirmed by these descriptions of compositional techniques and patterns. Such studies demonstrate the need to examine further the oral residue in the written stories. If the oral transmission stage had a significant impact on the scribal stage, then one could expect that many more specific oral characteristics would be found in the stories, even if they were set down in writing. Ong observes that the book of Genesis as a whole, with its long linear temporal sequence, would be impossible without writing: it belongs to a literary genre. But he points out that 'the paratactic mode of utterance in Genesis remains almost purely oral' (1981: 68 and 1982: 37-39). In the oral tradition, action succeeds action in an endless chain and the grammatical link of event to event is the general coordinator *and*. Oral stories are additive and aggregative with a great deal of lexical repetition. Ong further comments that 'a new technology of the word reinforces the old while at the same time

from oral tradition, although he cannot point 'to a particular compositional technique that is ... characteristically oral' (p. 209).

28. Wallace (1985: 43). Wallace highlights the fact that the transition from an oral literary stage to a written one is slow. This fact is backed up by various studies on Norse sagas, Tudor prose and early English literature. As a result, written style in its early stages is influenced by oral style: 'Since there is a long period of time before the full development of a written style of literary composition in a society where writing is introduced, early efforts at written composition will frequently reveal traits of oral compositional style. This is particularly the case when the writer is recording traditional material which he is accustomed to hearing in the traditional style. Also in the early stages of the development of written literature, the only standards of compositional technique known are oral ones' (p. 46).

29. Hendel explains (1987: 167): 'Stories of renowned figures were passed along, in ever changing form from generation to generation, from village to village, from mouth to mouth.'

transforming it' (1982: 153). A scribe writing a story would simply transcribe an oral performance since no other compositional devices were yet known. Moreover, writing would even accentuate the oral techniques of composition, since the new medium would enable the scribe to craft more carefully the oral story. These observations are of crucial importance for a correct understanding of compositional patterns in biblical stories. In an oral culture, compositional devices are shaped by the requirements of retention and recall of knowledge. These call for special noetic structures and procedures different from the ones needed in literate cultures. They are largely based on formulaicity and repetition and so affect the way a story is told. Ong makes an important observation for my discussion on plot: 'One of the places where oral noetic structures and procedures manifest themselves most spectacularly is in their effect on narrative plot, which in an oral culture is not quite what we take plot typically to be' (1982: 141). He further comments that 'an oral culture has no experience of a lengthy, epic-size, or novel-size climactic linear plot. It cannot organize even shorter narrative in the studious, relentless climactic way that readers of literature for the past 200 years have learned more and more to expect' (1982: 143).

All these findings call seriously into question the place and methodological role Longacre ascribes to plot in the organization of biblical stories. Tension and denouement are by no means the indispensable and universal ingredients of a story. Other compositional devices, derived from the needs of an orally effective and relevant presentation of events, are still present in many stories.

e. *Plot as a Linguistic Structure*

On a linguistic level, Longacre claims for plot the status of a structure, that is, a pattern of organization such that predictive linguistic or grammatical statements can be based on it: 'Variation in a text is not random but motivated. In brief, where the author has a choice in regard to a lexical item or a grammatical construction, his particular choice is motivated by pragmatic concerns of discourse structure' (Longacre 1989: xiii).

The discourse is seen as a grammatical level[30] like the clause or the sentence, with plot as its structure. The plot-structure creates the seven episode-slots which are filled by various paragraph types or embedded

30. Significantly, Longacre's theoretical work is entitled *A Grammar of Discourse*.

narratives and it also causes certain filler-paragraphs to be linguistically marked when they expound crucial episodes.[31]

In the light of all the observations made about the notion of plot in Old Hebrew stories, one is entitled to have doubts about the analytical validity of such a structure. Climactic plot has not the universality and clarity Longacre claims it has. All narratives are not recognizably organized in this way. Moreover, they may vary from highly plotted to tenuously plotted texts. Plot cannot be categorized as a linguistic structure because of its inbuilt instability and irregularity. To claim that such a configuration with its inherent elusiveness can function as a structural parameter for the determination of paragraph constituents is a mistake.

The linguist Hoey writes: 'structural statements claim to say what is possible; organizational statements claim to describe what is done' (1991: 193-94). On the basis of this comment, it is preferable and more accurate to hold with Hoey to an 'organizational' view of texts. Speakers and writers provide patterns in narrative texts which hearers and readers are able to perceive. These patterns are not obligatory and they may be of various types, with some more common and popular than others. They may vary from one genre to another, or from one text to another, and are culturally conditioned. But these patterns (a) cannot be construed as linguistic structures; and (b) do not exercise a grammatical/syntactic constraint on clauses or paragraphs.

f. *Peaking*

One of the goals of Longacre's framework is to point to some distinctive linguistic facts marking particular sections of a story.[32] Longacre distinguishes three types of devices used to mark 'peak' described as a 'zone of turbulence': augmented sequence, immediacy and maximum interlacing of participant reference (1983: 25-38). Augmented sequence is particularly relevant for Hebrew narratives. In it, the normal routine storyline is made to shift to a different pace through the use of means such as paraphrase of action, detailed description of action or

31. The paragraph types are described in Longacre (1989: 83-118).

32. Longacre (1989: 18-19) writes: 'It has been my contention for several years now that the cumulative development(s) of a discourse usually manifests itself in certain grammatico-lexical characteristics. I have therefore referred to *peak-marking features* ... It (i.e. the peak) represents a kind of gear shift in the dynamic flow of discourse ... In describing a text we can draw its profile once we identify its peak(s).'

fast-moving series of actions. All these devices result in a high use of verbs which Longacre calls 'a rush of vav consecutives'.[33] The problem with considering this augmented flow of waw consecutives as marking the peak of a story is that it is a criteria too general to be really useful. How many vayyiqtol must appear in sequence in order to indicate the marking of peak? It is easy to point to long sequences of vayyiqtol in many narratives which do not mark peaking. Longacre analyses Gen. 44.1-13, which describes how Joseph's cup is discovered in Benjamin's sack, as a peak episode. The crisis is underlined by a flow of waw consecutive verbs (1989: 37, 290-91):

> and they hastened
> and they lowered (each man) his sack
> and he searched
> and the cup was found in the sack of Benjamin
> and they rent their clothes
> and they loaded each man his donkey
> and they returned to the city.

However, in 2 Sam. 12.20, the end of David's period of mourning after the death of his son is described by a chain of ten waw consecutive verbs, when there is no question of there being a crisis:

> and David rose from the ground
> and he washed
> and he anointed himself
> and he changed his clothes
> and he went into the temple of Yahweh
> and he worshipped
> and he went to his house
> and he asked
> and they set food before him
> and he ate.

The comparison of these two extracts shows that it is not the use of long sequence of waw consecutive verbs per se which is a marking feature of

33. For the Joseph story, see Longacre (1989: 34-35, 37-39). See also, for example, Longacre (1989: 27, par. 3.1.5.) which analyses ch. 41 considered as a peak episode with 'special structural features'. The structural marking of peak in this chapter is detailed on p. 34. There, Longacre says that a narrative expounds this peak (embedded discourse). Within this narrative the following features of the peak episode are noted: a sandwich structure which is 'storyline–dialogue–storyline'; a crowded action line; a rush of waw-consecutives. Similarly the peak-episode, i.e. denouement (chs. 43–45), discussed p. 28, par. 3.1.7. and detailed p. 37, par. 3.2.7.

the peak of a story, but rather some special properties of the sequence of clauses, or the semantics of the verbs used. The same criticism could be addressed to the marking property of dialogue, classified by Longacre under immediacy. Dialogue is prevalent in biblical stories, and if it is the case that dialogues are peak-marking devices, it must be some special properties of these dialogues which qualify them as peak-marking devices.

g. *Conclusion*

In the end, the inadequacy of profile analysis, with its two central notions of plot and peak, lies in an excessive reliance on formal criteria to determine the construction of discourse. The following example shows how the presence of a formal marking can override the semantics of a passage in Longacre's analysis of a text.

In Gen. 39.1-12, Longacre discerns two episodes (Episode 2 and 3) on the basis of the presence, at the beginning of Episode 3, of the elements *way^{e}hî* + temporal phrase (*and it happened after these things*) which 'in general marks an episode break in Hebrew narrative' (1989: 224-27). Episode 2 describes Joseph's rise to a position of trust in Potiphar's house. Episode 3 is the account of Joseph's sexual harassment by Potiphar's wife. Longacre's Episode 2 finishes with a nominal clause describing Joseph as physically attractive: *Now Joseph was well-built and handsome*. This clause explaining why Potiphar's wife was attracted to Joseph and why she tried to seduce him, seems more naturally to belong to Episode 3. Longacre, however, classifies it as 'terminus of Episode 2' on the grounds that a boundary marker follows it.[34]

A last remark needs to be made. Accepting that a given story has a plot pattern, the possibility of the author highlighting sections other than peak must not be excluded. Details of a pre-peak episode might be very important to understand the peak and might need marking. Longacre's scheme does not allow for that.

34. It is interesting that modern translators of the text see no difficulty in absorbing the nominal phrase in the new episode: 'Now Joseph was handsome and good-looking. And after a time his master's wife cast her eyes on Joseph' (NRSV; also NIV). 'Now Joseph was well built and handsome, and it happened some time later that his master's wife looked desirously at him' (Jerusalem Bible). 'Now Joseph was handsome and good-looking, and a time came when his master's wife took notice of him' (NEB).

3. *The Storyline Scheme*

a. *Storyline and Macrostructure*

The centrality of the storyline in Longacre's method of analysis is seen in the claim he makes that the macrostructure of a story can be found by tracing its storyline and by applying reduction rules to the material thus obtained. The macrostructure of a text is a semantic global structure which corresponds to the intuitive notions of theme, topic or gist of a text. The reduction rules adopted are the ones proposed by van Dijk.[35] In Old Hebrew stories, the material processed is found exclusively in the vayyiqtol verbal chains: 'Crucial to the deduction of the macrostructure of a narrative in Biblical Hebrew is the assumption of the dominance of the preterite in narrative' (1989: 172).

In his analysis of the Genesis Flood story (1985: 169-85), Longacre abstracts all clauses with vayyiqtol verbs. He then deletes from this list all repetitions, consequent and presupposed actions, and all paraphrases. He further eliminates direct quotes. He is left with a summary to which further reduction is applied through the elimination of repeated material. The end product of this reduction is the abstract of the Flood story. The Joseph story has also a macrostructure, though the way it is derived is less clear:

> If the story of Joseph is to be considered a distinct entity within the overall unity of *toledot ya^{a}qob*, the life and time of Jacob—as is assumed in this study—then it must be considered to have a macrostructure of its own, that is, an overall meaning and plan (1989: 42).

One can only assume that here too van Dijk's method would be applied. This exclusive reliance on the vayyiqtol clauses to identify the gist of a story is flawed. By claiming that the meaning, or theme or gist of a story can be extracted from the backbone constructions with verbs in the preterite (vayyiqtol in Old Hebrew), Longacre excludes all other kinds of material which are often essential to the general meaning of a story. Not only does he ignore totally the important role played by dialogues which are so abundant in Old Hebrew stories, but he also

35. See van Dijk (1977: 143-48) for details. The macrostructure of a text is obtained through the application of a series of rules (construction, generalization, deletion). The text is reduced to a few statements which are the global meaning of the text.

reduces a story to its action. However, evaluative elements and comments made by the storyteller may be central to the meaning of a story. Such material is often found in what Longacre would view as background material. Additionally, it is important that the distinction between storyline and theme or gist of a story should be maintained. The tracking of events and the processing of vayyiqtol clauses result at best in a summary of the action of the story but can in no way be taken as providing its meaning, which should at least also include the notion of the point of the story.

b. *Storyline and Vayyiqtol Clauses*

Longacre makes three claims which need to be examined.

1. The vayyiqtol form introduces a fundamental distinction in grounding. Vayyiqtol clauses belong to the foreground of the story, other clauses serve to present background material.
2. Events narrated by vayyiqtol verbs form the storyline, moving the story forward; they are action advancing events. Among other things, this is a result of their punctiliarity.
3. Vayyiqtol clauses present events sequentially. An event reported by a vayyiqtol verb follows temporally the preceding event. In a chain of vayyiqtol clauses, events are ordered chronologically

This third claim will be examined in a section of its own (sect. 4), as it is crucial to the understanding of the meaning of vayyiqtol.

i. *Vayyiqtol and Foreground*

Longacre does not provide a definition of what he understands by the foreground of a story. However, taking into account the alternative terms main line (or backbone) together with his rank scheme for clauses, one may conclude that he understands foreground as referring to (1) the chain of central events which move the story forward and which, as such, are 'dominant'; (2) the formal signalling of this dominance: 'Sentences whose main verbs are storyline should be *dominant* sentences in the constituent structure of the paragraph and other sentences whose main verbs rank lower should be ancillary' (1990: 6). This description of dominance at paragraph level applies also to a discourse as a whole.

By associating unilaterally vayyiqtol clauses with the two notions of storyline and foreground, Longacre blurs the specificity of the storyline. In his view, all vayyiqtol events, without distinction, whether key events or trifling events, belong to the storyline. Given that statistically vayyiqtol forms represent 75 per cent of all verbal forms used in narratives,[36] this would mean that a massive amount of material would be dominant in narratives. This theory would also call into question the usefulness of the very notion of foreground represented by vayyiqtol verbs.

In fact, storyline must not be defined by vayyiqtol verbs but rather by the notion of key events, that is, events which are indispensable to the story development. Even a cursory consideration of some texts shows that vayyiqtol verbs describe events very different in nature and importance: from routine events which keep the story going or track the changes in location, or remove participants from the scene, or are simply accessory, to events which have a strategic importance in the story. To give an example, at the end of the story recounting how Elisha brought back to life a child, a number of vayyiqtol verbs are used to describe the reaction of the child's mother:

(2.1) 2 Kings 4.36-37

(1) She came to him
(2) and he (i.e. Gehazi, Elisha's servant) said:
(3) 'take your son.'
(4) ותבא (5) ותפל על־רגליו (6) ותשתחו ארצה
(7) ותשׂא את־בנה (8) ותצא
(4) She came in, (5) fell at his feet, (6) and bowed to the ground.
(7) Then she took her son (8) and she left.

(5) and (6) describe the respect and gratefulness of the mother. As for (8), it is here a routine closure verb dismissing the participant. Only (4) and (7) are key events describing how the mother is reunited with her child. Other verbs may be deleted without changing the meaning of the story's ending.

A comparison of the verb ותצא ('she left') in (8) with ויצאו ('they went out') in the story of the rape of Tamar, shows the difference in importance between the two events denoted by the same verb:

36. This figure is found in Schneider (1985: 182, par. 48.1).

(2.2) 2 Samuel 13.9

(1) And Amnon said: 'send out everyone from me',
(2) ויצאו כל־איש מעליו
So everyone went out from him.

The verb 'they went out' in (2) belongs to the storyline as it is a response to an order which itself is part of the strategy of the main protagonist. Amnon's plan is to be left alone with Tamar in order to rape her.

Often incidents described through a series of vayyiqtol verbs are relatively unimportant and could be omitted from the story without affecting its development. They are reported as anecdotal details. The deity makes a covenant with Abram and the incident recorded here takes place in the middle the ritual, after the slaughtering of some animals:

(2.3) Genesis 15.11

(1) וירד העיט על־הפגרים
(2) וישב אתם אברם
(1) And birds of prey came down upon the carcasses, (2) but Abram drove them away.

If, as Longacre would argue, vayyiqtol verbs report 'dominant' events, it remains to be explained why the events reported in (1) and (2) may be omitted from the story without affecting its development whatsoever. A similar example is found in the story of Noah:

(2.4) Genesis 8.9

(1) But the dove could not find a resting place for its feet,
(2) and it returned to him to the ark
(2a) for there was water all over the surface of the earth,
(3) וישלח ידו (4) ויקחה
(5) ויבא אתה אליו אל־התבה
(3) and he put out his hand, (4) and took her, (5) and brought it back to himself in the ark.

Clauses (3) to (5) describe the return of the dove to the ark, after its unsuccessful attempt to find dry land. The description of Noah welcoming back the dove in (3), (4) and (5), may be omitted from the story altogether, showing either that storyline and foreground do not overlap, or that vayyiqtol is not by nature a foregrounding form.

The other side of the question is that Longacre's initial categorization of non-vayyitol clauses as secondary and backgrounded, prevents him from considering whether key events which belong to the storyline are not reported through other clause types. A writer, in fact, is not restrained to vayyiqtol clauses to report storyline events, as some examples will demonstrate. Consider first:

(2.5) Genesis 41.1

ויהי מקץ שנתים ימים ופרעה חלם

Two years later, Pharaoh had a dream.

The verb חלם is a participle and the event it reports initiates a new episode in the story of Joseph, setting things in action. It is difficult to see how this clause could be left out of the main line or foreground of the story, as it reports a key event which will lead to Joseph meeting Pharaoh. Similarly:

(2.6) Genesis 41.8

(1) ויספר פרעה להם את־חלמו
(2) ואין־פותר אותם לפרעה

(1) And Pharaoh told them his dream, (2) but there was no one who could interpret (it) for Pharaoh.

(2) is a collateral event, indicated by a negation. It expresses what might have happened but did not. Although negative clauses are commonly categorized as backgrounded, there is a strong case for seeing (2) as an event which belongs to the main line of the story. Even though the nature of the event reported in the clause is a lack of success, this lack of success is an event in itself. Moreover, it is the failure of the magicians and sages of Egypt to interpret Pharaoh's dream which triggers the choice of Joseph as an interpreter. This event is a pivotal event in the story. Consider another example:

(2.7) Genesis 18.10c, 12

(10c) ושׂרה שׁמעת פתח האהל...
(12) ותצחק שׂרה בקרבה

(10c) Sarah was listening at the entrance of the tent ... (12) and Sarah laughed to herself.

Three strangers have arrived unexpectedly at Abraham's tent. Abraham offers them a meal. While they eat, one of the strangers announces that

Abraham's wife will have a son. (10c) recounts how Sarah heard the promise. The participial verb in (10c) is not a secondary but a main event. It is the fact that Sarah heard the promise which allows the narrator to report her reaction in (12) (the narrative being interrupted by a parenthesis in v. 11). A last example will be considered:

(2.8) Judges 11.32

(1)	ויעבר יפתח אל־בני עמון
(1a)	להלחם בם
(2)	ויתנם יהוה בידו

(1) Then Jephtah went over to the Ammonites (1a) to fight them, (2) and Yahweh gave them into his hand.

Longacre's theory demands that the subordinate nature of clause (1a) excludes it from the foreground on definitional and formal grounds. However, considered in their temporal ordering, the events 'he crossed over', 'to fight', and 'he gave them into his hand' are in sequence. So, in terms of the criterion of events temporally ordered in respect to each other, (1a) must be interpreted as belonging to the foreground of an episode comprising three events. Moreover, the fighting did take place as (2) makes clear and so (1a), in terms of what happened, must be seen as a main event, not an ancilliary one. This example illustrates well the fact that sometimes the various criteria for determining foregrounding are conflicting. The 'semantic' criterion, iconic temporal order, clashes with the grammatical and formal criterion, main or subordinate clause.

There are also examples of storyline events reported with qatal verbs. These will be discussed in sect. 5 below.

ii. *Vayyiqtol Verbs and Action Advancing Events*

Longacre's other claim is that events recounted through vayyiqtol contribute to the development of the action of the story. There are a number of counter-examples to this assumption, in which events/situations reported with a vayyiqtol can in no way be interpreted as moving the action forward. Vayyiqtol events which do not advance the action may be classified into three groups:

(1) Vayyiqtol verbs may be used descriptively to pick out a striking detail in a scene. The verbal construction is often characterized by the absence of a human agent.

(2) The same action may be reported twice through successive vayyiqtol.
(3) A series of vayyiqtol verbs describe a process unrelated to the movement forward of the main action of the story.

Group 1. The first category is best illustrated by the following examples:

(2.9) Judges 3.21

(1) Ehud reached (vayyiqtol) with his left hand, (2) he drew (vayyiqtol) the sword from his right thigh,

(3) ויתקעה בבטנו
(4) ויבא גם־הנצב אחר הלהב
(5) ויסגר החלב בעד הלהב
(6) כי לא שלף החרב מבטנו
(7) ויצא הפרשדנה

(3) and plunged it into his (i.e. Eglon's) belly. (4) The hilt also sank in after the blade, (5) and the fat closed over the blade (6) for (Ehud) did not pull the sword out of his belly. (7) and he (i.e. Ehud) went out *through the window*.[37]

Clauses (4) and (5) report a detail of the assassination of King Eglon by Ehud. They are vayyiqtol clauses, but are depictive and not essential to the plot of the story. The way the knife was stuck into Eglon's belly is of no importance at all to the development of the action and cannot be said to move the action forward.

In the following example the death of Asahel at the hand of Abner, a seasoned warrior, is described through three vayyiqtol clauses:

(2.10) 2 Samuel 2.23

(1) ויכהו אבנר באחרי החנית אל־ החמש
(2) ותצא החנית מאחריו
(3) ויפל־שם
(4) וימת תחתו

(1) Abner struck him in the belly with the butt of his spear (2) and the spear came out at his back. (3) He fell there (4) and died on the spot.

Clause (2), with its non-agentive S, does not convey a meaning of advancing action; on the contrary, the action is suspended while this gruesome detail is reported. The purpose of (2) is to describe the brutal

37. The meaning of the Hebrew word is uncertain.

strength of Abner and is suggestive of the violence of the blow inflicted to Asahel. Similarly:

(2.11) Genesis 7.17-19

(1) The flood continued for forty days on the earth,
(2) and the waters increased (vayyiqtol),
(3) and they lifted up (vayyiqtol) the ark,
(4) ותרם מעל הארץ
(5) ויגברו המים
(6) וירבו מאד על־הארץ
(7) ותלך התבה על־פני המים
(8) והמים גברו מאד מאד על־הארץ
(9) ויכסו כל־ההרים הגבהים
(4) and it rose above the earth (5) and the waters swelled, (6) and they increased greatly upon the earth, (7) and the ark went upon the waters (8) and the waters swelled much more upon the earth, (9) and all the high mountains were covered.

This example has a double interest. First, the flood is presented as a single event and the mounting of the water is dramatized by the repetition of four vayyiqtol verbs in (2), (5), (6), (8). Secondly, (7) has an activity V with a non-human agent as S. The activity goes on over an interval of time which is the duration of the flood. Although the verb ותלך ('she went') is dynamic, it does not advance the movement forward of the storyline which describes the increase of the flood. It is rather a process which occurs alongside the main event which is the swelling of the flood.

In the next example, Solomon is acclaimed as newly anointed king:

(2.12) 1 Kings 1.40

(1) ויעלו כל־העם אחריו
(2) והעם מחללים בחללים ושׂמחים שׂמחה גדולה
(3) ותבקע הארץ בקולם
(1) and all the people went up following him, (2) playing on pipes, and rejoicing with great joy, (3) and the earth shook at their noise.

(3) has a V with inanimate S. The clause does not belong to the main action which is the acclamation of the new king. The clause helps capture the intensity of the noise coming from the procession escorting the new king and has a descriptive character.

The story of Noah and the flood starts in this way:

(2.13) Genesis 6.11-12

(1) ותשחת הארץ לפני האלהים
(2) ותמלא הארץ חמס

(1) and the earth was corrupt before God (2) and the earth was filled with violence.

A new situation with a new 'participant', the earth, is introduced here. Two vayyiqtol clauses report the stative situation, the condition of the earth, with *the earth* occurring twice as S. The evil in which the world has engulfed itself provides the background against which to understand Yahweh's subsequent punitive action. The clause relation obtaining between (1) and (2) is not one of temporal sequentiality but one of clarification. (2) explains (1) by referring to acts of violence, but it does not advance the action.

Group 2. This group comprises cases of repetition of the same event using vayyiqtol verbs. The end of the creation story has three vayyiqtol clauses:

(2.14) Genesis 2.1-2

(1) ויכלו השמים והארץ וכל־צבאם
(2) ויכל אלהים ביום השביעי מלאכתו אשר עשה
(3) וישבת ביום השביעי מכל־מלאכתו אשר עשה

(1) and the heavens and the earth were finished, and all their array, (2) and on the seventh day God finished his work that he had done, (3) and on the seventh day he ceased from all the work that he had done.

Clause (3) repeats the meaning of clause (2): the two vayyiqtol verbs ויכל and וישבת are different but express the same meaning of cessation of work. (3) cannot be described as advancing the action; it does not present a new event, but merely restates (2). Consider now:

(2.15) Genesis 7.22-23

(1a) כל....
(1b) אשר נשמת־רוח חיים באפיו
(1c) ...מכל אשר בחרבה
(1a) ...מתו
(2) וימח את־כל־היקום
(3) אשר על־פני האדמה מאדם עד־בהמה...
(4) וימחו מן־הארץ

(1) And all that had the breath of life in its nostrils, all that was on dry land, died. (2) And he wiped out all existence on earth, man and beast ... (3) They were wiped out from the earth.

Clauses (1) to (3) describe the effects of the flood. (1) reports the death of every living thing and the two vayyiqtol clauses (2) and (3) say the same thing using the verbs וימח ('he wiped out') and וימחו ('they were wiped out'). The action does not progress from (1) to (3).

Parapharastic repetitions may have an evaluative effect as in the following example:

(2.16) Judges 10.7b-8

(1) And he (Yahweh) sold them into the hands of the Philistines and the Ammonites,
(2) וירעצו
(3) וירצצו את־בני ישׂראל בשׁנה ההיא
(2) and they shattered (3) and crushed the Israelites that year.

The vayyiqtol verb in (3) repeats the idea of the vayyiqtol verb in (2). Together the two clauses have the effect of measuring the enormity of the Israelites' defeat. But there is no progression of the action from (2) to (3). Similarly in:

(2.17) Genesis 32.8

(1) ויירא יעקב מאד
(2) ויצר לו
(1) And Jacob was in great fear (2) and he was distressed.

(1) and (2) are two stative sentences. The two vayyiqtol verbs do not mean that Jacob was fearful and then distressed. Rather, the two verbs are used descriptively, laying stress on Jacob's anguish.

Group 3. Finally, a series of vayyiqtol verbs may be used by the narrator to linger on a side-aspect of a situation for rhetorical purposes. In the story of the rape of Tamar by Amnon, Amnon pretends to be sick and Tamar is asked to come to her half-brother's bedchamber and prepare cakes for him. The details of the preparation is reported through a series of vayyiqtol:

(2.18) 2 Samuel 13.8-9

(1) Tamar went to her brother Amnon's house;
(2) he was lying down.
(3) ותקח את־הבצק
(4) ותלושׁ
(5) ותלבב לעיניו

(6) ותבשל את־הלבבות
(7) ותקח את־המשרת
(8) ותצק לפניו

(3) She took dough, (4) and she kneaded it, (5) and she made 'hearty' cakes in front of him. (6) She boiled the 'hearty' cakes, (7) she took the pan (8) and served him.

The minute description of Tamar's preparation of the delicacies through six vayyiqtol verbs constitute a non-essential element of the story. Rather than advancing the main action, the vayyiqtol clauses slow it down and delay the unfolding of the plot. The narrator would appear to use them to control the flow of time. This has the effect of injecting suspense in the story and it also contributes to characterization. The precise detailing of the scene brings out the hard-heartedness of Amnon who is waiting for the cakes to be served.

A similar example is found in Gen. 33.4 where the scene of Jacob meeting his brother Esau is recounted through a series of vayyiqtol verbs:

> Esau ran to meet him (i.e. Jacob), he hugged him, flung himself upon his neck, kissed him and they wept.

Each individual verb does not signal a progression of the action. The piling up of four verbs emphasizes that the meeting between the two formerly hostile brothers turns out to be an affectionate reunion.The main intention here is to provide a sympathetic portrayal of Esau.

These few examples demonstrate that vayyiqtol forms may be used in a much less rigid way than that envisaged by Longacre. The writers may use vayyiqtol clauses for dramatic purposes or the production of various rhetorical effects and these uses break down the assumed categories of foreground and advancement of the action.

4. *Vayyiqtol and Chronological Sequence*

The third claim made by Longacre is that vayyiqtol verbs report events which are ordered sequentially:

> Calling it (i.e. *vayyiqtol*) a *waw-consecutive* with the imperfect is better than calling it a '*waw conversive*'—provided we simply mean that the tense form expresses sequential actions in the past (and is viewed as punctiliar) (1992a: 178).[38]

38. The basic meaning of sequentiality for vayyiqtol is reiterated in many grammars, most recently in Gibson (1994: 95).

The claim here is that in successive vayyiqtol clauses, the events reported occur one after the other and so are chronologically ordered. Longacre, somewhat unexpectedly, departs from his careful distinction of temporal relations described in his *The Grammar of Discourse* (1983: 94-100). The explanation seems to be that, for him, vayyiqtol is a preterite tense and that vayyiqtol clauses move the action forward. He views vayyiqtol verbs as describing completed actions, and a chain of vayyiqtol verbs describes a succession of completed actions, a finished event being followed by another one. There are, however, some problems with this analysis. The first example illustrates how a sequential intepretation of vayyiqtol may lead to an impossible meaning:

(2.19) Genesis 5.6-7

(1) and Seth lived one hundred and five years,
(2) and he became the father of Enosh,
(3) and Seth lived (vayyiqtol) after the birth of Enosh 807 years,
(4) ויולד בנים ובנות
and he begot sons and daughters.

Clause (4) cannot be interpreted sequentially as happening after (3) in time. Rather, it is co-temporal with (3). In fact, a variety of temporal relations other than sequential might obtain between vayyiqtol clauses, and some relations might even be totally atemporal. The following sections will examine these cases.

a. *Temporal Meaning Other Than Chronological Sequence*

There are two specific non-chronological meanings: flashback and overlap. They will be considered in turn.

i. *Flashbacks*

Vayyiqtol clauses may be used as flashbacks reverting to events at an earlier point in time than the point currently reported. Although the use of vayyiqtol with pluperfect meaning is disputed by some scholars, it is difficult to refute examples such as these:

(2.20) Jonah 3.5-8

(1) Then he (i.e. Jonah) preached
(2) and he said: (3) 'Another forty days and Nineveh shall be destroyed'.

(4) ויאמינו אנשי נינוה באלהים
(5) ויקראו־צום
(6) וילבשו שׂקים מגדולם ועד־קטנם
(7) ויגע הדבר אל־מלך נינוה
(8) ויקם מכסאו
(9) ויעבר אדרתו מעליו
(10) ויכס שׂק
(11) וישב על־האפר

(4) But the men of Nineveh put their trust in God, (5) they proclaimed a fast, (6) and put on sackloth, from the greatest to the smallest. (7) For the message had reached the king of Nineveh, (8) and he had risen from his throne, (9) removed his robe, (10) he had put on sackcloth (11) and had sat down in the dust.

Clauses (4)–(6) provide a general description of the effects of Jonah's preaching in Nineveh: the whole population adopts an attitude of repentance. Clauses (7)–(11) constitute a flashback which explains more in detail how these penitential activities started. Jonah's message of doom had reached the king who had taken himself the attitude of a penitent. He had then an edict proclaimed instituting a nationwide period of fasting and repentance.[39] Clauses (7)–(11) use vayyiqtol verbs with a past perfect temporal meaning. The same kind of use of vayyiqtol occurs later in Jonah:

(2.21) Jonah 3.10c, 4.1 and 4.5

(1) God changed his mind about the evil
(1b) which he had announced he would do to them,
(1c) and he did not do it.

39. This is also the reading of Wolff (1986: 145) who considers vv. 6-9 as a flashback explanation which catches up with events that have already taken place. On the other hand, Sasson (1990: 247) writes: 'I rather imagine that the reactions of Nineveh's citizens and of its king are simply following a sequential order.' The argument which destroys this interpretation is that in the overall account, clause (6) says 'from the noble to the lowly'. This is a merismus which refers to the whole population, including king and nobles. Clauses (6)–(8) must be interpreted as an overview of the effects over the Ninevites of Jonah's warning. Later, the narrator goes back in time to offer a more detailed treatment of these events. This is confirmed by the fact that later, the king, in his edict, proclaims a decree of fasting (Jon. 3.7-8): 'Men or beasts, herds and flocks, are to taste nothing; they must not eat, they must not drink water. All are to put on sackcloth and call on God with all their might.' The proclamation would not make a great deal of sense if the people were already fasting and wearing sackcloth.

(2) וירע אל־יונה רעה גדולה
(3) ויחר לו
(4) ויתפלל אל־יהוה

(2) Jonah was terribly upset (3) and he was angry. (4) He prayed to Yahweh ... (5) And Yahweh said: 'Is it right for you to be angry?' (Jon. 4.4)

(6) (Jon. 4.5) ויצא יונה מן־העיר
(7) וישב מקדם לעיר
(8) ויעשׂ לו שׁם סכה
(9) וישב תחתיה בצל

(6) Jonah had gone out of the city, (7) and had stayed east of the city. (8) There he had made a booth for himself, (9) and had sat down in its shade [until he should see what would happen in the city].

The writer's narrative strategy is to focus first on the decisive events of the story. He then tracks back, recounting again and filling in the details. The immediate emotional effects on Jonah of God's change of plans are reported first in (2), (3) and (4), stripped of any unnecessary element. This has a dramatizing effect which is reinforced by Yahweh's question in (5). It is evident that the waiting period of forty days has passed, and the promised destruction of Nineveh has not happened. In (6), a vayyiqtol flashback brings us back to a time immediately after Jonah's warning to the city, that is, before the start of the countdown, and provides us with the setting of the end of the story (7-9). This is necessary as the end of the story will be centered around the booth. Another example is found in:

(2.22) Numbers 1.47-49a

(1) והלוים למטה אבתם לא התפקדו בתוכם
(2) וידבר יהוה אל־משׁה לאמר

(1) The Levites were not numbered among them by their ancestral tribe, (2) for Yahweh had spoken to Moses saying: (3) 'Only the tribe of Levi you must not enrol.'

Clause (2), with a vayyiqtol verb, refers to an earlier point in time when Moses had been given the order to exclude the Levites from the census of the tribes. It explains the situation described in (1). Consider also:

(2.23) Joshua 2.3-4

(1) The king of Jericho sent to Rahab to tell her: 'bring out those men who have come to you ...'

(2) ותקח האשׁה את־שׁני האנשׁים

(3) ותצפנו

(2) but the woman had taken the two men, (3) and she had hidden them, (4) so she answered: 'true, these men did come to me, but I did not know where they were from ... when the gate was about to shut, at the onset of darkness, these men went off.'

(5) והיא העלתם הגגה

(6) ותטמנם בפשתי העץ הערכות לה על־הגג

(5) but she had brought them upstairs on the roof, (6) and had hidden them under the stalks of flax laid out by her on the roof.

(2) and (3) are a narrative aside explaining why Rahab is able to lie to the king's messengers. Earlier, that is before she was questioned, she had hidden the spies. It would be hard to imagine a sequence of events in which the hiding of the men had taken place while the kings' envoys were waiting at the door. Later, clauses (5) and (6) supplement this aside by explaining more precisely that Rahab had hidden the spies on the flat roof of the house under the stalks of flax. (5) has a verb in the qatal conjugation, (6) has a vayyiqtol verb. Another example is found in:

(2.24) 1 Kings 9.14

וישלח חירם למלך מאה ועשרים ככר זהב

Now Hiram had sent to the king 120 talents of gold.

Earlier in the narrative we read that King Hiram of Tyre 'supplied King Solomon with cedar and cypress, timber and gold' (1 Kgs 9.11). Hiram is given 20 cities in exchange but is disappointed with the gift. The narrator adds this comment with a vayyiqtol verb to explain the king's discontent. As the gift of gold has been mentioned before this is a retrospective comment and the vayyiqtol has a past perfect meaning.

All these examples show that vayyiqtol forms can have a past perfect meaning. Chronological sequence is not a meaning which is inherent to the form, as claimed by Longacre.

ii. *Overlap*

Sometimes vayyiqtol clauses express events which are overlapping in time. The overlap might be partial or complete:

(2.25) Genesis 25.29

(1) ויזד יעקב נזיד

(2) ויבא עשו מן־השדה

(3) והוא עיף

(1) When Jacob was cooking a stew, (2) Esau came in from the open country. (3) He was exhausted.

(2) describes a punctual event and although following (1) does not indicate a movement forward in time. (2) begins and ends within the limits of (1) which depicts a state of affairs in progress when (2) takes place. (1) provides the immediate setting and circumstances for the story, with the action beginning in (2), when Esau comes back from the hunt exhausted and starving. A similar example is:

(2.26) Numbers 22.25

(1) ותרא האתון את־מלאך יהוה
(2) ותלחץ אל־הקיר
(3) ותלחץ את־רגל בלעם אל־הקיר

(1) The donkey saw the angel of the Yahweh (2) and pressed herself againt the wall, (3) squeezing Balaam's foot against the wall.

(2) and (3) represent two sequential predications with the same agent, but the two vayyiqtol verbs do not represent two temporally successive events. The relation is one of simultaneity: the two actions occur at the same time, the first resulting in the second one.

These examples show that vayyiqtol clauses may be used even when there is a shift of temporal order involving movement backward in time or the description of simultaneous events. A vayyiqtol clause may describe a situation which is not sequential to the vayyiqtol clause which it follows. Thus, it is inaccurate to limit vayyiqtol verbs to the expression of temporal sequentiality and chronology.

Vayyiqtol clauses involving relations which are non-temporal in nature will be considered next.

b. *Non-Temporal Meaning of Vayyiqtol*

A common non-temporal inter-clausal relation obtaining between two vayyiqtol clauses is enumeration. Moreover, a vayyiqtol clause may be related not to the preceding clause, but rather to a whole section of a story, or to a whole story. It is then used evaluatively or to provide a summarizing statement.

i. *Enumeration*

(2.27) Genesis 2.3

(1) ויברך אלהים את־יום השביעי
(2) ויקדש אתו
(1) And God blessed the seventh day (2) and he made it holy ... [(3) because on it God rested from all his work].

(1) and (2) occur at the end of the creation account, pointing to the distinctive character of the seventh day. The two clauses are in a parallel relation to each other. Blessing and sanctification are two interrelated ideas, two faces of the same coin. There is no indication of a temporal succession of the two events. Consider another example:

(2.28) Genesis 12.4-5

(1) וילך אברם כאשר דבר אליו יהוה
(2) וילך אתו לוט
(3) v. 5 ויקח אברם את־שרי אשתו ואת־לוט
(1) And Abram went as Yahweh told him, (2) and Lot went with him ...
(3) And Abram took Sarai his wife and Lot.

(1) and (2) are in a relation of enumeration. (2) completes what is missing from (1), that is the presence of Lot with Abram, but (2) cannot be said to refer to an event which succeeds (1) in time. (3) adds further to the list of people who went with Abram, using a vayyiqtol clause too. The event it reports does not follow (1) in time, but rather precedes it. This shows that the vayyiqtol V in (3) cannot have a temporal sequential meaning.

ii. *Evaluation*
Consider the two examples:

(2.29) Genesis 25.34

(1) Then Jacob gave Esau some bread and some lentil stew, and he ate and drank, and rose and went his way,
(2) ויבז עשו את־הבכרה
Thus did Esau spurn the right of a firstborn.

All the clauses in (1) have vayyiqtol verbs. (2), another vayyiqtol clause, occurs at the very end of this story which tells us how Esau sold his birthright to Jacob. It is a conclusive statement which gives an appraisal of Esau. The vayyiqtol clause is not sequentially ordered in time, but has an evaluative meaning.

In the description of the material splendour of King Solomon (1 Kgs 10.14-29), a series of vayyiqtol clauses are used which do not express temporal sequence. One of them is a summarizing clause:

(2.30) 1 Kings 10.23

ויגדל המלך שלמה מכל מלכי הארץ לעשר ולחכמה

King Solomon was greater in wealth and wisdom than all the kings of the earth.

This clause recapitulates the information given in the previous sections of the story about Solomon's wisdom and wealth.[40] The narrator passes judgement on the person of Solomon. It is to be noted that later in the text, two vayyiqtol clauses are used enumeratively:

And Solomon gathered together (vayyiqtol) chariots and horsemen (1 Kgs 10.26).
And the king made (vayyiqtol) silver as common in Jerusalem as stone (1 Kgs 10.27).

iii. *Summary*

This is the end of the account of Sarah's death and the purchase of a burial place for her by Abraham:

(2.31) Genesis 23.20

(1) After this, Abraham buried (qatal) Sarah his wife in the cave of the field of Makpelah, east of Mamre in the land of Canaan,
(2) ויקם השדה והמערה אשר־בו לאברהם לאחזת־קבר מאת בני־חת
And so the field and the cave that was on it, passed from the Hittites to Abraham, as a burial site.

(2) has a vayyiqtol verb but the event it reports does not follow in time the event reported in (1). The clause is a conclusion to the story, reiterating the fact that the plot of land with the burial cave belonged to Abraham, having been legally acquired. In fact, the acquisition of the plot was reported earlier in the story: 'the field with the cave ... was handed over to Abraham as a possession' (vv. 17-18).

40. These sections speak of Solomon's wisdom (1 Kgs 10.4: 'and when the Queen of Sheba had seen all the wisdom of Solomon') and wealth (1 Kgs 10.14: 'the weight of gold that came to Solomon in one year was 666 talents of gold.').

The next example is found in the story of the crossing of the Jordan by the Israelites:

(2.32) Joshua 5.9

(1) Yahweh said (vayyiqtol) to Joshua, 'today, I have rolled away from you the disgrace of Egypt',
(2) ויקרא שם המקום ההוא גלגל עד היום הזה
and so that place is called Gilgal to this day.

(2) concludes an etiological section in the story, associated with the place where the Jordan was crossed and which was called Gilgal. The naming of the place is reported through a vayyiqtol V, although the duration of the situation extends to the present of the narrator, as indicated by the expression 'to this day'.

5. *Storyline and Qatal Clauses*

In Longacre's scheme qatal clauses are secondary to the main storyline:

> Clauses that begin with a non-preterite (perfect) verb portray secondary actions, for example actions which are subsidiary to the main action, which is described by a following preterite (1989: 65).
>
> The perfect makes possible the inclusion of participant-oriented actions or backgrounded actions which are one or two steps removed from the primary storyline, which is carried by the preterite (1992a: 178-79).

Here, too, a reading of biblical narratives makes it very difficult to accept this description of the meaning of qatal clauses without reservations. There are qatal clauses that report events which are central to the development of the story. Consider:

(2.33) Genesis 25.34

(1) ויעקב נתן לעשׂו לחם ונזיד עדשים
(2) ויאכל
(3) וישת
Jacob gave Esau bread and lentil stew. He ate and drank.

Clause (1) depicts the high point of the story, when Esau is finally given the stew he so much wanted. Longacre's categorization of the qatal clause simply does not make sense when applied to clause (1).

In the following account, Tamar is accused of whoredom and condemned to be burnt. She is brought out to the city gate where justice was administered:

(2.34) Genesis 38.25

(1) הוא מוצאת
(2) והיא שלחה אל־חמיה

(1) As she was being brought out, (2) she sent a message to her father-in-law.

The qatal clause (2) introduces the highly dramatic denouement of the story, when Tamar confronts Judah with the evidence that she is not guilty. The message sent consists in the material evidence of Tamar's innocence. (2) cannot be construed as a secondary storyline. It is indispensable to the development of the story.

(2.35) Genesis 40.1

ויהי אחר הדברים האלה חטאו משקה מלך־מצרים
והאפה לאדניהם

Some time later, the cupbearer and the baker of the king of Egypt gave offense to their lord [the king of Egypt].

This clause introduces a new episode in the story of Joseph and the event it reports is crucial to the understanding of why the two courtiers have been thrown in jail. It is immediately followed by two vayyiqtol clauses: 'and Pharaoh was angry and he put them in custody'. The qatal clause can in no way be classified as a secondary line in relation to the two following clauses. The three clauses belong to the same main narrative line. Consider now:

(2.36) Judges 6.34

(1) ורוח יהוה לבשה את־גדעון
(2) ויתקע בשופר
(3) ויזעק אביעזר אחריו

(1) and the spirit of Yahweh came on Gideon, (2) and he blew the horn, (3) and the Abiezrites mustered behind him.

The information that the spirit of Yahweh came upon Gideon is central to the narrative. This event cannot be given secondary line status. It is the event which sets Gideon into action and which is, crucially, the fulfilment of a promise made by Yahweh to Gideon.[41] The promise-fulfilment articulation constitutes the backbone of the story. The classification of (1) as a secondary action would destroy the very thread of the story.

In the story of Naboth's murder, Queen Jezebel instructs elders and nobles of Samaria to hold a fast and to arrange for corrupt witnesses to accuse Naboth:

(2.37) 1 Kings 21.11-12

(1) The men of his city, the elders and the nobles who lived in the city, did (vayyiqtol*)* (2) as Jezebel had instructed them, (3) as it was in the letters (4) that she had sent to them,

(5) קראו צום
(6) והשיבו את־נבות בראש העם...
(7) ויבאו שני האנשים בני־בליעל

(5) they called a fast, (6) and they seated Naboth at the head of the people. (7) Two men, scoundrels, came in [and sat opposite him], (8) and the scoundrels brought charge (vayyiqtol) against Naboth.

Jezebel's orders sent in a letter are: 'Proclaim a fast, and seat Naboth in a prominent place among the people and seat two scoundrels opposite him and let them bring a charge against him' (1 Kgs 21.9-10). The exact carrying out of Jezebel's orders is reported through two qatal clauses in (5) and (6) and two vayyiqtol clauses in (7) and (8). (5) and (6) fulfil Jezebel's orders in the same way as do (7) and (8) and it cannot be said that one set of events is secondary in relation to the other one. All four clauses are critical elements in Jezebel's scheming.

(2.38) Genesis 26.25

(1) ויט־שם אהלו
(2) ויכרו־שם עבדי־יצחק באר
(3) ואבימלך הלך אליו מגרר

(1) There he pitched his tent, (2) and there Isaac's servants dug a well. (3) And Abimelek came to him from Gerar.

Abimelech had previously expelled Isaac (Gen. 26.6) from Gerar for fear of his power; now he is looking for him in order to make a treaty. Clause (3) is a main new event in the development of the story with one

41. Judg. 6.15: ' "But sir, how can I deliver Israel? ... I am the least in my family." Yahweh said to him: "I will be with you and you shall strike down the Midianites." '

of the main protagonists as S; it cannot be analysed as backgrounded in any way whatsoever.

In the story of Jacob's marriage with Leah and Rachel, Jacob arrives at a well and speaks with the shepherds:

(2.39) Genesis 29.9

(1) עודנו מדבר עמם
(2) ורחל באה עם־הצאן אשר לאביה

While he was still speaking with them, (2) Rachel came with her father's sheep.

The ongoing conversation is reported through a backgrounded participial clause but (2) represents the central event of the first meeting between Jacob and Rachel.

Often qatal and vayyiqtol are used interchangeably as the following passages show. The same idea is expressed first through a vayyiqtol and then repeated as a qatal.

In Gen. 18.6-8, Abraham is the subject of two similar and successive actions performed in a hurry ('he hurried to Sarah's tent' and 'he ran to the herd'). The first one is described with vayyiqtol, the second with qatal:

(2.40) Genesis 18.6-7

(1) וימהר אברהם האהלה אל־שׂרה
(2) ואל־הבקר רץ אברהם
(3) ויקח בן־בקר רך וטוב

(1) Abraham hurried to the tent to Sarah … (2) Then Abraham ran to the cattle, (3) and took a calf, tender and choice.

(1) and (2) form part of the same sequence of actions reporting Abraham's haste to prepare a meal. One is no less important than the other and the distinction in verbal form does not indicate a distinction in importance.

The standard way of describing the birth of a child in a family is through the use of a series of three verbs 'to know', 'to conceive', 'to give birth'.[42] The three verbs are equally important in the sequence. However one of them may be used in the qatal:

42. These sequences of verbs constitute knowledge structures which will be discussed in more detail in Chapter 6.

(2.41) Genesis 4.1

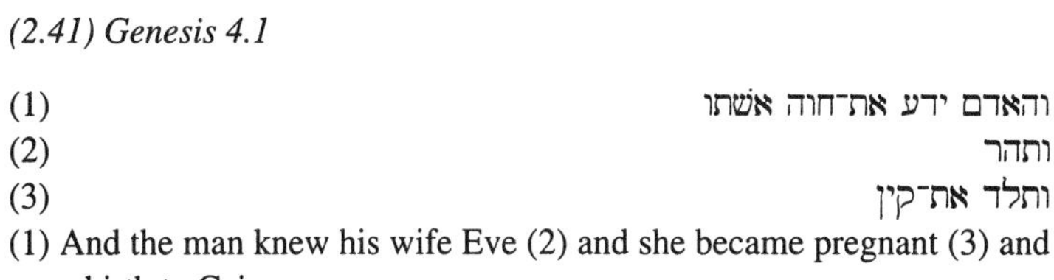

(1) והאדם ידע את־חוה אשתו
(2) ותהר
(3) ותלד את־קין

(1) And the man knew his wife Eve (2) and she became pregnant (3) and gave birth to Cain.

Qatal may be used here to signal a new beginning, but this discourse function does not downgrade the importance of the event reported. Elsewhere, in the same sequence using the three verbs, the first verb has a vayyiqtol form:

(2.42) Genesis 4.17

(1) וידע קין את־אשתו
(2) ותהר
(3) ותלד את־חנוך

(1) and Cain knew his wife (2) and she became pregnant (3) and gave birth to Enoch.

A comparison of (2.41) with (2.42) show that the qatal verb of (2.41) cannot be analysed in any meaningful way as a secondary verb. Another similar sequence involving Adam again confirms it:

(2.43) Genesis 4.25

(1) וידע אדם עוד את־אשתו
(2) ותלד בן
(3) ותקרא את־שמו שת

(1) And Adam knew his wife again, (2) and she gave birth to a son, (3) and called him Seth.

Thus, clauses using the qatal form of the verb may refer too to events which are essential to the story. The events/activities/actions reported do not always represent secondary information or do not always belong to a secondary storyline as claimed by Longacre (1989: 74).

A last example will illustrate how a questionable interpretation might be imposed on texts through Longacre's scheme. The story of Joseph starts with an expositional section explaining the hatred between Joseph and his brothers:

(2.44) Genesis 37.2b-3

(1) Joseph, being seventeen years old, was shepherding the flocks with his brothers. (2) He was a helper to the sons of Bilhah and Zilpah, his father's wives.

(3) ויבא יוסף את־דבתם רעה אל־אביהם

(4) וישׂראל אהב את־יוסף מכל־בניו

(3) And Joseph brought bad reports of them to their father. (4) Now Israel loved Joseph more than all his children.

(3), a vayyiqtol clause, follows one copular clause, (1), and one nominal clause, (2). Joseph is portrayed as a tale-bearer but nothing says that this contributes to the conflict with his brothers. By contrast, (4) is singled out later [43] as the key reason why the brothers sought to kill Joseph: it is Jacob's love for Joseph, as seen expressed especially in the gift of an ornamented robe, which sparks hatred in the brothers. Here the facts as expressed explicitly in the story go against Longacre's scheme. The significant event is expressed by qatal whereas a less important activity, which contributes to Joseph's characterization, is reported with vayyiqtol.

6. *Conclusions*

The following conclusions may be drawn form the above analysis.

a. *Circularity*

The foreground/background approach which relies upon vayyiqtol forms as indicators of the main plot-line of the story meets with a serious problem of circularity. The formal clue for deciding whether a clause is foreground or background is precisely the presence of the clue in the clause.

b. *One Form/One Function Model*

Longacre seems to adhere to a 'one form/one function' model. As a result, he forces some forms into the straitjacket of the functional categories he has established, thus ignoring altogether possible different functions. This deficiency is not removed by his use of a scalar

43. Gen. 37.4: 'But when his brothers saw that their father loved him more than all his brothers, they hated him.'

approach based on a verbal rank scheme (1989: 81) to refine kinds of background material. His account remains in fact a binary system as the foreground is represented by the vayyiqtol band only.

A further problem arises from the fact that each notional band is characterized by homogeneity of forms (one form only or one set of forms). No allowance is made for the functional skewing of forms. But the examples cited above have shown that sequenced events need not form a homogeneous category in terms of their formal grammatical representation.

c. *Discourse Description*

Longacre is guided by a structural view of discourse which places the discourse level in a hierarchy of structures. This encourages a rigid unitary way of describing language, from the level of morpheme to discourse, which ascribes to discourse the same formal regularities found at the lower clause and morpheme level of description. The counter-examples discussed above show that discourse structures are not of the same kind as those occurring at lower level of analysis. A discourse cannot be described as well-formed or ill-formed.

d. *Grounding and Temporal Sequence*

The actual use of verbal forms show that the notion of foreground/background is far more complex than Longacre suggests and throws partly into question the definition of foreground in terms of the main line of a story, characterized by temporal ordering and chronological sequence.

Such an interpretation imposes a specific and narrow meaning on the verbal form and in so doing, it often stretches the meaning beyond what is logically plausible or contextually allowed. Even if the prevalent tendency is towards using vayyiqtol for important events, there are many deviations and many discrepancies are found between the claims based on purely formal criteria and the linguistic data and their meanings.

e. *Grounding and Vayyiqtol*

One may choose to explain vayyiqtol in terms of foreground and main action as Longacre does, but this leads to a description so unfocused that its real value is doubtful, with too many inadequate explanations. Alternatively, one may choose to disentangle these notions and in this case vayyiqtol must no longer be considered as a unique foregrounding form.

To give a proper account of the facts, the notion of storyline must be detached from vayyiqtol and the notion of foreground cannot be seen as grammaticalized in Old Hebrew. It is also clear that temporal sequentiality and dominant events must be sharply distinguished.

f. *The Marking of Grounding*

In so far as grounding in discourse is a universal which has its origins in cognitive and psycholinguistic functions, we may expect this distinction to manifest itself in the linguistic structure of narrative. We need not, however, expect to find a universal consistent mapping of foreground and background on to grammatical categories or constructions across languages. The grounding function may have recourse to various strategies involving morphology (verb inflections, focal/non-focal pronouns) or clause types, but grounding can also be signalled by a number of different markers such as contrastive word-order patterns or repetitions of various types, or the semantics of a verb. In Old Hebrew, stories are played out largely through a syntax of coordinated main clauses. This fact tends particularly to favour grounding devices other than grammatical oppositions.

Chapter 3

TOPICALITY AND TOPICAL ENTITIES: AN ANALYSIS OF GENESIS 22

1. *The Notion of Topic*

Apart from the two statistical studies of Givón (1977) and Fox (1983), the question of topicality in Old Hebrew has not been the subject of detailed research.[1] No model to study the sentence articulation is readily available to be used or to build upon. For the analyst trying to understand these notions in the Old Hebrew narrative clause the problem is twofold. First, the general literature on topic-comment displays a great variety of perspectives and assumptions, the task of understanding these notions being complicated by the absence of homogeneity in the terminology. Secondly, most studies discuss the question on the basis of SVO languages. Old Hebrew is a VSO language, a factor which is to be taken into account when choosing and adapting a suitable model.

The procedure chosen here is inductive. A basic analytical model is applied to a story in order to define topicality and to describe the encoding of discourse topicality. Then the clausal articulation topic-comment is considered.

The basic idea behind the notion of topic-comment is that communication is 'about' something. Any utterance has a subject or topic and something is said about this topic, which is the comment. So the topic constitutes the starting point of an utterance. In her survey of 'sentence topic', however, Tanya Reinhart (1982: 4) comments: 'Although the linguistic role of the relation TOPIC OF is widely acknowledged, there is no accepted definition for it, and not even full agreement on the

1. Givón and Fox consider the question of continuity of topic over stretches of discourse with the aim of discussing factors affecting word order change at various stages of the history of the language. An article by G. Payne (1991: 62-82) is mainly concerned with trying to apply the functional sentence perspective (FSP) model to the Old Hebrew clause.

intuitions of what counts as topic.'

Historically, the groundwork on topic was started by the linguists of the Prague school who coined the terms theme and rheme.[2] Later, linguists seeking an entry point to study the question have focused their attention on one or the other aspect of topic described by Prague linguists.[3] One significant feature in the development of topic analysis has been the level at which individual authors choose to consider the question. Two groups are identifiable. Some linguists analyse topic at the level of the clause. Thus Halliday (1985: 39) writes: 'The theme is the starting-point for the message; it is what the clause is going to be about.' Other linguists such as Brown and Yule (1983), Gundel (1977), Allan (1986),[4] Reinhart (1982), Comrie (1981: 64) endorse this definition, while choosing to examine the notion rather at the level of the sentence and concentrating primarily on the correlation between topic and given information.

There seems to be a general consensus among linguists that clause topic is 'what the clause is going to be about'. This is the definition of clause topic which will be adopted in this chapter. Topic is the entity that the proposition communicated in the clause is about. As such the topic of a clause is the referential material which provides a plug-in point for the comment, the comment having the specific function of 'point-making'.

2. *Theme* was the term originally created by the functional linguists of the Prague School and it seems to be preferred by linguists working in this tradition. In general 'topic' is the term preferred by American linguists.

3. Functionalism came into existence between the world wars in Prague. The Prague school viewed language primarily as an instrument of communication. The emphasis on the instrumental character of language led them to formulate the principle that language cannot be analysed in isolation. This had the practical result of compelling linguists to look beyond the mere study of the structural organization of language. Especially, in seeking to explain the linguistic structures of a language, they had to take into account the external factors that contribute to its particular internal organization.

4. Gundel defines topic in the following way: 'An entity, E, is the topic of a sentence, S, if in using S the speaker intends to increase the addressee's knowledge about, request information about, or otherwise get the addressee to act with respect to E.' Such a definition captures 'the intuitive characterization of topic as what a sentence is about' (Gundel 1988: 210). Allan (1986: 82-83) writes: 'We reserve the term *topic* to describe what an utterance or a text is about, i.e. its subject matter; hence topic is essentially a narrative category.'

The Prague linguist Firbas (1987a: 142) defines the notion of topic in the following way:

> It may indicate that the sentence is about one of the central notions of the discourse, or simply about the same notion as the preceding sentence(s) has (have) been concerned with.
> It may indicate that the notion concerned will be dealt with from a point of view that has already been mentioned in the immediately relevant preceding context or from a point of view that has not been mentioned before.
> It may naturally also introduce an entirely new notion about which the sentence is to convey something either from a point of view already known or from one entirely new as well.

This definition is useful as it is concerned with relating clause topic to discourse topic. Such concern is at the centre of another approach to the study of topic represented by Givón and Tomlin. They examine sentence topic in the light of the context of the whole discourse.[5] Topicality is viewed not as a clause-dependent property only but as a discourse-dependent one as well: what makes a participant topical is not the fact that it is grammaticaly coded as topical in a sentence, but rather that it is the topic of the discourse or a stretch of discourse. The discourse-based approach will provide the starting point for the study which follows, a topic (what a sentence is about) being viewed as dependent upon the context of communication.[6]

The integration of the dimension of discourse in the analysis of sentence topic requires first that the notion of discourse topic should be explained. Tomlin has offered a valuable solution to the question of the determination of discourse topic. His approach will be first described and then adapted for and applied to Old Hebrew texts.

5. Givón (1990: 902) makes the following point: 'Put plainly and in operational terms, the topic is only *talked about* or *important* if it remains *talked about* or *important* during a number of successive clauses.'

6. Context dependence invariably renders an element topical. But it is necessary to point out that aboutness is not invariably linked with context dependence. If it is true that known information, that is information such as can be gathered from the verbal and situational context, is generally topical, the topic does not always exclusively convey such information. Sometimes it may also express new (i.e context-independent) information. An example of this would be a sentence used at the beginning of a story. This means that the two characteristics, context (given and new) and topic must also be kept separate and that the 'aboutness' feature is naturally hierarchically superior to the feature of context dependence.

2. *Tomlin's Model for Topicality*

Tomlin, who uses the terms theme and rheme, starts with two assumptions:

(1) The definition of topic must be empirically based. Tomlin refrains from providing any a priori theoretical definition of topic. Instead, the topical material in a discourse is identified by resorting to the analysis of a real-life situation.
(2) The identification of topic needs to be based on plausible cognitive factors.[7]

Tomlin (1986: 41-44) notes that there are three different methods of analysis which use a text independent methodology for identifying topical information:

(1) A descriptive analysis of text goals by informed subjects;
(2) The computation of cumulative referential density which he believes is an improvement on Givón's measuring of referential distance. Such statistical analysis is based on the fact that referents which are more important occur more often than less important referents;
(3) An experimental method which consists in examining the allocation of attention in discourse production.

The third method will provide the starting point for this analysis. It will be complemented later by the second one. Tomlin illustrates it through the use of a developed example: the reporting of an ice-hockey game (Tomlin 1983, 1985, 1986: 45-47). In his experiment, topical information is identified by using video-tapes of play-by-play reporting of an ice-hockey game. Two different types of information are in use during the report. *Shared information,* that is information which the speaker and hearer hold in common, and *Thematic information* which is also information that speaker and hearer hold in common, but which is also connected to the goal of the discourse: 'Thematic Information is that knowledge which the speaker assumes is relevant to the goal of the communicative event' (1985: 64). As such, topical/thematic information becomes necessarily a centre of attention for both speaker and hearer:

7. Givón (1989: 209, 213) also underlines the importance of cognitive factors.

> Thematic Information: information in an expression is thematic to the extent the speaker assumes the hearer attends to the referent of the expression ... Thematic information appears to help the hearer orient attention to specific information within the hearer's current mental model (Tomlin 1986: 39, 40).

In the ice-hockey game the goal of the reporting is to describe the action on ice. The verbal description of the game is organized by the extra-linguistic activity of viewing the hockey game unfolding on ice and so the organization of the linguistic material will depend upon the salient features of the game on which the reporter's attention is focused: the puck and the players. These salient elements in the extra-linguistic situation once encoded linguistically will constitute topical information. The puck is topical: it is a centre of attention because its movement and its fate determine the outcome of the game. The players are topical: they are a centre of attention because they seek to control the puck and thus the outcome of the game. Of the two centres of attention, attention to the puck is more basic than attention to the players. The spectators follow the puck, the players try to control it. When a player takes control of the puck the two centres of attention coincide and reference to such a player becomes 'more topical' than reference to the puck or another player without the puck. On this basis, a hierarchy of thematic information may be established:

> player in control of the puck > puck > player without puck > other.

The advantage of such a method is that the determination of levels of topicality takes place independently of the syntax. It is linked to centres of attention in the extra-linguistic situation.

3. *Adaptation of Tomlin's Model*

The same extra-linguistic context obviously does not obtain in Old Hebrew narratives. Nevertheless, it is possible to find the equivalent of Tomlin's thematic information connected to the goal of the discourse in stories which give clues as to their topical concerns through a brief statement or heading at the beginning. Such statements are not to be confused with headings used in news report which provide a gist or abstract of a text. Rather, they constitute what Brown and Yule call a 'topic framework' and function, as 'a particularly powerful thematization device' (1983: 139). This means that they list the topical elements around which the story is constructed. The 'title' establishes the participants mentioned as the topical participants and the action as the topical action. The topicalization of specific entities in a story through a heading results in the readers focusing their attention on the elements in question because they create an expectation and are linked to the goal of the discourse. Although a title is not an extra-linguistic contextual clue, it represents an indication by an external source, the author, as to what the topical elements in the story are. As a result, it ensures that some kind of objective criterion is used in the analysis and that the determination of topical information is established initially independently of the syntax, thus avoiding a circular argument in the analysis.

The remainder of the chapter will apply this model to a story and develop further some concepts.

4. *Application to Genesis 22*

The components of topicality are the following. At discourse level a discourse topic which refers to specific topical entities must be identified. A topical entity may become the topic of a clause and function at the level of the topic-comment articulation.

a. *The Topical Frame*

A story with a heading is the story of Abraham's near sacrifice of his son Isaac, in Genesis 22. The story begins with the sentence *After these things God tested Abraham*. Commentators of Genesis 22 agree that this clause functions as a heading given to the story which follows.[8] The heading announces the topic of the story: *God tested Abraham*. The discourse topic comprises one central action (*to test)* with two topical entities *Abraham* and *God*, which are topical participants. Through the heading these two participants are assigned the highest degree of topical importance and it is expected that such a feature should be reflected at clause level.

The topical action of the story is described in a nutshell by the verb

8. G.W. Coats (1973: 390) writes: 'The exposition defines the purpose of the action presented in the plot line as a test of Abraham.' F. Landy (1989: 4): 'The story introduces itself with a brief generic summary.' C. Westermann (1985: 356): 'The narrator who was responsible for the title intended the event to serve as a model.'

nissāh, 'he tested'. The verb establishes a general controlling framework. It describes how things are going to develop in the discourse and any possible entity (other participants, props, objects, place) associated with the notion of 'test' must be examined in terms of linguistic encoding. A particular, and for our purpose very helpful, feature of the story is that this topical framework is unpacked in more detail at the very beginning of the story. In a direct speech section, Yahweh, the speaker, gives an order to Abraham:

2b-d: 'Take your son, your only one, whom you love, Isaac,
2e: and go to the land of Moriah,
2f-g: and offer him there as a burnt offering, on one of the mountains which I will tell you.'

The topical action ('he tested') is spelt out: it takes the form of a sacrifice to which are associated two new topical entities: (1) a new topical participant, *Isaac*; (2) a topical location, a *mountain* in *the land of Moriah*. Moreover, the specific action (to sacrifice) involves here a particular religious and cultural knowledge schema with objects (props) associated with the schema. Thus we have three categories of topical entities: participants, schema related props and place. These may be classified in terms of importance in the following way:

(1) Main topical participants:	—Abraham —Yahweh
(2) Secondary topical entities:	
—participant:	—Isaac
—location:	—a mountain
—props:	—objects related to the sacrifice-schema
(3) Non-topical entities:	—a donkey, two servants

If a parallel is drawn with Tomlin's ice-hockey game, the discourse topic provides what Tomlin calls 'thematic information', that is information held in common by speaker and hearer and which is connected to the goal of the discourse. In an ice-hockey game, team A plays against team B, the aim being for one team to score more goals with the puck than the other one. The radio reporter describes the action on ice, focusing on the topical elements, the puck and the player controlling the puck. In our story, the action is a test which involves a sacrifice, with two entities directly associated with it, Isaac and the specific location. It is principally on the two main topical participants Abraham and God, that the speaker's attention is expected to be focused. This parallels

Tomlin's scale of thematic elements centered on players and puck. How these levels of topical importance are coded needs to be considered now.

b. *Determining the Topical Importance of Entities*

Topical importance is the central dimension of topicality and the title provides a good indication as to which entities are the main topical ones in a story. But it is also possible to evaluate an entity's topical importance in a more precise way, through computation.

Topical importance has a mainly cataphoric character: topical entities which are important persist in the developing discourse and so occur with greater frequency than less important ones. Various topic measurement techniques have been devised to rate the topical importance of entities. Tomlin proposes a calculation method which he calls 'computing of cumulative referential density', which works in the following way. The text examined is divided into paragraph units and the topical entities are identifed in each clause. For every clause, the number of references to the entity at a given point of the paragraph is worked out. This number is divided by the number of clauses up to that point in the paragraph. A ranking of each topical entity in each clause is established as well as a global ranking of all the entities.

One problem, when clause-level topic is considered from the angle of discourse, is which level of discourse should be selected as a suitable analytical unit. Textual units chosen to describe topicality, such as paragraph or episode, are not defined well enough in too many studies. The appropriate level at which discourse topic should be traced is the episode which is defined by the sustaining of attention on a particular paragraph level theme'.[9]

The identification of paragraphs may present difficulties in some written stories. In Chapter 2, this was a criticism that was made of Longacre's analysis of the Joseph story. However, in the Genesis 22 story, some noticeable paragraph boundaries appear. Paragraphs contain quoted conversations where stable procedures control turn-taking. The order, content and type of exchanges help to determine paragraph boundaries. Boundary markers are also used, characterized by features of hiatus or discontinuity. Adverbial phrases of location or time secure

9. 'Clause and sentence level thematic information is determined at the paragraph level' (Tomlin 1986: 43).

a connection between two different paragraphs. The dispersing of participants or the introduction of a new cast of participants mark an end or new beginning. The use of a noun as an explicit S or a summary statement may also be clues to boundaries. Finally events tend to be lumped together and form coherent blocks describing short self-contained action sequences.

c. *Analysis of Topical Importance*

The section presents the analytical data related to topical importance. Paragraphs and episodes are used here interchangeably. The non-topical entities have been included in the measurement tables for comparative purposes. The breakdown of the text with its references is found in the Appendix.

The analysis of topicality comprises direct speech sections and third person narration. Topical items mentioned in narration are indicated by (Nar). The letter m (for 'mention') indicates a reference to a topical item other than a first mention. Tables providing an analysis of the grammatical functions of the topical entities follow the frequency tables. These will permit an examination of the correlation between topical importance and syntactic encoding.

i. *Episode 1: Genesis 22.1c-2f. God's Command*

The first episode begins in 1c and finishes in 2f. It comprises a conversation which is marked by the direct discourse marker 'and he said' repeated three times (vv. 1c, 1e, 2a). The markers also delimit the turn-taking boundaries: they signal where one voice breaks off and the other begins. The turns of the exchange consist first of one adjacency pair with a 'summon' turn followed by a 'response' turn. One participant, God, uses the name of the other, Abraham, in order to establish contact before introducing the discourse topic (vv. 2b-2f). As vv. 1c-d and 1e-f include the syntactically necessarily very brief summon and response adjacency pairs, the direct discourse quotes (*Abraham* and *Here I am*) are analysed as belonging to the sentence created by the quoted speech marker.

Cumulative frequency table

		God	Abraham	Isaac	Moriah	Sacrifice	Mountain
1c-d	1	1.00	1.00				
1e-f	2	1.00	1.00				
2a	3	1.00	0.67				
2b	4	0.75	0.75 m	0.25			
2c	5	0.60	0.80 m	0.40 m			
2d	6	0.50	0.83 m	0.33	0.16		
2e	7	0.43	0.85 m	0.45 m	0.28 m	0.14	0.14
2f	8	0.50 m	0.87 m	0.37	0.25	0.12	0.25 m

Overall topical ranking: Abraham > God > Isaac > Moriah, mountain > sacrifice

Syntactic realization

Abraham:	S: 5 (1 Nar)	O: 1 (Nar)	A: 0
God:	S: 2 (2 Nar)	O: 0	A: 0
Isaac:	S: 0	O: 3	A: 0
Moriah:	S: 0	O: 0	A: 2
Mountain:	S: 0	O: 1	A: 1
Sacrifice:	S: 0	O: 0	A: 1

ii. *Episode 2: Genesis 22.3a-g. Abraham's Departure*

Cumulative frequency table

		Abraham	Morning	Donkey	2 Servants	Isaac	Wood	Place	God
3a	1	1.00	1.00						
3b	2	1.00	0.50	0.50					
3c	3	1.00	0.33	0.33	0.33	0.33			
3d	4	1.00	0.25	0.25	0.25	0.25	0.25		
3e	5	1.00	0.20	0.20	0.20	0.20	0.20		
3f	6	1.00	0.16	0.16	0.16	0.16	0.16	0.16	
3g	7	1.00	0.14	0.14	0.14	0.14	0.14	0.28m	0.14

Overall topical ranking: Abraham > place > morning, donkey, 2 servants, Isaac, wood, God

Syntactic realization

Abraham:	S: 6 (1 Nar)	O: 0	A: 1
Morning:	S: 0	O: 0	A: 1 (Nar)
Place:	S: 0	O: 1	A: 1 (Nar)
Donkey:	S: 0	O: 1 (Nar)	A: 0
Servants:	S: 0	O: 1 (Nar)	A: 0
Wood:	S: 0	O: 1 (Nar)	A: 0
Isaac:	S: 0	O: 1 (Nar)	A: 0
God:	S: 1	O: 0	A: 0

iii. *Episode 3: Genesis 22.4a-5e. Abraham's Order to his Servants*

Cumulative frequency table

		Abraham	3rd Day	Place	2 Servants	Donkey	Isaac
4a	1	1.00	1.00				
4b	2	1.00	0.50	0.50			
5a	3	1.00	0.33	0.33	0.33		
5b	4	0.75	0.25	0.25	0.50m	0.25	
5c	5	0.80 m	0.20	0.40m	0.40	0.20	0.20
5d	6	0.83 m	0.16	0.33	0.33	0.16	0.33m
5e	7	0.85 m	0.14	0.14	0.42m	0.14	0.42m
Overall topical ranking: Abraham > 2 servants, Isaac > 3rd day, place, donkey							

Syntactic realization

Abraham:	S: 6 (1 Nar)	O: 0	A: 0
2 servants:	S: 0	O: 1 (Nar)	A: 2
Isaac:	S: 3	O: 0	A: 0
3rd day:	S: 0	O: 0	A: 1 (Nar)
Place:	S: 0	O: 1 (Nar)	A: 1
Donkey:	S: 0	O: 0	A: 1

iv. *Episode 4: Genesis 22.6 a-d. Preparation for the Journey*

Cumulative frequency table

		Abraham	Isaac	Wood	Fire	Knife
6a	1	1.00		1.00		
6b	2	1.00	0.50	0.50		
6c	3	1.00	0.33	0.33	0.33	0.33
6d	4	1.00	0.50m	0.25	0.25	0.25
Overall topical ranking: Abraham > Isaac > wood, knife, fire						

Syntactic realization

Abraham:	S: 4 (Nar)	O: 1	A: 0
Isaac:	S: 1 (Nar)	O: 0	A: 1 (Nar)
Fire:	S: 0	O: 1 (Nar)	A: 0
Wood:	S: 0	O: 1 (Nar)	A: 0
Knife:	S: 0	O: 1 (Nar)	A: 0

v. *Episode 5: Genesis 22.7a-9d. Abraham and Isaac*

Cumulative frequency table

		Abraham	Isaac	Fire	Wood	Lamb	Sacrifice	God	Place
7a	1	1.00	1.00						
7b-c	2	1.00	1.00						
7d-e	3	1.00	1.00						
7f	4	0.75	1.00						
7g	5	0.60	0.80	0.20	0.20				
7h	6	0.50	0.66	0.16	0.16	0.16	0.16		
8a	7	0.57m	0.57	0.14	0.14	0.14	0.14		
8b	8	0.50	0.62m	0.12	0.12	0.25m	0.25m	0.12	
8c	9	0.55m	0.75m	0.11	0.11	0.22	0.22	0.11	
9a	10	0.60m	0.87m	0.10	0.10	0.20	0.20	0.10	0.10
9b	11	0.63m	0.63	0.09	0.09	0.18	0.18	0.18m	0.18m
Overall topical ranking: Abraham, Isaac > lamb, sacrifice, God, place > fire, wood									

Syntactic realization

Abraham:	S: 4 (Nar, 2 pl.)	O: 2	A: 0	- other: 1 (7b)
Isaac:	S: 3 (Nar, 2 pl.)	O: 0	A: 0	- others: 2 (7e, 8e)
God:	S: 2	O: 0	A: 0	
Lamb:	S: 0	O: 1; C: 1	A: 0	
Sacrifice:	S: 0	O: 0	A: 2	
Place:	S: 0	O: 1	A: 1 (Nar)	
Fire:	S: 0	O: 0	C of Presentative: 1	
Wood:	S: 1	O: 0	C of Presentative: 1	

vi. *Episode 6: Genesis 22.9c-f. Preparation for the Sacrifice*

Cumulative frequency table

		Abraham	Isaac	Place	Altar	Wood
9c	1	1.00		1.00	1.00	
9d	2	1.00		0.50	0.50	0.50
9e	3	1.00	0.33	0.33	0.33	0.33
9f	4	1.00	0.50m	0.25	0.50m	0.50m
Overall topical ranking: Abraham > Isaac, altar, wood > place						

Syntactic realization

Abraham:	S: 4 (Nar)	O: 0	A: 0
Isaac:	S: 0	O: 2 (Nar)	A: 0
Place:	S: 0	O: 0	A: 1 (Nar)
Altar:	S: 0	O: 1 (Nar)	A: 1 (Nar)
Wood:	S: 0	O: 1	A: 1

vii. *Episode 7: Genesis 22.10a-12f. Sacrifice Interrupted*

In this episode the divine messenger and God are identified as one topical entity.

Cumulative frequency table

		Abraham	Messenger-God	Isaac	Knife
10a	1	1.00			
10b-c	2	1.00		0.50	0.50
11a	3	1.00	0.33	0.33	0.33
11b-c	4	1.00	0.50m	0.25	0.25
11d-e	5	1.00	0.40	0.20	0.20
12a	6	0.83	0.50m	0.16	0.16
12b	7	0.85m	0.42	0.28m	0.14
12c	8	0.87m	0.37	0.37m	0.12
12d	9	0.77	0.44m	0.33	0.11
12e	10	0.80m	0.40	0.30	0.10
12f	11	0.81m	0.45m	0.36m	0.09
Overall topical ranking: Abraham > God/messenger > Isaac > knife					

Syntactic realization

Abraham:	S: 7 (3Nar)	O: 0	A: 1	- other: 1
God/Messenger:	S: 4 (3 Nar)	O: 1	A: 1	
Isaac:	S: 0	O: 3	A: 1	
Knife:	S: 0	O: 1	A: 0	

viii. *Episode 8: Genesis 22.13a-13f. Sacrifice of the Ram*

Cumulative frequency table

		Abraham	Ram	Sacrifice	His Son
13a	1	1.00			
13b	2	1.00			
13c	3	0.66	0.33		
13d	4	0.75m	0.25		
13e	5	0.80m	0.40m		
13f	6	0.83m	0.50m	0.16m	0.16m
Overall topical ranking: Abraham > Ram > sacrifice > his son (Isaac)					

Syntactic realization

Abraham:	S: 5 (Nar)	O: 0	A: 0
Ram:	S: 1	O: 2 (Nar)	A: 0
Sacrifice:	S: 0	O: 0	A: 1 (Nar)
Isaac:	S: 0	O: 0	A: 1 (Nar)

ix. *Episode 9: Genesis 22.14a-d. The Naming of the Place*

Cumulative frequency table

		Abraham	Place/Mountain	God	Today
14a	1	1.00	1.00		
14b	2	0.50	0.50	0.50	
14c	3	0.33	0.33	0.33	0.33
14d	4	0.25	0.50m	0.50m	0.25
Overall topical ranking: Place, God > Abraham, today					

Syntactic realization

Place:	S: 0	O: 1 (Nar)	A: 1
God:	S: 1	O: 0	A: 1
Abraham:	S: 1 (Nar)	O: 0	A: 0
Today:	S: 0	O: 0	A: 1

5. *Discussion: Grammatical Encoding and Topical Importance*

Two separate aspects will be considered:

(a) the role of grammatical function in the marking of the topical importance of a particular entity.
(b) the variable degree of topicality of a referent mentioned in a clause.

The first area examines the correlation between clause topic, discourse topic and grammatical function. The second considers the fact that in a clause a main topical entity has not always necessarily a uniform degree of topicality. How the degree of topicality may be altered from one clause to another is investigated. As mentioned earlier the entities referred to in God's command (direct speech, section vv. 2a-2f) are topical. They are: *your son* (or *Isaac*), *the land of Moriah*, *a mountain*, *a sacrifice*.

a. *The Role of Grammatical Encoding*

The measurements confirm the levels of topicality indicated in the title and its expansion in God's command. *Abraham*, the first main topical participant, is mentioned in all the nine episodes and is ranked at the top of the scale in eight episodes. The other main topical participant, *God*, is mentioned only in five out of nine episodes and the ranking of this mention is never as high as that of *Abraham*:

Episode 1: 2nd out of 4
Episode 2: 3rd out of 3
Episode 5: 2nd out of 3
Episode 7: 2nd out of 4
Episode 9: 1st out of 2

However, it must be noted that when the mention of *God* occurs at the second rank (episodes 1, 5, 7) it immediately follows Abraham.

An intriguing feature of the topical importance of *God* is that the item occurs comparatively less frequently in the episodes than the secondary topical participant *Isaac* which is mentioned in eight out of nine episodes. Moreover, a comparison of the ranking of the two entities in episodes where both occur shows that overall the two participants have the same ranking:

	Ep.1: 5 ranks	Ep.2: 3 ranks	Ep.5: 3 ranks	Ep.4: 4 ranks
God	2	3	2	2
Isaac	3	3	1	3

The question arises then as to which feature signals in the story that, in line with the title, *God* is a main topic and not *Isaac*. The syntactic encoding of these entities provides the answer. Altogether, *God* is encoded ten times as S, once as O and once as A. *Isaac* is encoded six times as S (four times only if the third person plural pronouns in vv. 6d and 8c are not included), but nine times as O and three times as A. These figures would seem to indicate that topical importance is not only simply connected to the persistence or the recurrence of an entity in the discourse, but is also significantly correlated to the S function of the entity. Although *God* is not referred to as topical across quite a long stretch of paragraphs, the topicality of the referent is asserted through the occupation of the S function whenever it occurs. A main topical entity may not always be realized as S, but topical importance would seem to coincide with S.

This is confirmed by thc fact that, as alrcady observed, the participant *Isaac* (secondary topic) is encoded principally as O and A. Other secondary entities, location and props follow this pattern. The following table gives a comparative view of the syntactic encoding of topical props:

	O	A	
Mountain/place	5	6	
Wood	3	1	C = 1
Fire	1	0	C = 1
Knife	2	0	C = 1
Sacrifice	0	4	
Altar	1	1	
Ram	(S = 1) 2	0	

The non-topical entities are encoded in the following way: *donkey* is once O and once A; *the 2 servants* is twice O and twice A.

One may conclude that the grammatical encoding of topical entities is a significant indicator of topical importance in Old Hebrew narrative.

b. *Levels of Topical Importance*

For Tomlin, topicality at clause level is linked to extra-linguistic centres of attention in the situation. Centres of attention can be ordered individually in a hierarchy of importance as seen above. But two centres of attention may also coincide. In such cases the topical participant described as 'in control' of a second one becomes more topical than when occuring in isolation. In the ice-hockey game report, Tomlin mentions a player in control of the puck as an example of a referent higher in topicality than a reference to the puck which has become loose (1985: 69). The same phenomenon can be observed in narrative. In Genesis 22, the main participant, *Abraham*, is sometimes referred to in a predication independently of any other topical entity, sometimes in combination with other topical entities. When this is the case, its topical importance increases as two centres of attention coincide. The reference to *Abraham* coinciding with another topical item is more relevant to the goal of the discourse than a reference to *Abraham* on its own. However, the notion of 'coincidence' of the two entities must be defined linguistically. It is at the level of the logical structure of the clause, that is the representation of its semantic content, that the notion of coincidence can be identified. The logical structure describes the system of semantic roles which participants may have within the proposition expressed in the clause.[10] Originally developed by Fillmore (1968) the system of

10. The heart of the meaning of a proposition is the predicate consisting of the V which describes an action, a state or a process. The other elements of the clause

possible roles have multiplied under the name of case grammar. The role and reference grammarians Foley and Van Valin (1984: 29) have proposed two macro-roles which are more basic than case roles. They are Actor and Undergoer. The Actor is the argument of a predicate which expresses the participant that performs, effects, instigates, or controls the situation denoted by the predicate. The Undergoer is the argument which expresses the participant which does not perform, initiate or control any situation but rather is affected by it in some way. These two arguments are generalized semantic relations related to, but not equivalent to, case roles. Case roles such as agent, experiencer, patient, benefactive, etc. belong to a derived system. The two macro-roles have the right level of precision for the purpose of this analysis.

Coincidence may be described semantically as occurring when the main topical participant and other topical entities are arguments of the same predication. The main topical participant is Actor and the other topical entity is Undergoer. Most of the time the case role of Agent (the animate entity who performs the action) is the primary choice for Actor and the case role of Patient (or Object; that is the entity which undergoes the effect of the action, or undergoes change) is the primary choice for Undergoer.[11] In such a distribution of roles the main topical participant with its role of Actor is represented as controlling the other topical entity. This typically occurs when verbs of action are used, that is verbs expressing a dynamic agentive event. Consider:

(3.1) Genesis 22.4a

ביום השלישי וישא אברהם את־עיניו

On the third day Abraham lifted up his eyes.

The verb describes a situation which is an accomplishment. But the Undergoer ('his eyes') is not a topical entity different from the Actor. Only the main topical entity is referred to in the predication and so there is no increase in topicality. The following clause is different:

are linked to the predicate as arguments called the predicate case frame. NPs function in a 'role' or 'case' with reference to the V which may have a variety of syntactic manifestations.

11. Other possibilities might arise. For example, when the verb is a verb of perception the Actor has the case role of Experiencer.

(3.2) Genesis 22.9

ויערך את־העצים

and he laid the wood in order.

The predicate has an action V. The main topical participant is Actor. The Undergoer is a topical prop as it is related to the sacrifice. Two topical items are brought together in the predication and as a result the topical participant in the role of Actor increases in topicality. Semantically this clause contributes more to the goal of the communicative event than the one in (3.1). The reference to Abraham in (3.1) may be said to be proportionately less relevant to the goal of the communication than in (3.2).

The types of clauses occurring in Genesis 22 illustrate well the variations in the degree of topicality which a main topical entity might bear.

(1) The main topical participant is the only argument in the predication. Its degree of topicality may be described as 'normal'. Attention is fixed on the item in a routine kind of way as in:

(3.3) Genesis 22.3a

וישכם אברהם בבקר

Abraham rose up early in the morning.

The verb is an action verb with the single argument of Actor. The level of topicality is not augmented. The temporal phrase is not an obligatory argument; moreover it is not topical.

(2) A main topical participant and a non-topical prop occur as arguments of a transitive clause:

(3.4) Genesis 22.3b

ויחבש את־חמרו

He saddled his donkey.

The main topical participant, *Abraham*, is Actor. The DO refers to a prop which has the role of Undergoer. But the prop does not belong to the topical frame. It is not important for the overall goal of communication. As a result, there is no increase in the level of topicality of the main topical participant.

(3) A main topical participant and a topical prop occur as arguments of a transitive clause:

(3.5) Genesis 22.3d

ויבקע עצי עלה

He cut the wood for the burnt offering.

The main topical participant, *Abraham*, has the role of Actor. The Undergoer is a prop related to the topical framework of the sacrifice. As a result, the topical entity which is Actor increases in topicality and is higher in topicality than in clause (3.4) above.

The following is a similar case:

(3.6) Genesis 22.6c

ויקח בידו את־האשׁ ואת־המאכלת

He himself took the fire and the knife.

The main topical participant is Actor. Two topical props associated with the topical frame of the sacrifice are Undergoers. The topical participant increases in topicality.

(4) The main topical participant occurs in a transitive clause with a secondary topical participant:

(3.7) Genesis 22.9e

ויעקד את־יצחק בנו

He bound Isaac, his son.

The main topical participant, *Abraham*, is Actor and the secondary topical participant, *Isaac*, is Undergoer. The two arguments are directly relevant to the goal of the discourse. They refer to the person tested and the object of the test. In such a clause the main topical participant Actor (case role of Agent) increases its degree of topicality. It reaches the highest degree of topicality and is described as a topical peak.

Similarly, in the following example, the same two topical entities are arguments of a predication. *Abraham* is Actor and *Isaac* is Undergoer, moreover a topical prop has the role of a Locative. The main topical participant is also a topical peak.

(3.8) Genesis 22.9f

וישׂם אתו על־המזבח ממעל לעצים

He laid him on the altar, on top of the wood.

In the next example the writer has delayed the mention of the secondary topical participant for particular effects:

(3.9) Genesis 22.3c

ויקח את־שני נעריו אתו ואת יצחק בנו

and he took two of his young men with him, and his son Isaac.

The main topical participant, *Abraham*, is Actor and there are two Undergoers. The first one, *young men*, is a non-topical entity; the second, *Isaac*, is a secondary topical entity which is mentioned after the non-topical entity. It is the mention of the last entity which makes the Actor a topical peak. By mentioning last the participant which is topically more important the writer produces an effect of surprise. The first argument seems to set the main topical participant (Actor) at an ordinary level of topicality, but unexpectedly the second resets it as a topical peak.

The following conclusions about levels of topical importance may be drawn.

(1) Discourse entities which are topical may be brought together as arguments of a predication. This phenomeneon may be exploited pragmatically.

(2) The main topical participant is usually encoded in the role of Actor (case role of agent) in the predication.

(3) When the main topical participant is mentioned in a clause with the role of Actor its level of topicality is susceptible to be increased.

(4) The increase in topicality is understood cognitively as an increase in attention on the entity in question.

(5) The increase in topicality varies in proportion to the topical importance of the entity which has the role of Undergoer in the predication.

(6) On the basis of the story in Genesis 22, a topical ranking of the main participant may be offered:

Main topical participant on its own:	1
Main topical participant + prop:	1
Main topical participant + topical prop:	2
Main topical participant + second. topical partic.	3 = topical peak

(7) The variation in degree of topicality from neutral to topical peak is exploited by the storyteller to create particular centres of interest which stand out in the middle of routine narration.

(8) The main centres of interests in the story, with the main topical participant as a topical peak, are the following:

(3.10) Genesis 22.3:

(3a) וישׁכם אברהם בבקר 1

So Abraham rose early in the morning,

(3b) ויחבשׁ את־חמרו 1

and saddled his donkey.

(3c) ויקח את־שׁני נעריו אתו ואת יצחק בנו 3

He took two of his young men with him and his son Isaac,

(3d) ויבקע עצי עלה 2

and he cut the wood for the burnt offering.

The main participant in (3c) is topical peak, in spite of being encoded as a clitic pronoun. The presentational order of the topical entities is significant as it is only with the mention of the item which comes last in the clause (secondary topical participant) that the Actor becomes topical peak.

(3.11) Genesis 22.9

(9c) ויבן שׁם אברהם את־המזבח 2

Abraham built an altar there

(9c) ויערך את־העצים 2

and laid the wood in order.

(9d) ויעקד את־יצחק בנו 3

He bound Isaac his son,

(9f) וישׂם אתו על־המזבח ממעל לעצים 3

and laid him on the altar, upon the wood.

In the last two clauses, the main topical participant and the secondary topical participant are Actor and Undergoer respectively. Attention is entirely fixed on the Actor, the sacrificer, 'in control' of his victim.

(3.12) Genesis 22.10

(10a) וישׁלח אברהם את־ידו 1

Abraham put forth his hand

(10b) ויקח את־המאכלת (10c) לשׁחט את־בנו 3

and took the knife to slay his son.

In the first clause, the Undergoer (*hand*) is a part of the main topical participant. The second sentence has a main clause followed by an infinitival clause. A topical prop is Undergoer in the predication of the main clause. In the infinitive construction, the Actor role is understood to be the the same as the Actor of the main predication. The Undergoer (*son*) differs, however, being the secondary topical participant. As a result, *Abraham* encoded morphologically as a clitic becomes a topical peak.

(9) No marked constructions such as forefronting or a change in word order are used to signal topical peaks. The only constraints are the case frames associated to the verb used.

6. *Topic and Basis*

In episode three, the first clause begins by a preverbal adverbial phrase *and on the third day* (v. 4a). It is not part of the discourse topic and cannot be categorized as a topical entity. Its forefronting is not for topicalization. Chafe has offered the following view of topic which will be useful to understand the role of this phrase:

> What the topic appears to do is to limit the domain of applicability of the main predication to a certain restricted domain. The topic sets the spatial, temporal or individual framework within which the predication holds (1976: 50).

This definition was proposed to describe the function of certain initial elements in Mandarin Chinese. But even when applied to the main predication of the clause only, the amalgamation of spatio-temporal setting and topical participant under the single notion of topicality is not very helpful. Topicality understood cognitively as the fixation of attention on an entity overlaps with what Chafe calls 'the individual domain'. But it is confusing to analyse temporal or locational expressions as topicalized items. Such constituents function pragmatically at a level which is different from the one at which topical participants operate. Topical entities are the essential elements around which a story is constructed; the main topical participants belong to the goal of the discourse. Spatio-temporal settings do not have such a role and cannot be categorized in such a way. A preverbal adverbial with vayyiqtol will be called a 'basis', using a concept first proposed by Benes (1962: 6-11) who defined basis as the opening element of the sentence which serves as a 'point of departure' and which is tied in with the context. Here, however, the term basis will be reserved for the spatial or temporal framework set by a preverbal adverbial and within which the ensuing stretch of discourse holds.

7. *The Morphological Encoding of Topic*

The last aspect of topicality which remains to be examined is how the topical entities are morphologically encoded and which factors influence various types of encoding.

Topicality is explained cognitively by the centering of the attention of a speaker and hearer upon a discourse entity. Givón has proposed describing the fixation of attention during discourse production and comprehension through a metaphor borrowed from computer programming (1989: 914-44). When an entity is mentioned it is moved in the 'active discourse file'. In terms of attention, it is maximally activated and serves as an address or file label which can receive incoming information (new information). When an entity is not mentioned for a while it gradually falls into the 'inactive discourse file'.

The centring of attention on an entity is correlated to its formal encoding in two ways. First, in order for an entity to show itself to be a centre of attention it must obviously be encoded linguistically. Secondly, as the centring of attention is affected by how accessible the entity is in terms of the preceding discourse context, the form of the encoding varies according to the accessibility or (predictability) of the entity.[12] Referential accessibility derives from the contextual sources of the speech situation or of the preceding discourse or of general knowledge. It has also to do with short-term memory and the ability of the hearer to keep track of the entity referred to. Referential distance from the previous mention of the entity in discourse and the complexity of the immediately preceding discourse are particular areas to be considered in the study of accessibility.

The basic principle guiding referent accessibility is that the less accessible a referent is the more morphological material will be used to encode it.[13] On this basis the following scale can be offered:

12. Accessibility depends on shared knowledge between hearer and speaker. The three major sources of shared knowledge are (1) the cultural context, generically shared; (2) the speech situation, deictically shared; (3) the preceding discourse or textually shared context. It is the last source which is of primordial importance in the study of written texts, where attentional activation is affected by the hearer's mental storage of the preceding (anaphoric) discourse context.

13. As proposed, for example, by Givón (1988: 249).

1. Zero anaphora 2. Clitic pron. 3. Independent pron. 4. Full noun

Most accessible referent ⟶ Least accessible referent

An examination of the morphological encoding of the topical entities in the story gives the following results:

	Abraham	Yahweh/messenger of Yahweh	Isaac	Abraham & Isaac
NP	13	2	1	2
PRO	17	3	2	

The proper noun Abraham is used a great deal in a relatively short story. Moreover, in the narrative clauses the full noun phrase occurs in 3a, 4a, 6a, 9c, 10a, 13a and 14d as S of the clause. This seems to go against the principle mentioned above as throughout the story *Abraham* is the main participant on stage and so is highly accessible. It could be argued that these clauses are episode initial: they start a new scene or open a new burst of closely related actions and so they function as reaffirming the topic for a new episode. But this explanation is not satisfactory in the light of what can be observed in other stories. For example, in the narrative describing King Ahaziah's reign (1 Kgs 22.52–2 Kgs 1.18) the topical participant *Ahaziah* is first introduced through a proper noun (2 Kgs 22.52). Then, it is referred to through the use of a clitic pronoun which is S of six vayyiqtol verbs. With the next vayyiqtol V a change of S occurs:

> Moab rebelled against Israel after the death of Ahab (2 Kgs 1.1).

This clause is followed by the opening of a new paragraph with the proper noun *Ahaziah* as S:

(3.13) 2 Kings 1.2

ויפל אחזיה בעד השׂבכה בעליתו אשׁר בשׁמרון

Ahaziah fell through the lattice in his upper chamber at Samaria.

This is the last time the main topical participant is referred to by a full noun.

The story which follows is rather intricate. A new main topical participant, *Elijah*, and secondary participants, *the messengers* and *the captains* are introduced. *Ahaziah* is often out of discourse and then reintroduced after a gap (e.g. 2 Kgs 1.5, 13). It is referred to at the beginning of a paragraph (2 Kgs 1.9, 11). Complexity of reference is also present (2 Kgs 1.5: *the messengers returned to him* [suffix pron] *and he* [clitic] *asked them*). In spite of these factors which normally encourage a stronger linguistic coding of the referent, all the twelve narrative verbs of the story with the participant *Ahaziah* as S use the clitic pronoun. This is in stark constrast with Genesis 22. The main participant *Abraham* is strongly attended to and is quite accessible and so should not require strong activation by massive coding. But this is in fact what happens.

The conclusion which can be drawn from a comparison of the two stories is that accessibility (referential distance or referential complexity in the preceding discourse) does not seem to be the only factor which has a bearing on the way entities are encoded in Old Hebrew stories. Commenting on the Ahaziah story, Jacob Licht writes:

> Neither the accident, nor the sin of having recourse to Baal-Zebub, nor the historically important event of a king's death, seem to have interested the narrator very much. The theme he is concerned with is the power of Elijah's prophecy (1978: 55).

If what Licht says is true, then it may be concluded that a weak morphological encoding of one of the main participant makes the other main participant, *Elijah*, to stand out. When in a story with two main topical participants, one acts as a foil to the other one, for example in terms of action–reaction as exemplified in the Ahaziah story, the participant made salient is subject to more morphological encoding than the other one who is being kept track of mainly through pronouns.

Morphological encoding would not be then merely related to questions of attention and accessibility, of keeping track of participants. It could also be used as a special highlighting device of one of the main participants.

8. *Conclusion*

The following important points have emerged from the analysis:

(1) Topicality is best described cognitively as the centring of attention of speaker and hearer on discourse entities which are the main concern of the story.[14] In written narrative, the choice of topical participants

14. The confusion to which the absence of cognitive criteria in the analysis of topicality leads can be observed in Payne's article (1991: 62), where he claims that the theme of the Hebrew clause is the verb.

is unilaterally made by the writer. Once the topical entities have been introduced they become the centre of attention of writer and reader.

(2) A cognitive understanding of topicality allows one to detect various kinds of importance which are signalled in different ways in the story.

(3) The first type of importance is controlled by the discourse topical framework which, in most stories, is unveiled in the course of the narration, but which sometimes is provided in a title, as is the case in the Genesis 22 story.

(4) The importance of entities belonging to the topical framework is conveyed through the persistence of the entity in discourse, and is marked by the grammatical coding of the entity. A main topical participant will persist throughout the story and will be found mostly in the grammatical function of S, which corresponds to the main topic having the case role of agent. The repeated occurrence of an entity in a clause with a DO or A function indicates that the entity is a secondary topical entity, either a secondary participant or a prop.

(5) The second kind of importance affects a main topical participant only. It is linked to the organization of the semantic roles (types of arguments) in a given predication. When a predication merges the main topical participant and another topical entity into one centre of attention, the main topical participant increases in topicality. This is usually happening in transitive clauses with the main topical participants as Actor and the other topical entity as Undergoer. A participant with the highest degree of topicality is a topical peak.

(6) A participant which is a topical peak is salient in terms of attention: the attention of both speaker and hearer is maximally focused on the main topical participant who is 'in control' of the other topical entity, as it contributes more directly to the goal of the story.

(7) The use of such salient constructions throw a very different perspective on two aspects of Longacre's analysis of biblical stories:

(a) Concerning his foreground–background distinction, it can no longer be claimed that all the vayyiqtol clauses have a uniform foregrounding value. If clauses have as arguments of their predications participants which may vary in their degree of topicality, it means that those with a reference to a participant with a higher degree of topicality (a topical peak) and contributing more to the goal of the discourse, are more salient than those who do not contain a similar reference.

(b) Concerning his description of story profile as a plot, it can no longer be claimed that only the peak or climax of a story is highlighted for prominence. Rather, a storyteller has the freedom to introduce salient constructions with a topical peak at any point in the narration. These clauses break the routine recounting of events and the routine reference to participants. They stand out as their predication brings together topical entities which fix the attention of the hearer in a greater degree.

Chapter 4

DISCOURSE REFERENTS AND TOPICALITY

1. *Preliminaries*

Chapter 3 has considered the question of topic from the perspective of the centring of attention on a discourse participant. This chapter will examine topicality from a different angle. It will analyse how the deployment of information in discourse and the mental representation of entities during discourse influence the choice of clausal forms. The analytical framework has taken into account the works of a number of linguists,[1] but the overall influence of Lambrecht's ideas predominates.[2]

a. *Discourse Referents and their Cognitive Status*

The question of topic is directly related to the question of how entities are represented in the mind. An initial distinction must be made between linguistic expressions and the entities denoted by these expressions in utterances. The entities are called referents. The referents are represented abstractly in the minds of speaker and hearer. For the purpose of this analysis, it is not necessary to make a distinction between referent as such and their abstract mental representation. When the term referent is used, it is the mental representation of the referent which is designated by the term.

The mental representation of referents is affected by two informational categories: identifiability and activation. Together, these two notions refine the concept of 'shared knowledge' used in many pragmatic studies, and which is too general to account adequately for what takes place cognitively in discourse. Knowing something is different from thinking of something and in discourse production and comprehension particularly, this last mental state is extremely important too.

1. Notably Givón (1988, 1990), Gundel (1985, 1988) and Horn (1986).

2. His theory, developed over many years, has been described in various articles published in the 1980s. It is now published in a book (1994).

Chafe explains that 'our minds contain very large amounts of knowledge or information, and only a very small amount of this information can be focussed on, or be 'active' at any one time' (1987: 22).

To explain the two categories of identifiability and activation, it is useful to return to Givón's 'discourse file' metaphor mentioned in Chapter 3, sect. 7. When speakers want to make an assertion about an entity which is assumed to be not yet represented in the hearer's mind, they must create first a mental representation of the entity in the hearer through linguistic description. The creation of such representation can be compared to the opening of a referent 'file', and the opening of the file is directly connected to the referent's *identifiability*. A referent is *identifiable* when its representation exists in the hearer's mind. Once a referent is *identifiable*, new incoming information may be added to the referent's file.

Every entity mentioned during discourse has its file stored in the hearer's mind. However, a referent is not necessarily always at the forefront of the hearer's consciousness. There are various degrees of activation of referents. An entity is activated to the extent that it is 'lit up' in the consciousness of the hearer. Chafe distinguishes three different activation states:

> An *active* concept is one that is currently lit up, a concept in a person's focus of consciousness. A *semi-active* concept is one that is in a person's peripheral consciousness, a concept of which a person has a background awareness, but one that is not being directly focused on. An *inactive* concept is one that is currently in a person's long-term memory, neither focally nor periphally active (Chafe 1987: 25).

The notions of active and inactive referent do not need more explanations. As for semi-active ('accessible' is the other word sometimes used), a referent has this status when it is deactivated from an earlier active state. In this case, it is textually accessible. But it may also be semi-active because it belongs to a set of expectations associated with a knowledge schema; it is then inferentially accessible. The terminology used will be the following:

not-yet-activated: the referent has no activation state.
activated: the referent has an activation state which may be:

inactive
semi-active
active

Inactive or semi-active referents are *non-active* referents, in contradistinction to referents with an *active* status.

The degree of activation of a given referent at a specific point in discourse is reflected in a variety of ways across languages. Part of the aim of this study is to examine how activation correlates to grammar. One known area of correlation is (apart from prosody) morphological: activation states play a role in the selection of nouns or pronouns. Pronominal reference is inadequate if the activation state of the referent is insufficient, for example. But referent activation also influences the establishment of a referent as topic, as will be shown in the analysis.

b. *Types of Information and the Pragmatic Roles of Topic and Focus*

The traditional distinction between old and new information is redefined in terms of pragmatic presupposition and assertion. The typical sentence is characterized by the coexistence in it of a presupposition, evoked lexically and grammatically, and an assertion. The presuppositional component consists of a set of propositions[3] which the speaker believes the hearer knows or is ready to take for granted. To make an assertion is to establish a relation between the presupposed set of propositions and a non-presupposed proposition. The assertion is the proposition which the hearer is expected to know or take for granted as a result of hearing a sentence (Lambrecht 1994: 52). By 'knowing' is meant here 'to have a mental representation of' the proposition.

The definitions of topic and focus in terms of presupposition and assertion correlate with their pragmatic roles. Pragmatically, the term topic denotes a referent (usually the discourse topical entity referred to in Chapter 3) which has a particular relation to a proposition expressed in a clause. The referent is the topic of the proposition if the proposition is about the referent, that is, if it communicates information which is relevant to the hearer's knowledge of the referent or increases it. This relational definition means that topics are presuppositional. They must be taken for granted as elements of the pragmatic presupposition evoked by a sentence. As for focus, it is the part of an utterance whereby the presupposition and the assertion differ from each other.

The topic referent is encoded in a clause through a linguistic expression, a noun phrase or pronoun which must not be confused with the

3. Lambrecht (1994: 53) is aware that this term is ambiguous but he explains that what is meant by 'proposition' are the situations or events *denoted* by a proposition.

referent itself. A pronoun, for example, will be a topic expression when its referent has a topic relation to the proposition.

c. *Sentence Types*

Sentences can be categorized according to their communicative functions in discourse, and the information structures which enable them to fulfill these functions.[4]

The *topic-comment* sentence presupposes that the topical entity is a focus of current interest. The topic is shared and the comment answers the question *what did x* (i.e. the topic) *do next?* making an assertion about a topical referent. The statement in the comment aims at increasing the hearer's knowledge about the topical entity as in the question–answer pair:

(1) What did Tim do?
(2) He fixed himself a stiff drink and put a blues CD on.

(2) presupposes that *Tim* is the item of current concern between hearer and speaker. The two comments of (2) predicate some property of *Tim*.

The *identificational* sentence has a predicate which is presuppositional. Its communicative function is to provide the identity of the referent sollicited by the question. Consider:

(3) Kate heard the telephone ring (4) and picked it up.

(3) and (4) may be used as a reply to the question *Who picked up the telephone?* In this case both clauses are identification clauses, with focus on the N *Kate*. The presupposition is *someone heard the telephone ring and picked it up.*

The *event-reporting* sentence does not answer the question *What happened to x?* with *x* presupposed. It has no pragmatic presupposition, except a general proposition evoked in the question *what happened?* Consider the sentence:

(5) My son fell from a ladder.

(5), said by a speaker explaining why he has arrived late at work, will be understood as informing the hearer of the event which delayed him

4. This classification is inspired by a group of linguists using the functional sentence perspective model of analysis, notably Firbas (1979; 1986a; 1986b; 1987a; 1987b; 1992), Vande Kopple (1986), Papprotté and Sinha (1987); but it is principally guided by Lambrecht's model (1994) which is more precise in its use of pragmatic notions.

or her. The participant *son* is mentioned because he was involved in this event, not because he is the topic of discourse. The purpose of such an utterance is to answer the question *what happened?* In this kind of clause, the hearer usually assumes that the referent of the noun *son* can be identified in a minimal way by the hearer.

In English the non-topical status of the NP subject is not distinctly marked, but in some languages it is. In spoken French (5) is:

(5a) *Y'a mon fils qui est tombé d'une échelle.*

Importantly, Lambrecht has noticed that a sentence such as (5a) has also, what he calls, a 'presentational' meaning; that is, it is used to indicate the existence or coming into existence of a referent (1994: 137-146). Consider the sequence in spoken French:

(6a) *Qu'est-ce qu'il y a?*
(6b) *J'ai la tête qui me tourne.*
(6a) What's the matter?
(6b) I feel dizzy.

Given a context in which (6a) is said by speaker A who has noticed that a friend B looks unwell, (6b) introduces *tête* into the discourse. Lambrecht explains: 'in the presentational sentence proper the newly introduced element is an ENTITY (a discourse referent) while in the event-reporting sentence it is an EVENT' (1994: 144).

The event-reporting clause proper and the presentational clause have in common that they have a 'non-topical' character. In spoken French, this is indicated grammatically by the post-verbal placement of the noun, as illustrated in (6b) above. In both of them the information conveyed is entirely new. The presentational clause is used to present a referent as non-topic; the event-reporting clause is used in an utterance in which the referent is a necessary participant in an event, without being a topic.

The main purpose of the analysis which follows is to examine the correlation between activation states of referents, their encoding as topics and the sentence types in which they occur. Activation states of referents change in discourse. A brand-new referent may have the state of 'not-yet-activated' state. In the unfolding of discourse, a referent might be absent from discourse for a while and become semi-active, before being reintroduced. A referent might simply persist without interruption over a discourse span, having an active status. These various possibilities will be taken into account.

For a predication about a referent to make sense, the referent must be identifiable. Establishing identifiability is the particular concern of a speaker introducing a brand-new referent in discourse. How a referent is made identifiable will be considered in the section which deals with the first mention of a referent in discourse.

The term 'referent' used in a narrative context mainly designates the participants in a story. So, the terms *referent* and *participant* will be often used interchangeably in this chapter.

2. *First Mention of a Referent in a Story*

When a referent is first mentioned in a story, the speaker assumes that it is either identifiable or not identifiable by the hearer. Typically, a not-yet-activated referent is also not identifiable. In this case, the speaker has to make the referent identifiable.

Identifiability has to do with a speaker's assessment of whether a discourse representation of a referent is already stored in the hearer's memory or not. If a referent is identifiable the hearer has a certain mental representation of the referent in his mind which corresponds to the representation of the referent the speaker has in his mind. If a hearer cannot identify the referent, it is impossible for them to decide whether the predication made about the topic is true or not. Consider the examples:

(1) A car is red
(2) Isabella is ill.

(1) is unaccepable because it does not make sense to predicate 'redness' of a topic which is an unidentifiable referent. The hearers are not able to understand the proposition they are presented with properly. In (2), the mention of the referent *Isabella* activates it in the mind of the hearer, but *Isabella* could refer to a horse, a cat, a queen or a little girl. Satisfactory activation requires the establishment of identifiability.

As a preliminary note, it is important to know that a great number of Old Hebrew stories recount the lives of the great heroes of Israel's past. These figures are assumed by the storytellers to be identifiable because in the universe of discourse of the speaker and hearer, or of the community to which they both belonged, there existed only one referent which could be named by these NPs. *Abraham*, *Moses*, *David*, *Solomon* need not be identified every time they appear in a new story. The hearer or reader is assumed to know who they are in a unique way. In terms of activation, when these referents are first mentioned, they are inactive referents stored in the long-term memory of the hearer.

a. *Making a Referent Identifiable*

When a referent is brand-new, the first task of the speaker is to make it identifiable. A variety of devices may be used to establish a referent's identifiability. They are: anchoring, anaphoric reference, generic reference and deictic reference.

i. *Anchoring*

Anchoring consists in linking the NP which represents the non-identifiable referent to another discourse entity which is identifiable. Consider:

(4.1) Genesis 3.1

והנחש היה ערום מכל חית השדה

The serpent was more crafty than any other wild animal [that Yahweh God had made].

Serpent is a brand-new referent. It is anchored to another referent *animal (of the field)* through a comparative construction. This last referent has been mentioned earlier in the creation story (Gen. 2.19, 20). As a result *serpent* is uniquely identifiable as a specific representative of a class of entities; this explains the presence of the definite article.

(4.2) 2 Kings 5.1

ונעמן שׂר־צבא מלך־ארם היה איש גדול לפני אדניו

Naaman, army commander to the king of Aram, was a great man in the sight of his master.

The brand-new referent *Naaman* is linked to another referent *the king of Aram* which is not mentioned in the context. However, the referent *the king of Aram* is considered as an identifiable referent in the universe of discourse shared by speaker and hearer. *Naaman* is made identifiable through its anchoring to *the king of Aram.*

ii. *Anaphoric Reference*

This is a form of anchoring through anaphoric pronoun. A referent is identifiable when it is linked through an anaphoric pronoun to a participant mentioned in the previous discourse. Consider:

(4.3) 1 Kings 22.40

(1) וישכב אחאב עם־אבתיו
(2) וימלך אחזיהו בנו תחתיו

(1) Ahab rested with his fathers (2) and his son Ahaziah reigned in his stead.

The referent *Ahaziah* in (2) is brand-new and not-yet-activated. Its identifiability is established through the anaphoric phrase *his son*, which anchors it to *Ahab*, a participant which is identifiable.

Anaphoric reference is the usual device to introduce a brand-new female character in a story. The phrase *wife of* makes the new referent identifiable through reference to the husband, an already known referent. Consider:

(4.4) 1 Samuel 25.3

(1) ושם האיש נבל
(2) ושם אשתו אבגיל

(1) The name of the man was Nabal (2) and the name of his wife Abigail.

Nabal is an identifiable referent, having been mentioned in the prior context. The way the new participant *Abigail* is introduced is unusual. (2) does not predicate that *Nabal had a wife*, as is usually the case in Old Hebrew stories (see example *(4.5)* below). Instead, the referent *wife* is mentioned almost incidentally, the topic of the clause being *the name*. However the anaphoric reference is present in ישתו, *his wife*.

The two main female participants in the story of the birth of Samuel are first introduced in a similar way:

(4.5) 1 Samuel 1.1-2

(1) There was a certain man from Ramathaim, a Zuphite from the hill country of Ephraim. (2) His name was Elqanah, son of Jeroham [the son of Elihu, the son of ...]

(3) ולו שתי נשים

He had two wives.

In (3) the referent *wives* is a brand-new referent. It is made identifiable through the expression of possession. The anaphora *to him* refers backs to the identifiable referent *man (from Ramathaim)*.

iii. *Generic Expressions*

When a brand-new referent is expressed through a generic NP, it is considered as uniquely identifiable, because identifying a whole class of similar things is to identify also a unique referent.

(4.6) 2 Kings 7.3

וארבעה אנשים היו מצרעים פתח השער

There were four men with leprosy at the entrance of the city gate.

The complement of the copular V, *leprous*, establishes the indefinite NP *four men* as expressing an identifiable referent. *Leprous* is a generic expression which describes the *four men* as a representative set of members of the class of leprous people, which is identifiable.

iv. *Deictic Reference*

In establishing identifiability through deictic reference, the storyteller has recourse to aspects of the text's external situation. A referent can be made identifiable through deictic reference because the deictic referent is identifiable in the speech situation. This is the main device found in the stage-setting sections of stories. It might seem, in fact, that stage-setting sections are brought into play when the other devices (particularly anchoring and anaphoric reference) cannot be used because the brand-new referent cannot be hooked on to another identifiable participant in the world of the text. The deictic expressions denote location, membership of an ethnic group and possession. The expressions are often combined. Consider:

(4.7) 1 Samuel 1.1-2

ויהי איש אחד מן־הרמתים צופים מהר אפרים

There was a man from Ramathaim, a Zuphite[5] from the hill country of Ephraim.

The indefinite NP *one man* is anchored to a NP referring to a town first and then to the clan of the man. Identifiability here is obtained through a semantic process parallel to generic reference. *Ramathaim* denotes the whole population of the town and *a man* is a specific member of the group.

5. I choose to read here צופים as צופי, a Zuphite on the basis of the later mention of the area in which Samuel lived (1 Sam. 9.5). The Masoretic text provides a reading which is grammatically impossible and probably corrupt. The final ם of צופים is a dittographic repetition of the first letter of the following word.

(4.8) Judges 17.1

(1) ויהי־איש מהר־אפרים (2) ושמו מיכיהו

(1) There was a man from the hill country of Ephraim (2) and his name was Micah.

The first reference to the brand-new participant in (1) is conveyed by an indefinite NP. Its identifiability is provided simply through reference to an identifiable geographical area.

The new referent may be made identifiable through deictics denoting location, followed by tribal membership:

(4.9) Judges 17.7

ויהי־נער מבית לחם יהודה ממשפחת יהודה

Now there was a young man of Bethlehem in Judah, of the clan of Judah. [He was a Levite and he was residing there].

The brand-new and indefinite referent *a young man* is assumed to be identifiable through the text external reference *Bethlehem in Judah* which is complemented by a deictic phrase denoting kinship: *the clan of Judah*.

In some cases the locational deictic is text internal and anaphoric, providing a back reference to a location previously mentioned in the text:

(4.10) 2 Kings 4.8

(1) ויעבר אלישע אל־שונם
(2) ושם אשה גדולה

(1) Elisha was passing through Shunem (2) and there, a wealthy woman lived.

The deictic *there* is linked anaphorically to an identifiable locational antecedent *Shunem* and so the referent *woman* is made identifiable.

The following example combines identifiability through the use of a possessive expression and deictic reference:

(4.11) 1 Kings 21.1

(1) After these events,
(2) כרם היה לנבות היזרעאלי

There was a vineyard belonging to Naboth the Jezreelite.

In this introduction two referents are introduced at the same time: a topical prop and a topical participant. The referent *vineyard*, which is inanimate, is identified through mention of its owner, *Naboth*. As for the referent *Naboth,* it is made identifiable through a reference to his place of origin, *Jezreel*.

v. *Frame*

Finally a referent is identifiable because it belongs to a class of items evoked by a previously mentioned referent. Fillmore defines this structural context as follows:

> By the term 'frame' I have in mind any system of concepts related in such a way that to understand any of them you have to understand the whole structure in which it fits; when one of the things in such a structure is introduced into a text, or into a conversation, all of the others are automatically made available (1982: 111).

Consider:

(4.12) 2 Samuel 17.19

(1) They came to the house of a man at Bahurim, who had a well in his courtyard...

(2) ותקח האשה

and the woman took [and spread a covering over the well's mouth].

In (1) the referent *man* is made identifiable through a locational deictic. In (2), the referent *woman* is mentioned for the first time. It is considered identifiable because of the presence of a knowledge frame. Once the referent *man* has been mentioned, a 'family' frame is created and the referents included in this frame are considered as identifiable. As a result, the referent *woman* can be immediately encoded in a definite NP. The definite article also indicates that the referent is semi-active (see 1a above).

Another type of frame is used in:

(4.13) 2 Samuel 18.24

(1) David was sitting between the two gates,

(2) וילך הצפה אל־גג השער אל־החומה

and the sentinel went up to the roof of the gates by the wall.

The referent *sentinel* is identifiable through the knowledge frame provided by the referent *gate*. It is encoded in a definite NP.

vi. *Conclusion*

The examples fall into two distinctive groups. Referents which are brand-new but have an activation state may be introduced while involved in the action, i.e. as subject of a vayyiqtol verb. This is the case of those referents which are inactive (and identifiable) because they belong to a frame (cf. 4.12 and 4.13). These referents, although newly introduced in discourse, do have an activation state. Through the frame, they are stored in long-term memory, ready for retrieval, though inactive. In (4.12), the referent *woman* is accessible through inference from a frame provided by the referent *house of a man*. In (4.13), the referent *sentinel* is accessible through the frame provided by the referent *gate*.

Referents which are brand-new but are not-yet-activated are not immediately used as topics of vayyiqtol clauses. They are also made identifiable in a special stage-setting section which uses verbless or copular clauses. In these clauses, the function of the predicate, usually an adverbial phrase or a prepositional phrase, is to make the referent identifiable by expressing its identity or some of its property or attribute.

However, (4.3) with its vayyiqtol verb, is an obvious a counter-example. It will be discussed on page 142 below.

b. *Definiteness, Indefiniteness and Identifiability*

Definiteness embraces the class of reference items such as the definite article, definite pronouns, proper names and possessed noun phrases. How the identifiability of a referent and its active state is correlated to the encoding of the referent in question as a definite NP has been noticed in the preceding section. This section will examine a few more examples of referents encoded as NP with the definite article.

In Old Hebrew indefiniteness is grammatically marked by the absence of the article. Definiteness is indicated by the article *ha-* prefixed to the noun. That the definite article marks identifiable referent is confirmed by many examples such as:

(4.14) 1 Samuel 25.2-3

(1) ואיש במעון

(2) ומעשׂהו בכרמל

(3) והאיש גדול מאד

(1) There was a man in Maon, (2) and his property was in Carmel. (3) The man was very rich.

In (1) the indefinite *a man* introduces a brand-new referent which is made identifiable through a locational NP. In (3) the now identifiable referent is expressed through a definite NP. The absence of article in (1) shows that the speaker, on first mentioning the participant, does not expect the hearer to identify which man is meant. The presence of the article in (3) indicates that identification is expected.

Similarly, in the episode recounting Samson's marriage (Judg. 14.1-19), Samson first *saw a woman* (אשׁה, v. 1) and later he *talked to the woman* (לאשׁה, v. 7) and his father *went down to the woman* (אל האשׁה, v. 10).

So as a general rule, an unidentifiable (brand-new) referent is expressed by a NP without the article. However, the NP may be preceded by a numeral as in:

(4.15) 1 Kings 2.39

ויברחו שׁני־עבדים לשׁמעי אל־אכישׁ

[Three years later] two of Shimei's slaves ran off to king Akish.

But the correlation between definiteness and its cognitive counterpart, identifiability, is not absolute. An indefinite NP does not signal automatically unidentifiability. The semantics of the NP used has a role to play too. A generic referent is identifiable, although used without the article:

(4.16) 1 Samuel 2.27

ויבא אישׁ־אלהים אל־עלי

A man of God came to Eli [and said to him].

The indefinite NP *a man of God* is a generic description used often to designate an oracle-giver or prophet. The referent is identifiable as a member of the class *men of God*. The storyteller does not need to use any other device to establish its identifiability.

In conclusion, if it is true that there is a correlation between definiteness and identifiability, it is also true that it is not absolute. Non-identifiable referents are generally encoded as indefinite forms or various other reference items such as number modified nouns. But identifiable referents may be encoded as indefinite NPs. The semantic class of a referent plays a role in whether a referent will be definite on first mention.

c. *First Mention of a Referent: Activation and Topicality*

A referent is activated when it is at hand in the hearer's consciousness. On its first mention in a story, a referent is either:

(a) Not-yet-activated; such a referent would be brand-new, not known to the hearer. The first task for the speaker is to activate the referent. As seen earlier, this goes hand-in-hand with the task of making it identifiable.

(b) Activated; and in this case two activation states are possible. The referent may be inactive, if it is in the hearer's consciousness but has been unused so far in discourse. It may be semi-active, if the referent occurred in discourse and then was removed from it for a while, or if it belongs to a knowledge frame used in discourse.

We noted in the conclusion at p. 139 above, that only an activated referent (for example, semi-active referent created by a frame) seems to be allowed to be introduced in discourse in a vayyiqtol clause, with the pragmatic role of topic. The process is delayed with a not-yet-activated referent. Such a referent usually appears for the first time in discourse (and is also identified) in a non-vayyiqtol clause. The next section will explore more in detail the correlation between the activation state of a referent, its establishment as topic and the type of clauses in which it occurs. As topical referents are the primary concerns, the emphasis will be on clauses with brand-new referents encoded as subjects. Brief mention will be made of referents which are encoded as DO noun phrases, too.

i. *Not-Yet-Activated Referent Introduced in a Vayyiqtol Clause*

There are examples of not-yet-activated (brand-new) participants introduced in a vayyiqtol clause and encoded as S, that is a topic of the sentence. At first sight, it seems that the topical participant is immediately involved in the action denoted by the V, and its identifiability is established while the action goes on, so to speak. However, upon closer examination, it appears that the question is not as straightforward as first appears: these vayyiqtol clauses reveal features which set them apart from other vayyiqtol clauses. The following analysis identifies these particular features. Some of the examples analysed have already been cited earlier. They are 1 Kgs 22.40 and 2.39, and 1 Sam. 2.27. Consider first (4.3) repeated here:

(4.3) 1 Kings 22.40

(1) וישכב אחאב עם־אבתיו
(2) וימלך אחזיהו בנו תחתיו

(1) Ahab rested with his fathers (2) and his son Ahaziah reigned in his stead.

Ahaziah is a brand-new referent; it has no activation state and yet is established as topic in a vayyiqtol clause, which seems to go against the conclusions of p. 139. The explanation lies in a particular feature of this clause. It is a standard notice of succession which belongs to a larger formulaic regnal summary (Long 1984: 157-67). Such formulaic resumés are widely used throughout the book of 1 Kings (for example, in 14.20, 31; 15.8, 24; 16.28), and constitute framing devices. The succession notice has the role of introducing the new king on to the scene, and so the vayyiqtol clause has in fact a presentational value.

(4.17) 1 Samuel 17.4-5

(1) ויצא איש־הבנים ממחנות פלשתים
(2) גלית שמו מגת

(1) and an infantryman came out of the camp of the Philistines; (2) his name was Goliath, he was from Gath.

The referent *infantryman* has no activation state and is brand-new in the story. It is expressed by a NP which is S and also apparently topic of the clause. However, the clause uses an intransitive verb of motion, which can be interpreted as having the main role of introducing Goliath, a new participant, into the narrative. The function of the clause is not to predicate something about the new referent, but rather to present the referent in the world of the discourse. As such, the clause has a presentational role. Significantly, after the introduction, and once the new participant has been introduced, it is immediately made identifiable more fully in (2), using a verbless clause.

(4.18) Exodus 1.8

(1) ויקם מלך־חדש על־מצרים
(2) אשר לא־ידע את־יוסף

(1) A new king (2) who did not know Joseph (1) arose over Egypt.

The referent *king* has no activation state when introduced in (1). It is encoded as S of the intransitive verb קום ('to arise'), used here with the presentative meaning of 'to come on the scene, to appear'. It is difficult to maintain that, in this clause, there is a topic about which something is predicated. Rather, the not-yet-activated referent is introduced into the discourse through a vayyiqtol clause which has a presentational role.

(4.16) is looked at again, as my next example:

(4.16) 1 Samuel 2.27

ויבא איש־אלהים אל־עלי

A man of God came to Eli [and said to him].

The referent *man of God* has no activation state and its identifiability is established through a generic designation. It is the S of an intransitive vayyiqtol V denoting movement. Here too the clause can be interpreted as taking on a presentational role, through the meaning of its V of motion. At the same time as it denotes a visit of the *man of God* to *Eli*, the clause is also used to introduce the new referent in the narrative. Similarly:

(4.19) Exodus 2.2

(1) וילך איש מבית לוי
(2) ויקח את־בת לוי

A man from the house of Levi went and took to wife a daughter of Levi.

The referent *man* has no activation state; it is made identifiable in (1) through anchoring to *house of Levi*. The NP expressing the brand-new referent is S of an intransitive verb which, semantically, has lost its denotation of movement. The verb is a 'dummy' vayyiqtol V, with the grammatical function of a verb, but without the meaning of 'motion towards'. The clause here too has a presentational role: it introduces the not-yet-activated referent into the discourse.

Another verb of movement, עלה ('to go up'), is used in the next example:

(4.20) 1 Samuel 11.1

ויעל נחש העמוני ויחן על־יבש גלעד

Nahash the Ammonite went up and besieged Jabesh-Gilead.

The new referent has no activation state. It is made identifiable through the mention of ethnicity (*Ammonite*). The V, *he went up*, is intransitive and has lost its literal meaning. No adverbial phrase indicates source, direction or goal. It is used only to introduce the new referent into the discourse and the clause has a presentational role.

In all the examples above, it is significant that intransitive verbs of movement are used. These verbs do not report literally the movements of the new referents mentioned but, rather, they are used as presentational devices, introducing the not-yet-activated referents in discourse. As a result the newly introduced referent is no longer seen as a 'topic' about which a predication is being made.

These observations strongly suggest that a vayyiqtol clause may be used to introduce a referent with a not-yet-activated state only if the referent mentioned for the first time has not the pragmatic role of topic in the clause in which it occurs. Although they are encoded as subjects of verbs, as these verbs are intransitive verbs of movement which tend to loose their literal meanings, the referents are divested of their role of topical agent. Such vayyiqtol clauses must be seen as having a special presentational function.

A second group of vayyiqtol clauses exhibit a different set of peculiarities. In them, the referents encoded as subjects may be categorized as secondary participants or even props. They have a local role in the story and are maintained as clausal topics only over a very short discourse span (a few clauses at the most). Significantly, their identifiability is established through a minimum amount of information; such participants are not given a name, a title or a function. This is exemplified in (4.15), repeated here:

(4.15) 1 Kings 2.39

ויברחו שני־עבדים לשמעי אל־אכיש

[Three years later] two of Shimei's slaves ran off to king Akish.

The context of the story shows that the referent *two slaves* is topical only in this clause. In the rest of the story, the two slaves are not involved as main participants in the events recounted. The clause reports an incident in Shimei's life, who is, in fact, the main participant.

Consider also:

(4.21) 2 Samuel 18.10

וירא איש אחד ויגד ליואב

and one man saw it and told Joab.

The referent *one man* functions only as an informant. He brings the news that Absalom is caught in a tree and he is the initiator of a dialogue with Joab. The topical participant is clearly Joab who is going to strike Absalom dead.

Similarly the unnamed participant is an informant in:

(4.22) 2 Samuel 17.18

וירא אתם נער ויגד לאבשלם

and a lad saw them and told Absalom.

The context of this sentence is that Jonathan and Ahimaaz are carriers of vital information for the safety of King David. They are spotted by a youth sympathetic to Absalom, the king's enemy. The referent *lad* has a very local role and function as a prop. It soon disappears out of discourse.

All these referents have no activation state when mentioned for the first time in the narrative. The NPs which encode them are subjects of vayyiqtol clauses and the referents are topics. However, as the minimum of information provided for their identifiability confirms it, these participants do not have a topical role overall in the story.

The findings relating to the examples examined in this section can be summarized as follows. When a vayyiqtol clause is used to introduce a not-yet-activated referent in a story, there is a tendency to break down the tasks of activation and topicality. To illustrate with a rendering in English, instead of saying:

And Agur, from Beth-Shemesh, killed the king.

an Old Hebrew storyteller will use the sequence:

(1) And a man came (vayyiqtol clause)
(2) and he was from Beth-Shemesh (verbless clause)
(3) and his name was Agur (verbless clause)
(4) and he killed the king (vayyiqtol clause)

When the referent is a primary participant in discourse, the vayyiqtol clause has a presentational role (and form, with V of movement) which divests the referent encoded as S, of its topicality in the clause. The vayyiqtol clause may be used with a referent with no activation state encoded as a topic of the clause, only when such a referent plays no major role in the story. These facts seem to point to a preference which is motivated by cognitive factors: introducing a not-yet-activated referent and giving it at the same time the role of topic must be avoided. This is confirmed by an examination of the use and role of the NP + qatal clause.

ii. *Not-Yet-Activated Referent Introduced as S in a NP + Qatal*
Referents with no activation state are also introduced in a NP + qatal clause. The referent is encoded as the N, and is subject. Consider the following examples:

(4.23) 1 Kings 20.35

ואיש אחד מבני הנביאים אמר אל־רעהו
A certain man of the sons of the prophets said to his fellow companion.

The referent *man (of the sons of the prophets)* is brand-new in the story and has no activation state. It is S and persists as topical participant in the story. (It is made identifiable through the generic term *the sons of the prophet.*)

(4.24) 2 Kings 4.1

ואשה אחת מנשי בני־הנביאים צעקה אל־אלישע
A certain woman, the wife of one of the sons of the prophets, cried out to Elisha.

The new referent is not-yet-activated and also encoded as S. It persists as topic in the discourse.

(4.25) 2 Kings 2.23-25

(1) He went up from there to Bethel,
(2) והוא עלה בדרך
(3) ונערים קטנים יצאו מן־העיר
(2) While he was going up on the way, (3) some young boys came out of the city.

The main participants, *young boys*, are brand-new in the story and have no activation state. They are also the main referents in the story.

These three examples illustrate an alternative way of introducing in discourse brand-new referents with no activation state. Significantly, the participants introduced in this way are topically more important than the referents mentioned in (4.15), (4.21), (4.22). They remain the main topical referents in the story in which they are involved.

Two types of clauses introduce brand-new referents with no activation states, and so perform the same function. One may assume that one clause type has a role which the other has not. The explanation proposed here is that the NP + qatal clause is in fact a presentational clause. A not-yet-activated referent should not immediately be encoded as a topic, for cognitive reasons. In the presentational NP + qatal construction, all the constituents are viewed as 'new' information and all the constituents of the clause are in focus. There is no topic-comment articulation. So, although the new referent is encoded as the N subject, it is not the topic of the clause.

The understanding of the NP + qatal clause as presentational solves a number of syntactical and pragmatic puzzles such as the function of the first clause in Gen. 14.18. Longacre has attempted to identify the function of this clause through a mixture of rather equivocal notions such as 'action preliminary to the main action', 'surprising development', 'part of the staging' (Longacre 1992b: 213-14):

(4.26) Genesis 14.18

(1)	ומלכי־צדק מלך שלם הוציא לחם ויין
(2)	והוא כהן לאל עליון

Melchizedek king of Salem brought out bread and wine. He was priest of God most high.

(1) introduces *Melchizedek*, a brand-new referent with no activation state, into the discourse. It is a presentational clause. The NP subject must not be construed as the topic of the clause, rather the whole clause is in focus. The identifiability of the new referent is established through the NP *king of Salem* and the storyteller makes it even more identifiable through the nominal clause in (2). After this clause, the referent becomes the topic in vayyiqtol clauses.

To summarize, when a NP + qatal clause is used in narrative discourse with its NP designating a brand-new referent, the clause is presentational. Its function is to introduce the not-yet-activated referent into the discourse. Once the referent has been activated (and made identifiable), it takes the role of topical participant in the following vayyiqtol clauses.

The reason for the use of the presentational clause has been mentioned earlier. To activate a new referent and to give this referent the role of topic about which a predication will be made, must be done separately. Doing two cognitive operations at the same time, in the same clause, must be avoided (Lambrecht 1988: 146-49), as this would result in a too important cognitive effort. A presentational clause should be used first and then a clause providing information about the new referent may follow.

That the NP + qatal clause with a new not-yet-activated referent is a presentational clause, finds its confirmation in a very similar construction, the הנה + NP + qatal clause. This is a construction whose presentational value is given by the particle הנה.[6] Very often the verb is in the participle, but a few times it is in the perfect (qatal), as in:

(4.27) 1 Kings 20.13

והנה נביא אחד נגשׁ אל־אחאב

And a certain prophet came to Ahab...

King Ahab is besieged in the city of Samaria by the Arameans, refusing to surrender. The sudden arrival of a prophet carrying instructions for the king, is introduced by a והנה + NP + qatal clause. The new referent has no activation state. The והנה could be dropped, with a resulting NP + qatal clause which would function exactly as the ones examined in the examples cited above.

The description of the presentational clause as having a NP + qatal form with the NP as subject does not mean that all NP + qatal clauses are presentational, as will be seen in Chapter 5. The general criterion for distinguishing presentational NP + qatal from other uses of the clause is provided by the activation state of the referent encoded in the NP. A presentational construction is required when the referent needs to be 'presented' in the discourse, that is when it is not-yet-activated. Before leaving the question of first mention of brand-new referents with no activation state, it is necessary to have a brief look at referents introduced as non-subjects.

iii. *Not-Yet-Activated Referent Introduced as DO in a Vayyiqtol Clause*

The analysis of the story of Abraham and Isaac (Gen. 22) given in Chapter 3 showed that, in general, secondary participants tend to be coded as DOs. Secondary participants may also be encoded as DOs in a vayyiqtol clause when they are first mentioned in a story and have no activation state. A vayyiqtol clause can be used because these referents do not occupy the position of topic.

6. Most examples of hinneh clauses have a verb in the participle but a few occurrences display NP + qatal construction which follow the particle. Kogut (1986) observes that vehinneh in most instances follows a verb of seeing. The clause which complements the verb is an object content verb. Sometimes the verb of seeing is omitted but the shortened formula vehinneh is maintained. This object content is in fact a presentative clause. This is how Waltke and O'Connor analyse the clause too (1990: 675-77).

In the story of King Ahaziah, three captains in charge of 50 men are sent to capture Elijah the prophet. The first captain is introduced as a direct object NP:

(4.28) 2 Kings 1.9

וישלח אליו שׂר־חמשים וחמשיו

He sent to him [i.e. Elijah] a captain of 50 with his company of 50 men.

The topic is the pronominal S *he* whose referent is active in discourse. The introduction, in the comment of the clause, of a referent with no activation state poses no cognitive problems. Similarly:

(4.29) 1 Samuel 8.1-2

(1) When Samuel grew old,
(2) וישׂם את־בניו שׁפטים לישׂראל
He appointed his sons as judges for Israel.

The referent *sons* is brand-new, with no activation state, and is introduced as DO, that is in a non-topical role. Samuel's sons are secondary participants in the story.

Consider also:

(4.30) 2 Samuel 14.2

(1) Joab sent to Tekoa
(2) ויקח משׁם אשׁה חכמה
And he fetched from there a wise woman.

The new referent *wise woman* will be a main topical participant in the story. It has no activation state and it is introduced as an indefinite noun phrase DO; that is, it does not occupy the role of topic. The active referent and topic is encoded as the clitic pronoun *he*.

A brand-new participant may also be encoded as IO:

(4.31) 2 Kings 4.12

ויאמר אל־גיחזי נערו

And he said to Gehazi his servant ...

The referent *Gehazi* has no activation state and is suddenly introduced in the discourse as an IO. Gehazi is a main participant in the story.

d. *First Mention of a Referent: Non-Active Referent*

When a referent is first mentioned, it may have a non-active status if it is inactive or semi-active.The cognitive problem identified concerning the introduction into discourse of not-yet-activated referents does not affect non-active referents, as they have already an activated status. As a result, non-active referents can be encoded in vayyiqtol clauses, as in:

(4.32) Genesis 34.1

ותצא דינה בת־לאה

Dinah, the daughter of Leah [whom she had borne to Jacob] went out.

The referent *Dinah* is semi-active: it has occurred four chapters earlier, in the story of Jacob (Gen. 30.21). This is the beginning of a new story and *Dinah* is mentioned for the first time in a vayyiqtol clause.

However, examples are found in which the introduction into discourse of a non-active referent takes place in a NP + qatal clause.

i. *Non-Active Referent in a NP + Qatal clause*
Consider:

(4.33) Judges 6.34

ורוח יהוה לבשה את־גדעון

And the spirit of Yawheh came over [clothed] Gideon.

Gideon has been asked by a messenger to rescue Israel from the attacks of the Midianites. This clause occurs in the middle of the account of a new threat on the part of the Midianites. The referent *spirit of Yahweh* is inactive, assumed by the speaker to be stored in the hearer's long-term memory. It is introduced into the story out of the blue, as it were, in a NP + qatal clause. In spite of the activated state of the referent, the clause must not be construed as having a topic *spirit of Yahweh* about which something is predicated. It is not a presentational clause either. The purpose of the clause is not to bring into the discourse the referent *spirit of Yawheh*. This is confirmed by the non-continuation of the referent in discourse. Rather, what matters here is the fact that an 'empowering event' takes place involving two participants, *the spirit of Yahweh* and *Gideon*. This event caused Gideon to be ready as a military leader.

A similar event-reporting NP + qatal clause is:

(4.34) 2 Kings 1.3

ומלאך יהוה דבר אל־אליה התשבי

and a messenger of Yahweh told Elijah the Tishbite …

King Ahaziah is injured and has planned to consult the god Baal-Zebub in order to be healed. An unexpected event takes place which will interfere with the king's plan. The referent *messenger of Yahweh* has an inactive status and occurs as S. As in the preceding example, the clause's purpose is not to present the referent *messenger of Yahweh* in the world of the story,[7] but to recount the specific event of the delivery of a message to the prophet Elijah, in which the two referents are necessary participants.

ii. *Non-Active Referent as Topic: NP + Vayyiqtol + PRO*

There is a syntactic construction which allows a speaker to encode a referent with a non-active state as S and topic on its first mention. In it, the NP designating the referent is placed in an detached position, before the clause containing the information about the referent in question. The referent encoded as topic is then also encoded as grammatical S through a resumptive clitic pronoun. Consider the example:

(4.35) 1 Samuel 11.11

ויהי הנשארים ויפצו

And those who survived were scattered.

The clause is used at the end of a battle report. The referent designated by the detached expression *those who survived* is semi-active. It is inferentially accessible, belonging to the expectation created by the 'battle' knowledge frame. The personal pronoun *they* is attached to the verbal form.

The detached construction is relatively rare in Old Hebrew narratives (other examples are found in Gen. 22.24; 1 Sam. 10.11; 14.19). The referents are construed as being unused or accessible through inference from the discourse context. Moreover, in all the examples the referent is topic only in the clause concerned and is not maintained as topic in the ensuing discourse.

7. Although not a decisive criterion, it is significant that the referent does not persist in discourse.

iii. *Non-Active Referent: Multiple Topic in a Vayyiqtol Clause*

Another construction resembling the one just mentioned, and not very often used too, must be mentioned for the sake of exhaustivity. Through it, a non-subject constituent is given the role of topic. Consider:

(4.36) 1 Kings 13.11

(1) The words that he had spoken to the king,
(2) ויספרום לאביהם
They told their father.

The referent *words* is semi-active and inferentially accessible from the context. It is encoded as a N placed in a detached position or 'topicalized'. The clause may be described as a multiple-topic clause, as it has more than one topic. The first semi-active referent *words* is encoded in the role of topic as a pre-vayyiqtol NP. The second active referent, encoded as a pronoun S, has the role of continuing topic.

Two other examples are found in 2 Kgs 24.16 and 1 Kgs 9.20-21. In these two cases the referents detached in pre-verbal position have also an activated status.

Whether the referent is encoded as a forefronted NP subject or object, the examples of pp. 151-53 show that the referent is mentioned as a 'point of departure' for the predication which follows. For these specific cases, the notion of 'point of departure' is helpfully explained by the definition of topic given by Chafe (it was already referred to in Chapter 3, sect. 6: *Topic and Basis*). It can be said with him that 'the topic sets the ... individual framework within which the predication holds' (Chafe 1976: 50).

The forefronted elements refer to some participant or some concrete entity which are topic-like in the sense that their function agrees with the intuition that the element is what the predication is about. The domain of the point of departure is restricted to the clause only.

iv. *Conclusion: Referent and Topic*

Among referents mentioned for the first time in discourse, it is the brand-new and not-yet-activated referents which are subject to a cognitive constraint. The constraint may be expressed as the principle that

> a not-yet-activated referent cannot be introduced into the discourse in a clause in which it has also the pragmatic role of topic.

It follows from this principle that:

(1) the vayyiqtol clause with its topic-comment articulation tends not to be used for introducing not-yet-activated referents. It may be used only if its verb allows a presentational interpretation of the clause.

(2) instead of the vayyiqtol clause, a special presentational clause which has the form NP + qatal is preferred to introduce such a referent into the discourse. In the presentational clause, the not-yet-activated referent, encoded as the N, is not the topic of the clause. The whole clause is in focus.

Finally, taking into account the observations made in section 2, it is possible to establish a classification of clause types used for introducing not-yet-activated referents (participants) into the discourse.

At one end of the spectrum, verbless or copular clauses used in descriptive introductions of the participants are the most acceptable constructions (cf. 4.1, 4.2, 4.5, 4.6, 4.7, 4.8). This is explainable in cognitive terms. Even if a not-yet-activated referent is encoded as topic in these types of clauses, the predication about the topic helps, in fact, to make the referent identifiable. Descriptive clauses fulfil a cognitive function rather than a narrative one.

At the other end of the spectrum is the vayyiqtol clause, with the not-yet-activated referent encoded as topic. This is the least acceptable option as two operations, one cognitive and the other pragmatic, are required of the hearer at the same time.

In the middle of the spectrum, the presentational NP + qatal (also, but more rarely the הנה + NP + qatal) introduces the new referent into the discourse by divesting it of its topicality.

3. *Continuation of a Referent in the Story*

By continuing referent is meant a referent which persists in discourse in the pragmatic role of topic and which, as a result, is encoded as S. A continuing referent is characterized by its active state. It remains lit up in the consciousness of the hearer during the unfolding of discourse. This section looks at the correlation between the active state of the referent, its topicality and its grammatical encoding.

A typical sequence of clauses with continuing topical referent is illustrated by:

(4.37) Exodus 2.15

(1) וישמע פרעה את־הדבר הזה
(2) ויבקש להרג את־משה
(3) ויברח משה מפני פרעה
(4) וישב בארץ־מדין
(5) וישב על־הבאר

(1) When Pharaoh heard of it, (2) he sought to kill Moses (3) Moses fled from Pharaoh (4) and stayed in the land of Midian (5) and he sat down by a well.

A lexical NP encodes the two referents, *Pharaoh* in (1) and *Moses* in (3). The following clauses (2) and (4)–(5) encode the referents in active state as pronominal clitic morphemes. This shows that there is a correlation between active referent and morphological pronominal coding. Moreover, as each referent is also topic of the clause, it is possible to say that clitic pronouns encode continuing topic. Thus, there is a very strong link between grammatical devices marking referent continuity and topic continuity. The two kinds of continuity are tied together. A continuing referent is active and encoded as PRO; such a referent has habitually the role of topic. However, it is important to note that continuity of topical participant is not connected to the vayyiqtol clause type. In (3) a vayyiqtol clause is used when there is discontinuity of referent.

(4.37) implies that all pronominal expressions encode active referents. But this does not mean that all active referents are expressed pronominally. Consider:

(4.38) 2 Samuel 12.19

(1) וירא דוד כי עבדיו מתלחשים
(2) ויבן דוד כי מת הילד
(3) ויאמידוד אל־עבדיו

(1) David noticed that his servants were whispering together. (2) David perceived that the child was dead (3) and David said to his servants …

In (2) the active referent satisfies the condition for pronominal coding but it is designated through a lexical NP. The threefold repetition of the proper name *David* cannot be accounted for cognitively. Commentaries on the passage do not provide a literary explanation of the phenomenon. One could suggest that the effect sought by the narrator is to break down an almost instantaneous event into its three separate phases. The pace of narration is slowed down and the attention is centered on the main participant *David*.

Interestingly, other examples can be found with verbs of perception and cognition (*to notice, to perceive)* which are followed by a cognitively unnecessary repetition of the lexical NP as subject. Consider:

(4.39) 2 Samuel 10.6

(1) ויראו בני עמון
(2) כי נבאשו בדוד
(3) וישלחו בני־עמון
(4) וישכרו את־ארם
(1)The Ammonites saw (2) that they had become odious to David (3) and the Ammonites sent [messengers] (3) and hired the Arameans.

Sometimes, the repetition of the lexical NP has a clearer rhetorical motivation:

(4.40) 2 Samuel 15.16-17

(1) ויצא המלך וכל־ביתו ברגליו
(2) ויעזב המלך את עשר נשים פלגשים...
(3) ויצא המלך וכל־העם ברגליו
(1) And the king marched out with all his household at his heels. (2) The king left ten concubines [to keep the house]. (3) The king marched out with all his servants at his heels.

In middle of a civil war caused by Absalom, King David is threatened and has to abandon his capital city in haste. The threefold repetition of the NP *the king* is best explained in terms of a narrator wanting to underline the dramatic importance and emotional impact of the situation described.

4. *Reintroduction of a Referent*

A referent (participant) may be removed from discourse for a while, remaining unmentioned, and reintroduced subsequently. The referential gap may be more or less important. Measured in clauses, it may vary from one clause to thirty or more. When a referent is removed from discourse, its state of activation changes from active to semi-active (accessible). Cognitively, the referent remains in the hearer's consciousness but is not directly focused on. A referent may be reintroduced in two ways: in a vayyiqtol clause or a NP + qatal clause. Only cases of reintroduction of a referent as topic, that is encoded as S, will be considered here.

a. *Reintroduction of a Referent in a Vayyiqtol Clause*

The story of King Ahaziah (1 Kgs 22.40–2 Kgs 1.18) offers an example of immediate reintroduction:

(4.41) 2 Kings 1.2

ויפל אחזיה בעד השׂבכה בעליתו אשׁר בשׁמרון

Ahaziah fell through the lattice in his upper chamber at Samaria.

The narrative with the referent *Ahaziah* as topic has been interrupted by a clause with a different referent: *Moab had rebelled against Israel after Ahab's death* (2 Kgs 1.1). The deactivated referent *Ahaziah* is reintroduced through a lexical NP for identification, in a vayyiqtol clause.

The referential gap in the following example is more important:

(4.42) 2 Samuel 11.6c-7

(1) וישׁלח יואב את־אוריה אל־דוד
(2) ויבא אוריה אליו
(3) וישׁאל דוד לשׁלום יואב...

(1) Joab sent Uriah to David (2) and Uriah came to him. (3) David asked if Joab was well.

The three referents are the main protagonists of the story. Out of the three, two are textually accessible and have a semi-active state. The referent *Joab* in (1) is reintroduced in a vayyiqtol clause, having been active two clauses before. The referent *David*, in (3), is reintroduced after a gap of ten clauses, also in a vayyiqtol clause. As for the referent *Uriah,* it is mentioned in the immediately preceding clause as DO, and its full lexical coding is for disambiguation.

Finally, in the next example, there is a referential gap of over 35 clauses. The referent *Abraham* is reintroduced at the beginning of a new episode and after a whole independent account in which Abraham was not a participant.

(4.43) Genesis 20.1

ויסע משׁם אברהם ארצה הנגב

Abraham journeyed from there into the region of the Negeb.

The deitic *from there* points anaphorically to a location given earlier and, at the same time, to an earlier story involving the referent *Abraham. Abraham* has a semi-active status, being textually accessible, and is introduced as a NP in a vayyiqtol clause. This example shows that a vayyiqtol clause may also be used as the initial clause in a new section, reintroducing a semi-active referent.

In (4.41), (4.42) and (4.43) the referents reintroduced take on immediately the pragmatic role of topic. No special topicalization construction is needed for reintroducing a participant absent from discourse, even after a gap as important as more than 30 clauses. Reintroduction of a topical referent is effected in a vayyiqtol clause and through the use of a full lexical NP in the postverbal position of S. The vayyiqtol clause is indifferent to continuity or discontinuity of participants.

b. *Reintroduction of a Referent in a NP + Qatal Clause*

There are examples of a NP + qatal clause used to reintroduce a referent in discourse. Given that the reintroduction of a participant after a gap is routinely effected through a vayyiqtol clause, one has to find the distinctive role played by the NP + qatal clause.
Consider:

(4.44) Jonah 1.4

ויהוה הטיל רוח גדולה אל־הים

But Yahweh hurled a great wind upon the sea.

The referent *Yahweh* is semi-active, having been mentioned at the very beginning of the story. It is reintroduced in this clause but does not continue as topic. The purpose of the clause is not to assert something about the referent *Yahweh* in a topic-comment articulation. This could be achieved in a vayyiqtol clause. The context reveals that it is the 'wind-hurling' event which counts at this point. The ensuing discourse is about the storm and its effects, not about *Yahweh.* The clause must be categorised as an event-reporting clause. The whole proposition is asserted, answering the implicit question *what happened?*

In another case the NP + qatal clause has a passive V with an inanimate referent encoded as S:

(4.45) 1 Samuel 4.11

וארון אלהים נלקח

And the ark of God was taken.

The clause occurs at the end of the account of a battle between Israel and the Philistines. Israel is routed and their battle palladium is captured. The referent *the ark* is semi-active. The purpose of the clause is to inform the hearer of the event of the capture of the ark. The speaker does not continue to give information about the ark, but informs us of another event, the death of the two sons of Eli, and goes on telling the story of a survivor who escapes and brings news of the defeat to Eli. As an inanimate S, the *ark*, in fact, is a very unlikely candidate to retain the role of topic.

Later in the story, the news of the capture of the ark is reported to Eli, the priest, by a survivor of the battle. The dialogue between the survivor and Eli is of particular interest. It has a question–answer form, with Eli asking the question:

(4.46) 1 Samuel 4.16-17

(1) [Eli] What has happened, my son?
(2) The messenger replied: Israel has fled before the Philistines, the army has been utterly routed,
(3) וגם־שני בניך מתו...
and your two sons are dead...
(4) וארון אלהים נלקחה
and the ark of God has been captured.

In this direct speech section, (3) and (4) are both NP + qatal clauses, repeating the clausal forms used in the third person narrative account. In particular, (4) is an exact copy of (4.45).[8] The context shows that this is a typical event-reporting account and, significantly, the event-reporting clause (4) has a NP + qatal form. Clause (3), which is also event-reporting, has the NP + qatal form too.

In the next example, the inanimate S is personified:

(4.47) Jonah 1.4

(1) And there was a great storm upon the sea,
(2) והאניה חשבה להשבר
and the ship expected itself to break up.

The referent *the ship* is semi-active. The figure of speech (personification) must not conceal the fact that, in this clause, there is not a topic (the ship) about which a comment is made. Rather it is the whole event of the ship's fast approaching disintegration which is reported. In fact, the storyteller no longer mentions the ship in the following discourse,

8. The only change is that *the ark* is now considered a fem. noun and that there is a corresponding mark of agreement in the V.

but attention is shifted to the sailors and their reactions in face of the impending disaster.

An event-reporting clause may also be found at the beginning of a story:

(4.48) 2 Kings 9.1

ואלישע הנביא קרא לאחד מבני הנביאים

The prophet Elisha called a member of the company of prophets [and said to him ...]

This is the initial clause in a story whose hero is Jehu, a military commander who will overthrow the reigning king. The topical referent *Elisha* is semi-active. It has not been mentioned in the preceding episodes and it does not persist as a topic in the following development. The clause does not mention Elisha to predicate something about him. The assertion extends over the entire proposition, reporting the initiating incident in Jehu's story.

All these examples help us to determine more precisely the characteristic features of an event-reporting clause. An event-reporting clause tends to occur in isolation, surrounded by a series of vayyiqtol clauses. This formal isolation finds its counterpart in the isolated mention of its referent. The referent, seen as being involved in the event, is not maintained as a discourse topic in the ensuing clauses. To summarize, the clause is used to describe an event which happens suddenly and unexpectedly. It is a clause for recounting abrupt changes or sharp starts.

c. *Reintroduction of a Referent as S, with Topicalization*

The construction is similar to the one used with a non-active referent mentioned for the first time (p. 152). In (4.36) the semi-active referent was mentioned for the first time in the story, here the semi-active referent is reintroduced in the discourse:

(4.49) 1 Samuel 17.24

וכל איש ישׂראל בראותם את־האישׁ
וינסו מפניו

All the men of Israel, when they saw the man, fled from him.

The referent *men (of Israel)* has become semi-active; it was mentioned earlier (v. 19) and then left out of the story. The reintroduced referent has a full nominal form and it is also topicalized through forefronting. This element represent the point of departure of the clausal predication (see comments on p. 153).

5. *Conclusions*

This chapter has examined how the cognitive status of a referent affects its assignment as topic (or not), and how this is reflected in the surface constructions. Some conclusions can be drawn now, related more directly to the notion of foregrounding. The description of the types of clause used shows that the narrator has the possibility of making certain pragmatic choices related to the activation state of the referent mentioned.

(1) When a not-yet-activated referent which is going to be a main participant is first introduced in a story, a special type of clausal encoding is preferred, if not required. The presentational construction, a NP + qatal clause, with its not-yet-activated referent as NP (cf. [4.23], [4.24], [4.25], [4.26], [4.27]), signals that a totally new participant is introduced into the world of the story.

(2) A participant with a non-active status may be introduced for the first time into the discourse in a vayyiqtol clause. But the narrator may choose to use a NP + qatal clause which is event-reporting. The referent is not encoded as a topic, but the whole clause is in focus, the event being at the centre of attention.

(3) The usual way of reintroducing a participant into the discourse is through a vayyiqtol clause. But there is a marked form of participant reintroduction which uses the event-reporting clause NP + qatal. In that, the referent is reintroduced not with the role of topic, but as being involved in the event reported. The purpose of the choice of this type of clause is to focus on the event in which the reintroduced referent is involved.

As can be noticed, this analysis results in conclusions which do not agree with the traditional explanation which sees the NP + qatal clause as having a backgrounding function. First, it would seem that the event-reporting NP + qatal clauses are in fact foregrounded. But secondly, the choice of this form is not dictated by a general notion of backgrounding, as Longacre says, but rather by identifiable cognitive and pragmatic factors. In the course of narrative discourse, a speaker is always making assumptions about the hearer's state of mind at the time of an utterance, particularly as to whether or not the hearer is aware of the referent. The cognitive states of referents are always implicitly assessed and the speaker may choose a particular pragmatic structuring in the light of this assessment.

Chapter 5

FOCUS IN DIRECT SPEECH CLAUSES AND FOCUS IN THE NARRATIVE VERBAL CLAUSES

1. *Introduction*

The purpose of this chapter is to examine the role which is played by the pragmatic articulation presupposition-focus in the shaping of the narrative clauses (vayyiqtol and NP + qatal clauses) and the influence the articulation has over the way these clauses are used. In the study of Old Hebrew, various types of preposing constructions related to the question of focus (but not specifically analysed as such) have been identified and described through such terms as *casus pendens* or nominative absolute.[1] However, no systematic exploration of the question of focus in Old Hebrew has so far been undertaken. It follows that these analyses are exploratory and that it has been necessary to provide first a theoretical framework, as well as to examine the role of focus in non-narrative clauses.

2. *A Descriptive Framework for Focus*

a. *Focus and Presuppositions*

The focus-presupposition articulation is a well-known pragmatic articulation, but in view of the various ways in which the terms have been

1. Consult Blau (1977), Khan (1988), Geller (1991) for details. Walter Gross (1987) lists and classifies the forms of the *casus pendens* constructions in Old Hebrew, which covers a variety of fronting such as left dislocation, hanging topic, topicalization, but the analysis of the various discourse functions of these forms is not the concern of his work. To my knowledge, there are only short studies of the question of focus in Old Hebrew by Buth (1992) and van der Merwe (1991, 1993). The latter offers an analysis of the use and role of the particle gam (1990), which is syntactic and semantic, but not pragmatic. The pragmatic notion of focus, in fact, does not seem to have influenced the study of Old Hebrew. Hebraists seem to be content with maintaining the general vague category of 'emphasis' without breaking down the category into 'emphasis for what purposes?'

understood by linguists,[2] it needs to be clearly defined.

Pragmatically, a clause is characterized by two articulations: topic-comment and presupposition-focus. As noted in the two preceding chapters, a clause topic is understood from the angle of discourse. It is a discourse entity (referent) which is at the current centre of attention of speaker and hearer, and about which a proposition is asserted.

Like topic, focus can also be characterized in terms of assertion and presupposition. As was observed in Chapter 4, pragmatic presupposition[3] is described as the proposition or set of propositions[4] which the speaker assumes the hearer to be aware of and to take for granted at the time of utterance, and which is relevant in the context of the utterance. Consider the utterance said by a schoolboy to a teacher trying to find out who, among several boys, made little Sarah fall. Andy tells the teacher:

> Tony pushed her.

The presupposition evoked by the answer is *someone pushed Sarah.* Andy assumes that the referent of *her* is at the forefront of the teacher's consciouness and that she is able to identify the referent of the pronoun. Also presupposed is that the speaker can identify the referent of *Tony.*

The presuppositions evoked in a sentence are of two main types. Some concern the state of knowledge of the hearer, that is the states of affairs or situations evoked in the sentence, which the speaker assumes

2. Comrie (1981: 63) describes focus as 'the most important piece of new information mentioned by the speaker, relative to the pragmatic information existing between speaker and hearer'. According to Halliday (1985: 278) focus assigns special salience only to those parts of the sentence which are not presupposed: 'Other things being equal, a speaker will choose the theme from within what is given and locate the focus, the climax of the new, somewhere within the new.' This means that there is always an overlap between the topic-comment and the focus-presupposition articulations. There are also psychological definitions of focus in which focus is understood as 'focus of attention' (Linde: 1979). Gundel, Hedberg and Zacharski write (1993: 279): 'In focus, the referent is not only in short-term memory, but is also at the current center of attention.' Although focus has a psychological dimension, the psychological parameter cannot provide a working definition for analysis.

3. Pragmatic presuppositions are part of the broader 'pragmatic universe of discourse' which comprises the set of propositions which constitute the speaker and hearer shared knowledge. See Lambrecht (1994: 36-43).

4. 'Proposition' refers to what is denoted by a proposition, things such as situations, states of affairs, events.

are known or taken for granted by the hearer. Some others are 'consciousness' presuppositions that is, they are linked to the activation of referents in the clause (cf. Chapter 4). The coding of referents through a N or a PRO exemplify this type of presupposition. All presupposed assumptions must be evoked lexically or grammatically in the sentence. Non-evoked presuppositions cannot be used for the purposes of the analysis because they are linguistically irretrievable.

To make an assertion is to relate a presupposed set of propositions to a non-presupposed proposition. Consider the example:

> Q: Where did you go yesterday?
> A: We went to the *beach*.

The assertion is the proposition which is added to or superimposed on the pragmatic presupposition in the utterance. It is a combination of the two propositions (in Q and A) which results in the abstract proposition *the location we went to yesterday was the beach.* The referent *the beach* is said to be in focus as the predicate of this proposition.

In other words, the referent is in focus because it stands in a pragmatic relation to the proposition in such a way that its addition to the proposition produces an utterance which is a piece of new information. Focus is thus seen in terms of conveying information through a pragmatic relation between a referent and a proposition. Lambrecht explains:

> The focus of the proposition expressed by a sentence in a given utterance context, is seen as the element of information whereby the presupposition and the assertion DIFFER from each other ... The focus is what makes an utterance into an assertion (1994: 207 and 213).

As focus is a relational pragmatic category, the property of being new in discourse, i.e. not previously mentioned, is not defining of focus. A constituent may be in focus even if its referent cannot be described as new in this sense. The 'newness' required for focus is not the newness of the constituent, but the newness of the role of the constituent in the abstract presupposed proposition. In contrast to the notion of 'newness of the constituent', such property is pragmatically not recoverable from the context and is unpredictable.

Presuppositions are linked to the pragmatic information derivable from the context. This contextual knowledge may be classifed in three categories: (1) general knowledge of the world and the culture; (2) situational knowledge, that is the background facts assumed by speaker and not open to challenge at the time of the utterance; (3) knowledge derivable from the linguistic context, that is the language which surrounds or accompanies the utterance. It is the third type of knowledge which will be particularly relevant in this analysis.

The entity or state of affairs designated by the linguistic expression in focus is called the *denotatum*. The term *referent* may equally be used when entities or states of affairs are designated. However, these entities may be attributes or relations and the term 'denotatum' covers such cases as well.

b. *Focus Structures*

There are a broad focus and a narrow focus. In broad focus, the focus domain (that is the syntactic domain which expresses the focus components of the proposition) extends over more than one constituent. In narrow focus, it is limited to a single constituent. Focus domains are phrasal categories such as NP, VP, and not lexical ones.

A clause has one out of three possible types of focus structure. These structures differ in terms of the broadness of their focus. Broad focus (BF) and narrow focus (NF) are illustrated by the following English examples:

(1) *Debbie visited Venice.*
BF
(2) Debbie *visited Venice.*
BF
(3) Debbie visited *Venice.*
NF
(4) *Debbie* visited Venice.
NF

The three categories of structures are: predicate, sentence and argument structure. Predicate focus and sentence focus are broad foci and argument focus is a narrow focus.

The *predicate-focus* structure is exemplified in (2). Such a structure would be used as a response to the question *What did Debbie do?* It is the usual unmarked focus type, with a NP available as topic and the predicate realizing the comment. The purpose of the assertion is to predicate some property of the topic.

The *sentence-focus* structure is exemplified in (1). Such a focus structure answers the question *What happened?* As observed in Chapter 4, the originality of Lambrecht's treatment of such a clause lies in his view that such a construction has no established topic. Both the subject NP and the predicate are part of the assertion and the focus domain is the whole sentence. Sentences of this type may have a presentational role (see Chapter 4, p. 132).

The *argument-focus*[5] is illustrated by (3) and (4). The focus structure of (3) could be found in an answer to the questions *Which town did Debbie visit?* or *I heard Debbie visited Venice?*; (4) might come as an answer to *Who visited Venice?* or *Which one of the girls visited Venice?* The assertion establishes a relation between an argument and a presupposed proposition and the focus domain is a single constituent.

In these focus structures, the denotata capable of producing assertions when added to presuppositions are predicates, arguments or propositions.

The ways the focus constructions are indicated grammatically vary from one language to another. The devices used may be morphological, syntactical, prosodic or a combination of several of these. In a spoken language, the basic mechanism is accentuation, an element of an utterance being made to stand out through stress.[6] In the analysis of a written language the prosodic component is absent. One has to rely on morphology or syntax, together with an analysis of the context.

c. *Focus, Context and the Dominant Focal Element*

Consider again Andy's answer to his teacher:

> Tony pushed her

This utterance might be said with a stress on the following elements:

> (1) *Tony* pushed her.
> (2) Tony *pushed* her.
> (3) Tony pushed *her*.

5. Argument is a cover term for any non-predicating expression in a proposition. 'It is neutral with respect to the issue of the valence of the predicates and the argument-adjunct distinction' (Lambrecht 1994: 224).

6. For spoken English, Halliday (1985: 274-77) sees the information unit realized by a pitch contour or tone which extends over the whole tone group. Within the tone group one element carries tonic prominence which indicates information focus. Leech and Svartvik (1975: 169-71) use the notion of tone-unit which they describe as a unit of information containing a nucleus. The nucleus marks the focus of information, i.e. 'the part of the unit to which the speaker especially draws the hearer's attention' (1975: 171). The focus is normally at the end of the tone-unit.

Each utterance reflects a different context and the selection of focus structure depends upon the context in which the sentence occurs. The context types may be illustrated by question-answer sequences such as:

(1Q) *Who* pushed Sarah?
(1) *Tony* pushed her.

(2Q) What did Tony do to Sarah?
(2) Tony *pushed* her.

(3Q) Who(m) did Tony push?
(3) Tony pushed *Sarah*.

The difference given by prosodic stress might be marked by special constructions such as:

(1a) It's *Tony* who pushed her.

(3a) It's *Sarah* (whom) Tony pushed.

In spoken French (3a) is:

(3b) *C'est* Sarah *qu'il a poussée*.

In order to have the full set of contextual possibilities, the following question and answer pairs must be added:

(4Q) What did Tony do?
(4) Tony *pushed Sarah*

(5Q) What happened?
(5) *Tony pushed Sarah*.

(4) has a predicate-focus structure, the focus domain extending over several constituents. One element of the predicate is more important than the other one; this is indicated in spoken language by an accent on it.[7] Consider the sentences:

What did Gary do?
Gary *went to the* **theatre**.

The denotatum of the NP *theatre* is the element which makes the answer informative; it constitutes the point of the assertion. In this analysis, it will be called the dominant focal element (DFE). A constituent is the DFE when its corresponding denotatum represents the

7. Lambrecht (1994: 226, 304) calls this principle 'the principle of predicate-focus interpretation'. VPs accented sentences have a predicate-focus structure.

informationally pivotal element of the assertion.[8] All things being equal, the DFE in (4) is likely to be the NP direct object:

(4) Tony *pushed Sarah*
DFE

In spoken language, the NP would have received a stress.

d. *Focus and Information Denotation*

Before embarking on the analysis, it is necessary to a have brief look at a more traditional approach to the notion of focus, with particular reference to the notion of contrastiveness. Various categories of focus have been described, without always making clear whether these categories must be envisaged as inferences which a hearer draws within a discourse context when hearing sentences, or whether they are grammatical categories.

In functional grammar, focus is subdivided into various sub-types on the basis of the information denoted by the focal element and the communicative goals which the speaker is trying to achieve. Dik (1981: 69-73; 1989: 282), following an original classification offered by Watters (1979), mentions six different types of focus. The first main distinction is between completive focus and contrastive focus. In completive focus the speaker provides salient 'new' information which fills a gap in the pragmatic information of the hearer. This information is presented by the speaker as not being recoverable from the verbal or situational context. It is news to the hearer and in English is affected by the principle of end-focus (Leech and Short 1981: 212):

Kevin played outside the whole *day*.

In contrastive focus, the speaker offers information in conflict with some other information. The speaker contradicts or opposes a previous statement, or presents information which corrects, or differs or diverges from the information the speaker thinks the hearer might entertain. A comparative element is present, if only to show the difference between pieces of infomation:

My brother is a *gentleman*. You are *vultures*.[9]

8. In English the stress is on the constituent which is in clause-final position: see Leech and Short (1981: 212-14), who identify a 'principle of end-focus'.

9. Gaetano Riina to the Italian Press, after the arrest of his brother, reputed mob boss Salvatore Riina. *Newsweek*, 1 February 1993, p. 7.

The two postverbal constituents *gentleman* and *vultures* are contrastive foci.

Contrastive focus comprises two sub-groups: parallel focus and counter-presuppositional focus. Parallel focus is illustrated by the last example mentioned. It occurs when paired referents are contrasted. In counter-presuppositional focus the hearer's presuppositions come into play. A contrast is achieved because the information presented by the speaker goes against the hearer's presupposition. There are four types of counter-presuppositional focus: replacive, expanding, restrictive and selective.[10]

In replacive focus, there is focus on one constituent when one piece of incorrect information is first rejected and then replaced by another one which is correct:

> John is in *Birmingham* today.
> No, he isn't in *Birmingham*, he's in Norwich.

Expanding focus occurs when the speaker is aware that the hearer possesses one piece of information, but also knows that it is incomplete. A new relevant piece of information is added:

> (1) Not only are you *funny*, but you're actually *witty* as well.
> (2) Sandy is clever and also *hard-working*.

In restrictive focus, the hearer possesses a partially correct piece of information, and the speaker places the focus on the part of it which is appropriate or correct:

> (1a) Tomba does not seem in top condition this season.
> (1b) He made one big mistake at the *start*, but he skied ever so well in the *last part* of the race.

In selective focus, the hearer possesses information in the form of a list of alternatives. The speaker selects one of them which becomes focused and by so doing eliminates alternatives:

> (1) Is the tube strike still *on*, or is it *over*?
> It's still *on*.
> (2) Only a *radical* economic reform will save this country.

Although these categories are useful in the analysis of focus, they will not be considered as grammatical categories. Instead of being categorized in terms of contrastiveness, restrictiveness and so on, the clauses

10. The terminology is proposed by Anna Siewierska (1991: 176-80).

will be explained in terms of their various focus structures. The types of contrastiveness listed above will be envisaged as inferences a hearer draws on the basis of a discourse context, so that contrastive interpretation may be inferred from a predicate-focus construction or from an argument-focus construction. A factor which militates strongly against a grammatical interpretation of these categories is the fact that the constrastive notions are not as clear-cut as the classification offered might lead us to think. There are instances where it is difficult to decide which kind of contrast can be inferred, or even if there is any contrastive meaning intended at all.

3. *Focus in Direct Speech Clauses*

In order to understand focus in the Old Hebrew narrative clause, a good starting point is to look at the morphosyntactic marking of focus structure in direct speech. In both groups the focal role of a constituent may be encoded in an unmarked form or a marked one. Unmarked form refers to the more usual form although not necessarily the more frequent one in any given discourse. Marked forms have a narrower range of distribution in the language.

In the absence of prosodic clues, these are the devices which can be looked at :

(a) Word order
As in many other languages the encoding of focus in Old Hebrew uses word order shift. The forefronting of NPs must be analyzed and interpreted in the light of presuppositions in the clause.

(b) Focusing particles
The main ones are:

> רק, 'only', which introduces a selective or restrictive focus.
> אך, 'only', is restrictive.
> גם, 'also', introduces an expanding focus.
> כי אם, 'except', is selective.

The focal constituent always immediately follows the particle. Sometimes the use of focusing particles is accompanied by a formal symmetry of the adjacent clauses. The symmetry reinforces the focussing effect of the particle.

a. *The Predicate-Focus Clause*

In a predicate-focus structure, a presuppositional topic is available which is related to the assertion denoted in the predicate. Functional grammar calls this focus completive focus. It is illustrated in a transitive declarative clause:

(5.1) Jeremiah 12.7

(1) עזבתי את־ביתי
(2) נטשתי את־נחלתי
(1) I have abandoned my house, (2) I have deserted my possession.

(1) and (2) are Yahweh's utterances communicated through his prophet Jeremiah. The referent *Yahweh* is coded as a first person S clitic pronoun and so as topic. The two predicates *have forsaken my house* and *have left my possession* are the focus domains. There are no morphological or syntactic marks to indicate focus and the word order is not disrupted. This is an example of unmarked focus and is the most common form of focus in Old Hebrew.

Within the predicate focus domain, the denotatum expressed by the object NP is informationally more important than the V. One can surmise that in spoken Old Hebrew, ביתי, *my house,* and נחלתי, *my inheritance,* would have received a stress. These NPs are the DFEs. The informational importance of the direct object NP in a transitive clause is confirmed by the fact that when the predicate-focus structure is marked through forefronting, it is the direct object NP which is forefronted, as in the following example:

(5.2) Isaiah 1.2

(1) Hear, o heavens, and listen, o earth, for Yahweh speaks:
(2) בנים גדלתי ורוממתי
(3) והם פשעו בי
(2) Children I have reared and raised up, (3) but they have rebelled against me.

This is part of a legal dispute in which Yahweh is the plaintiff and the adversaries are Judah and Jerusalem, metaphorically portrayed as children. In (2) the topic encoded as the clitic pronoun *I*, is presuppositional. The predicate is the focus domain but the N בנים does not appear in its expected postverbal position. It is the DFE which occupies a marked initial position. In (3), the anaphoric PRO subject refers to the DFE of (2), and is the new topical participant. Its forefronting, however, is not for focus but indicates a change of topic. It is the prepositional object בי, *against me*, which is the DFE.

Consider another example of DO forefronting:

(5.3) Jeremiah 12.13

(1) זרעו חטים (2) וקצים קצרו

(1) They have sown wheat (2) and reaped thorns.

(1) and (2) have the same topic expressed by the clitic pronoun *they*. (1) has a predicate-focus structure with unmarked word order. The DFE is *wheat*. In (2) the N direct object is the DFE and is forefronted as marked focus. The inferential meaning derived in (2) is counter-expectation. The harvest of thorn goes against the expectations created by the proposition of the first clause.

A forefronted DO is also found in:

(5.4) Genesis 14.21

(1) תן־לי הנפש

(2) והרכש קח־לך

[Then the king of Sodom said to Abram.] (1) Give me the people, (2) but keep the goods for yourself.

Abram has defeated four kings, and returns to its rightful owner, the king of Sodom, the booty that the enemy kings had carried away during their campaign. Aware that Abram has the right to keep all the spoils to himself, the king of Sodom specifies in (1) what he wishes to have back. (1) has an unmarked predicate-focus structure with הנפש, *the people,* as the DFE. (2) has a marked predicate-focus construction with the NP which is the DFE forefronted.

The DFE of the predicate in a transitive clause may be only one of the element of the direct object NP:

(5.5) 2 Samuel 13.30

הכה אבשלום את־כל־בני המלך

Absalom has killed all the king's sons [and not one of them is left].

The crown prince has been killed by assassins. A garbled version of the event, claiming that all the king's sons have been killed, reaches King David. The topic encoded as S is presuppositional. The focus domain is the predicate. Within the direct object NP the predeterminer כל, *all of,* is the DFE: it is the crucial piece of information in the rumour which reaches David. This is confirmed by the sentence which follows and which strengthens the assertion negatively: *not one of them is left* .

The NP direct object which is the DFE tends to be always forefronted when it is preceded by a focusing particle:

(5.6) Deuteronomy 2.34-35

(1) לא השארנו שׂריד
(2) רק הבהמה בזזנו לנו

(1) We left not a single survivor, only the cattle we kept as spoil for ourselves.

רק, only, is a restrictive particle. The presuppositional topic is the first person plural clitic PRO. The focus domain is the predicate (*kept only the cattle as spoil for ourselves*).The DFE is preceded by a restrictive particle and is forefronted. The clause has a marked focus form.

The following example illustrates the use of another restrictive particle, אך:

(5.7) Genesis 9.3-4

(1) As I gave you the green plants, I give you everything.
(2) אך־בשׂר בנפשׁו דמו לא תאכלו
Only flesh with its life, its blood, you must not eat.

In (2), the topic is the clitic plural PRO *you*. The focus domain is the predicate (*not eat flesh with its life, its blood*) and the direct object NP is the DFE. The particle אך imposes a restriction on the general statement made in (1) and the whole restrictive NP is forefronted in a marked construction.

So far in the clauses considered, the predicate contained only a NP direct object. The importance of the DFE becomes more manifest when ditransitive clauses or clauses with ADVPs are considered. The postverbal position occupied by the constituent in focus becomes crucial to understand the pragmatic meaning of the utterance. Two types of clauses, one with a predicate-focus structure (5.8) the other with an argument-focus stucture (5.9), will be compared.

(5.8) Deuteronomy 4.26

העידתי בכם היום את־השׁמים ואת־הארץ
I call heaven and earth as witnesses against you this day.

In this ditransitive clause, an indirect object PRO suffixed to a preposition is placed immediately after the verb. This conforms to the expected neutral order of postverbal phrases, which is PRO followed by NP.[11] The ADVP *today* precedes the NPs direct object which become clause-final. The normal order of the VP constituents is for the object NP to follow the V and any ADVP to come after it. Here, the order ADVP and DO is switched. The discourse context provides the explanation for this switch. A covenant has been made between Yahweh and Israel. The summoning of witnesses to the agreement was a normal part of treaty ceremonies in the ancient Near East. But here, it is the identity of the witnesses summoned, *heaven and earth,* which is pivotal. These are remarkable witnesses which, unlike human witnesses, are everlasting and will always testify in the future of the warning given to the people. The two NPs are the DFEs. The fact that they are moved to the clause-final position would suggest that this position has a determining role in designating the DFE when there is an adverbial phrase in the clause. This is upheld by the clues provided in an argument-focus structure clause, where the focus is on the ADVP:

(5.9) 1 Samuel 15.28

קרע יהוה את־ממלכות ישׂראל מעליך היום

Yahweh has torn the kingdom of Israel from you this very day.

Samuel has announced to Saul that he has been rejected from being king because of his disobedience. He turns to leave and Saul grasps his robe in supplication. Samuel's response constitutes a reiteration of the decision reported earlier: *Yahweh has rejected you from being king over Israel* (v. 26). It follows that the predication *Yahweh has torn the kingdom of Israel from you* is presuppositional and that the clause has an argument-focus structure. Saul knows that he has been rejected as king. Samuel reiterates the assertion with a temporal indication, היום, *this very day*, whose point is to make clear that there is no room for further argument. The focus of assertion is on the temporal ADVP, which is left in its normal clause-final position. This example shows that the clause-final position is the position of the unmarked DFE.

Another set of examples with switches of adverbial and object will confirm the importance of the final position in predicate-focus constructions:

11. See Lars Lode (1984: 121-40) for more details.

(5.10) 2 Samuel 13.6

ותלבב לעיני שתי לבבות

[Let my sister Tamar come] and make before my eyes a couple of heart-shaped dumplings.

The topic is encoded as PRO subject in a clause with a predicate-focus structure. The ADVP is fronted, whereas the direct object NP which is the DFE, is moved to the clause-final position. The discourse context explains why this word-order switch takes place. Amnon is in love with his half-sister Tamar and wants to sleep with her. He feigns to be sick, obtains that Tamar should come to his room and cook special cakes for him. (5.10) is Amnon's request made to the king. The shifting of the NP object, לבבות, to end position has the effect of highlighting the particular feature of the cakes Amnon wants Tamar to prepare. Whether the meaning is 'heart-shaped' dumplings or 'enheartening' dumplings, that is, giving strength to a sick person, Amnon insists that it is a very special kind of cakes he wants to eat. This is the information which is stressed in the request.[12] By contrast, the ADVP *before my eyes* is non-focal. Again, the context explains the pragmatic motivations for down-playing this detail. On the one hand, Amnon has to mention the locational indication crucial to the success of his plan in his request to the king, but on the other hand, as the request is part of a ruse, he must pretend that what is most important to him is the type of cakes he wants to eat.

In the next example the ADVP also introduced by לעיני, in the sight *of*, is left in its clause-final position:

(5.11) Hosea 2.12

ועתה אגלה את־נבלתה לעיני מאהביה

And now I will expose her lewdness in the sight of all her lovers [and noone shall rescue her out of my hand].

The speaker, Yahweh, describes metaphorically how he will deal with unfaithful Israel (the wife), who has affairs with her lovers (a reference to Canaanite fertility gods). He will humiliate the lovers by showing that they are powerless creatures. The predicate referring to the exposure of the woman's lewdness to public shame is not the focus domain. Rather, it is part of the presupposition as the earlier context makes

12. The storyteller makes his character, Amnon, exploit the erotic sense of the word, signalling through a pun Amnon's sexual desire for his half-sister Tamar.

clear: *I will take away my wool and my flax which were to cover her nakedness* (v. 11).[13] The clause has an argument-focus structure and it is the ADVP which is the focus of assertion. It refers to the testing of the woman's lovers to protect her. The detail is significant as the aim of the action is to prove the lovers' helplessness. The next clause confirms this meaning negatively: *No one shall snatch her from my hands*. The lovers will stand by like helpless watchers.

The focal importance of the clause-final position will be considered in a last example:

(5.12) Jeremiah 12.7

נתתי את־ידדות נפשׁי בכף איביה

I have delivered the beloved of my soul into the hands of her enemies.

This clause follows the two clauses of (5.1) above. It has a predicate-focus structure and its topic is the first person singular PRO. It is also ditransitive, with two obligatory arguments, the DO and the IO. The IO, *into the hands of her enemies*, is informationally the most important element of the focus domain. This is backed up by a consideration of the context. Together with the clauses of (5.1), (5.12) forms a crescendo of which the very last piece of information in the series, the NP indirect object, constitutes the climax. It is reasonable to deduce that the piece of information which constitutes the culmination of a series of assertion must also be the dominant focal element of the clause comprising it. The indirect object NP is the DFE. It is to be noted that the two NPs of the predicate could be switched, with the NP indirect object preceding the NP direct object. In this case, the direct object would become the DFE, but the crescendo effect would be lost.

The analysis of direct speech clauses with predicate-focus structure show that the constituent placed in clause-final position is the dominant focal element. Whether it is a NP direct object, indirect object or adverbial, it represents the most important piece of information of the clause in the context of communication. A speaker has the option of backshifting any constituent encoded as a full NP to establish it as the DFE. All these shifts occur postverbally and do not affect the clause-initial position of the V. They may be described as unmarked options for the establishment of a DFE. Examples have been considered where,

13. Also earlier (2.5): 'I will strip her naked and expose her as in the day she was born'.

however, a NP was forefronted, occurring as clause-initial as a result. These are marked forms of the DFE.

b. *The Argument-Focus Structure Clause*

In examining these clauses, it is important not to confuse the semantic and the pragmatic level. An argument-focus structure clause is a clause in which the referent which is the focus at the informational level functions as an argument at the semantic level of the proposition. Consider the exchange:

Q: I heard your keys were stolen?
A: My *chequebook* was stolen.

In (A) the semantic argument required by the predicate is encoded as a NP subject. However, the pragmatically structured proposition is *the thing that was stolen is my (the speaker's) chequebook.* The referent encoded as a subject in the semantic proposition is in fact predicate in the pragmatic proposition. The non-identity of pragmatic predicate and semantic predicate is clearly marked in some languages. In spoken French, this happens through an obligatory clefted construction which reproduces the pragmatically structured proposition:

A': *C'est mon carnet de chèques qui a été volé.*

The argument which is the pragmatic predicate, *carnet de chèques*, is encoded as a syntactic predicate (complement of the copula) while the semantic predicate *a été volé* is expressed in a relative clause which encodes the presupposed proposition. The relation between the pragmatic subject and the pragmatic predicate is one of identification.

In Old Hebrew the argument-focus construction may occur in three different contexts. It may arise in a question-answer sequence. It may follow certain focusing particles. Finally, it may be determined by the discourse context.

i. *Question-Answer and Argument-Focus*

WH-questions followed by an answer will be considered here. It is well known that when a question-answer sequence is used, the element brought to the fore in the answer is the focus. Comrie writes:

> The use of question and answer sequences is particularly useful in illustrating focus distinctiveness, since the nature of the question forces the answerer to select a particular part of his reply as focus (1981: 63).

WH-questions are themselves a type of argument-focus constructions. When the WH interrogative is removed from the interrogative clause, the proposition left is pragmatically presupposed in the discourse. As for the answer, it provides the argument missing and so the referent encoded in the NP is in focus. A number of such question-answer sequences will be examined.

The Argument is a NP Subject

(5.13) Judges 6.29

(1) מי עשׂה הדבר הזה
(2) גדעון בן־יואשׁ עשׂה הדבר הזה
(1) Who did this thing? [They searched and they inquired and they said:]
(2) Gideon, son of Joash, did it.

In (1) the presupposition is: *x did this thing*, where *things* refers to the desecration of an altar to the god Baal. (2) has an argument-focus structure which provides the identity of the culprit. The focus is on the referent encoded as the forefronted NP. Here the WH-question evokes a presupposition derived from the external context: the question is about the destruction of a religious installation.

Some WH-questions, however, do not necessarily evoke a presupposed proposition. Consider:

(5.14) 1 Samuel 26.6

(1) מי־ירד אתי אל־שׁאול אל־המחנה
(2) אני ארד עמך
(1) Who will go down with me into the camp, to Saul? [Abishai said:]
(2) I will go down with you.

The presupposition of (1) is the proposition *x will go with David into Saul's camp*. The referent identifying the person encoded as a PRO is forefronted as in the previous example.

The Argument is a NP Direct Object

(5.15) 1 Samuel 28.13

(1) מה ראית
(2) אלהים ראיתי עלים מן־הארץ
[The king said]: (1) What do you see? [And the woman said to Saul] (2) I see a god coming up out of the earth.

The presupposition elicited in the question is: *the woman* (the witch of En-Dor) *saw an identifiable entity x*. The assertion made in the answer identifies *x*. The referent in focus is encoded as a NP direct object which is in clause initial position. Similarly in:

(5.16) 2 Kings 20.15

(1) מה ראו בביתך
(2) את כל־אשר בבתי ראו
(1) What have they seen in your house? [And Ezekiah answered] (2) They have seen all that is in my house.

The question presupposes the proposition *the vistors saw an identifiable thing x in the house of King Hezekiah* (the addressee). The answer (2) identifies the referent encoded as the indefinite pronoun כל, which is forefronted. The PRO is followed by a relative clause, forefronted too as it must follow its antecedent.

In all the examples considered so far, the argument in focus, whether S or DO, was forefronted. For comparative purposes the following example has an argument-focus clause with the V in the present participle:

(5.17) Genesis 37.15-16

(1) מה־תבקש
(2) את־אחי אנכי מבקש
(1) What are you seeking? [He said] (2) My brothers I am seeking.

Hebraists categorize the participial clause as nominal or verbless. Although its normal word order is debated[14] (some suggest S-PRED, others PRED-S), the two unmarked word order possibilities would be S-V-O or V-S-O. The question of (5.17) presupposes the proposition *the addressee is looking for an identifiable entity x*. The argument in focus in the answer is a forefronted NP.[15]

14. See Muraoka (1985: 20-28) for explanations.

15. The same question ('what do you see?') is found twice elsewhere, in Jer. 1.13 and 24.3, and in each case the NP direct object in focus is forefronted. It is also found in Amos 7.8 (Q: 'Amos, what do you see?' A: 'A plumb line.') and Amos 8.1 (Q: 'Amos, what do you see?' A: 'A basket of ripe fruit.'), but there is ellipis of the V in the answer and so only the NP is left.

The Argument is an Adverbial NP
Consider the example:

(5.18) 2 Kings 20.14

(1) ומאין יבאו אליך
(2) מארץ רחוקה באו מבבל

(1) and whence did they come to you? (2) From a far country they have come, from Babylon.

The presupposition taken for granted is *envoys came to you from x*. (2) has two locational phrases, one forefronted and the other in its normal postverbal position. It is the semantically more general NP which is forefronted and is the marked focus. A look at the discourse context explains why the focus is the NP which indicates a more imprecise location. The answer is given by King Hezekiah to a question asked by the prophet Isaiah. Hezekiah had welcomed to his palace envoys from the king of Babylon and had unwisely shown them his treasures. Isaiah's question is accusatory. Hezekiah seeks to lessen the seriousness of the matter by making the vaguer NP informationally more important than the second locational NP.

The next example comprises two questions which evoke two sets of presuppositions:

(5.19) Genesis 16.8

(1) אי־מזה באת
(2) ואנה תלכי
(3) מפני שׂרי גברתי אנכי ברחת

[Hagar, maid of Sarai,] (1) where have you come from (2) and where are you going? [She said] (3) from Sarai, my mistress, I am fleeing.

The pragmatic presuppositions evoked in the two questions are that Hagar has come from somewhere and is going to somewhere else. The first question sets an expectation for a reply whose focus will be the indication of the place Hagar has left. The forefronted locative phrase in (3) provides the referent inquired about through the interrogative *where* in (1). But the referent is not a location but a person, Sarai. The pragmatically structured proposition of (3) is *the person I am fleeing from is Sarai.* In this argument-focus structure clause the referent which is the focus of assertion is forefronted, as marked focus.

Conclusion. All the examples show that in the argument-focus structure clause, when the focus is forced through a question, the NP which encodes the referent in focus in the answer, whether subject, direct object or adverbial, is always placed before the V, thus becoming clause-initial. This forefronting of the NP is a marked form of focus.

ii. *Argument-Focus Constructions with Particles*
Examples will be examined in which the particles רק, גמ and כי אמ are used.

Focus with רק *and* גם

(5.20) Exodus 10.24

(1) Go, worship Yahweh,
(2) רק צאנכם ובקרכם יצג
(3) גם־טפכם ילך עמכם
Only your flocks and your herds shall remain behind. Also your children may go with you.

The larger presuppositional context to the two utterances is in fact the whole of the plagues narrative: Pharaoh hesitates between freeing the Israelites or keeping them in Egypt. The two predicates (*shall remain* and *may go*) are presupposed and the two clauses give the precise identification of the entities which are prohibited from going or allowed to leave. (2) begins with a restrictive focus particle whose scope is the forefronted referent *flocks*. (3) begins with an expanding focus particle, גם, whose scope is another forefronted referent, *children*.

(5.21) 2 Samuel 19.30-31

(1) 'You and Ziba shall divide the land.'
(2) Mephiboshet said to the king:
(3) גם את־הכל יקח
Even all of it, let him take (it).

David had given Saul's lands to Zibah, servant of Mephiboshet (2 Sam. 16.4), thus depriving Mephiboshet, Saul's grandson, of his rightful inheritance. David, having discovered that he had wrongly suspected Mephiboshet of subversion, takes the decision to give him back part of the land in (1). Mephiboshet replies in (3). The pragmatic presupposition is clear: *Ziba takes x of the land*. In his response, Mephiboshet identifies *x* through the N הכל, *the whole*. The N is forefronted, preceded by an expanding particle.

Focus with כי אם

(5.22) Deuteronomy 12.14

(1) You must take great care that you do not offer your burnt offerings in every place that you see.

(2) כי אם־במקום אשר־יבחר יהוה באחד שבטיך שם תעלה עלתיך

At the place that Yahweh will choose in one of your tribes—there you shall offer your burnt offerings.

The presupposition expressed in clause (1) is: *burnt offerings must be offered not everywhere, but in x*. The rightful location for offering sacrifices needs to be indicated. The compound particle כי אם occurs after a negative clause and introduces a replacive focus. The wrong piece of information having been eliminated, the particle introduces the information which is the correct one.[16] The referent *the place* is forefronted for marked focus. After the relative clause, it is reiterated in the form of another forefronted adverb, *there*.

In the next example, only the forefronted focus is left in an elliptical clause, in which כי אם is shortened to כי:

(5.23) Genesis 45.8

(1) ועתה לא־אתם שלחתם אתי הנה

(2) כי האלהים

(1) So then, it was not you who sent me here, (2) but God.

Joseph explains to his brothers that underlying the trials he went through is the providence of God. In (2) the presuppositional proposition is *the identity of the person who sent me here is x*. Joseph replaces the wrong piece of information, **you** *sent me here*, by the disclosing the correct identity of the agent: **God** (*sent me here*).

The forefronting of the NP in focus, when it follows a particle, is a marked form of focus. This is confirmed by contrasting the construction with examples where no focusing particle is used and where no forefronting occurs as a result:

16. The interpretations of כי־אם offered by Waltke and O'Connor (1990: 671, examples 16, 17, 18) are unsatisfactory. They interpret the particle as having a restrictive role.

(5.24) Genesis 17.5

(1) ולא־יקרא עוד את־שמך אברם
(2) והיה שמך אברהם
Your name shall no longer be Abram, but your name shall be Abraham.

In the two adjacent clauses coordinated by the conjunction waw, the V remains clause-initial. The two nouns in focus, אברם and אברהם, are both in clause-final position, the unmarked position for a referent in focus.

c. *Symmetrical Constructions*

Symmetrical constructions involving semantic repetition generate argument-focus structures. John Haiman (1988: 319) has called this phenomenon the 'focussing effect of parallelism'. Symmetrical or parallel constructions are used to compare, to contrast, or to express antithesis. In direct speech, focusing particles are often integrated in such symmetrical constructions. Consider:

(5.25) 1 Samuel 8.7

(1) כי לא אתך מאסו
(2) כי־אתי מאסו ממלך עליהם
(1) For they have not rejected you (2) but they have rejected me from being king over them.

The symmetry is created by the repetition in (2) of the V and the subject found in (1) *(they rejected)*. The pragmatic presupposition in (2) is *the one they rejected is x*. The argument in focus, encoded as a PRO direct object in (2), is forefronted.

The symmetrical construction with an argument-focus structure, as illustrated in *(5.25)*, must not be confused with symmetrical constructions in which the clauses have a predicate-focus structure, as in:

(5.26) Genesis 3.15

(1) הוא ישופך ראש
(2) ואתה תשופנו עקב
(1) He shall bruise your head (2) and you shall bruise his heel.

The two clauses display symmetry in the order of their constituents (S-V-O) and in the repetition of the verb *to bruise*. However, here, the two referents encoded as S are presuppositional, pragmatically available as topic for discussion. They are also presented in a contrastive relationship. The focus domain is the VP which happens to have the same lexical V. The two NPs subject have the pragmatic roles of contrastive topics. The DFEs are the two direct object NPs *head* and *heel*, which are contrastive foci.

A third type of symmetrical construction can be identified:

(5.27) Genesis 41.13

(1) אתי השיב על כני
(2) ואתו תלה
(1) Me, he restored to my position (2) and him, he had hanged.

Pharaoh's cupbearer compares his fate to the fate of the chief baker. The symmetry is centered on two antithetical VPs with parallel order of the constituents DO-V. The forefronted PROs cannot be construed as providing the missing argument of a presupposed proposition, as no background knowledge is taken for granted in (1) or (2): the propositions minus their forefronted arguments, *me* and *him*, are not pragmatically presupposed. As a result, the two direct object NPs must be explained not as contrastive foci but as contrastive topics. Both of the referents are pragmatically available as topics for discussion and they are contrasted.

That a referent encoded as DO may have the role of contrastive topic is further demonstrated in the following example:

(5.28) 1 Samuel 25.29

(1) If anyone should rise up to pursue you and to seek your life,
(2) והיתה נפש אדני צרורה בצרור החיים את יהוה אלהיך
(3) ואת נפש איביך יקלענה בתוך כף הקלע
(2) My lord's life shall be bound in the bundle of the living, in the keeping of Yahweh, your god, (3) but the lives of your enemies he will sling away in the pocket of a sling.

Abigail describes how, in her eyes, David's life is protected by his god in a special way. The symmetry is given by the referents *lord's life* and *the lives of your enemies*, which are contrasted. In (2) the referent *lord's life* is encoded as S and has the role of topic. In (3) the referent *the lives of your enemies* is encoded as DO and with the role of topic too. That it is a topic may be deduced form the fact that in (3) the proposition without its forefronted argument is not pragmatically presupposed and so the DO cannot be an argument in focus. The two referents are contrastive topics.

d. *Forefronting for Focus or Topicalization*

Formally, nothing distinguishes forefronting for focus from forefronting for topicalization. The examples discussed have already shown that a correct understanding of the presuppositions evoked by the context is all important to identify the pragmatic role of the forefronted PRO or NP in a direct speech clause. Some more examples will be discussed now which serve to underline this point.

(5.29) Isaiah 3.14

(1) Yahweh comes in judgement with the elders of his people and its princes:
(2) ואתם בערתם הכרם
'And you, you have devoured the vineyard, [the plunder of the poor is in your houses.']

(2) is part of a prosecution speech spoken by Yahweh before a court as (1) shows.[17] It is a rebuttal addressed to the corrupt rulers of Israel because the poor of the land suffer and experience harsh conditions. This charge is worded metaphorically through the expression *to devour the vineyard.* Within this context, the clause must be construed as having an argument-focus structure. The pragmatic presupposition of (2) is *those who have devoured the vineyard are x.* Yahweh identifies the culprits: the leaders. The very persons appointed to protect the poor have exploited them for their own gain (cf. v. 15: *what do you mean by crushing the people?*). The argument in focus is encoded as a forefronted PRO subject. Without an adequate analysis of the context and presuppositions, the forefronted pronoun could be wrongly interpreted as a marked topic.

Another case where presuppositions and context play a crucial role is:

(5.30) Jeremiah 15.6

את נטשת אתי
It is you who have forsaken me.

17. Also v. 13: 'Taking his position to contend (is) Yahweh, standing to judge peoples.'

The speaker is Yahweh. The clause is found in the following context. It is preceded by a description of the numerous tragedies which will befall Jerusalem[18] and an ironic question implying a negative answer: 'So who will pity you, Jerusalem, who will grieve for you, and who will turn aside to ask about you well-being?' (Jer. 15.5). Moreover, earlier a plea had been made by the people of Judah: 'Do not spurn us, for your name's sake. Remember, do not break your covenant with us!' (Jer. 14.21).[19] In the light of this context, the proposition pragmatically presupposed for (5.30) is *x is forsaking y*. In Judah's accusation, it is Yahweh who is in focus. When Yahweh contests the accusation, he replaces the incorrect piece of information *you* (i.e. Yahweh), *have forsaken us* by the correct one: *you*, i.e. the people of Judah, *have forsaken me*. The clause has an argument-focus structure and the PRO has the pragmatic role of replacive focus. The PRO is not forefronted for topicalization but because its referent is in marked focus (even though it is old information).

In the next example, the forefronted NP does not encode a referent in focus, but a topic:

(5.31) Jeremiah 12.10

רעים רבים שחתו כרמי

Many shepherds have destroyed my vineyard.

The utterance is found in the middle of a description of the land of Judah devastated through military invasions. Foreign rulers are portrayed through various metaphors such as birds of prey or spoilers. Here the subject NP introduces them again on to the scene as *shepherds,* the referent remaining the topic of the next three clauses.

e. *Conclusion*

Whether a clause has a predicate-focus structure or an argument-focus structure, the unmarked construction in both cases follow the normal word order. In addition, in both cases, the marked focus construction is characterized by the forefronting of the NP in focus resulting in its clause initial position.

Quoting the linguist Jespersen who strongly believed in a principle of

18. These are described in Jer. 15.3-4.

19. The plea followsYahweh's decision to abandon his people, cf. Jer 12.7: נטשתי את־נחלתי, 'I have forsaken my possession.'

'actuality' to explain word-order shifts, Haiman thinks too, that 'what is uppermost in the speaker's mind tends to be first expressed' (1985: 238); this principle, in particular, provides the reason for having focused elements in sentence-initial position. With the reservation that it applies only to marked focal constructions, it can be said that Jespersen's principle of actuality explains well the cases where the focal element is forced through a question-answer sequence, through particles or the context. These are situations in which the speaker is required to express 'what is uppermost in his/her mind'.

4. *The Third Person Narrative Clause: Predicate-Focus Structures*

a. *Introduction*

The purpose of this section is to examine the questions of types of foci, of focus structures and of the position of the dominant focal element in the two verbal narrative clauses, the vayyiqtol clause and the NP + qatal clause. The method of inquiry has to be adapted to the data available, a written text without prosodic marking. As a result, the main clue relied upon to identify the dominant focal element in a clause will be the identification of presupposed referents in a given sentence, through the context and the lexical and grammatical clues available in the text.

b. *The Predicate-Focus Structure in Vayyiqtol Clauses*

As already noted above in pp. 166-67, one of the elements comprised in the focus domain is always more important informationally than the rest; it is the DFE which, in spoken language, would have received a stress.

i. *Transitive Clauses*

The predicate-focus structure is found in its simplest form in a clause in which the vayyiqtol V is followed by a direct object only. A typical example with a lexical noun as subject, is:

(5.32) 1 Samuel 7.12

ויקח שׁמואל אבן אחת

And Samuel took a stone.

The proposition answers the question *then what did Samuel do?*, the question being determined by the narrative situation. The presuppositional referent *Samuel* is encoded in the role of topic. The assertion is the predicate (*took a stone*) and the NP direct object which is non-presuppositional, is the dominant focal element. It is to be noted that the DO is a necessary argument of the V.

The object in the transitive clause may be introduced through a preposition as in the next two examples:

(5.33) Genesis 49.1

ויקרא יעקב אל־בניו

And Jacob called his sons…

(5.34) Genesis 2.16

ויצו יהוה אלהים על־האדם

And Yahweh God commanded the man.

Both clauses have a VSO order but the objects are introduced by the prepositions אל and על respectively. The focus domains are the predicates and the NPs object are presuppositional. These NPs, which are obligatory arguments of the V, are the DFEs.

In the three preceding examples, the object (DO or prepositional O) is a NP and the DFE is in the clause final position. When the object is pronominal there is a constraint on the PRO which must occupy the immediate postverbal position,[20] whether used with a direct object marker (5.35) or a preposition (5.36):

(5.35) Genesis 12.15

ויראו אתה שׂרי פרעה

Pharaoh's courtiers saw her.

(5.36) Genesis 37.10

ויגער־בו אביו

His father rebuked him.

The pronominal as well as presuppositional nature of the objects in (5.35) and (5.36) makes it hard, even with the help of the context, to decide whether the PROs are really DFEs. It would seem that in instances such as these, the verb and its object form a semantic unit, exemplifying the 'Verb-Object Bonding' principle offered by Tomlin

20. See p. 173 and example (5.8); also Lars Lode (1984: 121-40).

(1986: 74).[21] The DFE is the element of the VP which is not presuppositional (i.e. entirely new) that is, the V. This analysis would explain why, when the speaker wants to have the object NP as the DFE instead of the V, it is indicated by a shift in word order and by the replacement of the pronoun by a full NP, in spite of the informationally redundant nature of the NP. This is exemplified in:

(5.37) Genesis 26.9

(1) King Abimelech ... saw him (i.e. Isaac) fondling his wife Rebekah,
(2) ויקרא אבימלך ליצחק
And Abimelech called for Isaac.

The use of the full NP *Isaac* in (2) is semantically not required. The expected clause ויקרא לו אבימלך (*and Abimelech called for him*), with the PRO in immediate postverbal position is not used because the speaker wishes to have the O and not the V as the DFE. The full NP must occur in end position.

One may conclude that in a transitive clause with a single object, when the object is a full NP, whether presuppositional or not, its referent is the DFE. Such a DFE is automatically in clause-final position.

ii. *Clauses with Ditransitive Verbs*
When the verb is ditransitive the speaker may choose to have either the direct object or the indirect object as DFE. Consider:

(5.38) 1 Samuel 17.38

וילבשׁ שׁאול את־דוד מדיו
Saul clothed David with his garments.

The predicate (*clothed David with his garments*) is the focus domain, and the referent *Saul* is the topical participant. Within the predicate, one of the two object arguments, *David,* is presuppositional; the second one, *his garments*, is non-presuppositional. The context does not allow the referent *David* to be construed as the DFE. A stress on *David* would be interpreted as contrastive in meaning, in a context in which the referent *David* would be selected out of several other referents. This is not the case. It would also leave the pragmatic role of the non-presuppositional

21. The principle is used to discuss word-order universals. It states: 'the object of a transitive verb is more tightly bonded to the verb than its subject', and 'the object and verb form an immutable whole'.

referent *his garments* totally unexplained. The only satisfactory interpretation is that *his garments* is the DFE.

The question arises as to whether the clause final position of the NP *his garments* has anything to do with its DFE status. A priori, it seems that this is not the case, as to invert the order of the DO and the instrumental object NPs in (5.38) would be ungrammatical. But a look at other examples is needed. Consider:

(5.39) 1 Samuel 8.1

וישׂם את־בניו שׁפטים לישׂראל

He made his sons judges over Israel.

The focus domain comprises the V with its two obligatory arguments and a non-obligatory ADVP, *over Israel*, which is presuppositional. Within the VP, the referent *his sons* is presuppositional and the referent *judges* is non-presuppositional. That this last referent represents the point of the assertion is confirmed by the ensuing discourse which describes the sons as unworthy of the new rank they have been appointed to. The NP is the dominant focal element. This is not indicated by word order. In fact, the move of the NP to a clause-final position is impossible as the placement of the NP *Israel* before *judges* would be ungrammatical.
The next example is the opposite of (5.39). The direct object NP is non-presuppositional and the indirect object NP is presuppositional:

(5.40) Exodus 2.21

ויתן את־צפרה בתו למשׁה

And he gave Moses his daughter Zipporah in marriage.

To construe the referent *Moses* as the DFE of the clause is not tenable. It would require a context in which the interpretation of the clause would be: *he gave his daughter* **to Moses** (*and not to X*). This cannot be the case, and so the new referent *Zipporah* must be the DFE. The normal word order of the clause is not changed. The consideration of these examples enables us to answer the question asked above. In clauses with a V-S-DO-IO order, with either the DO or IO non-presuppositional, it is the non-presuppositionality of the referent which is the determining factor for the NP of the predicate to be established as the DFE. Word order is not exploited to signal the DFE, and the clause-final position of a referent is not significant in itself. Cases in which both objects are presuppositional must now be examined. Consider:

(5.41) 2 Kings 22.8

ויתן חלקיה את־הספר אל־שפן

And Hilkiah gave the scroll to Shaphan.

The two referents in the predicate, *scrolls* and *Shaphan* are presuppositional. They are encoded as NPs which are two obligatory arguments of the V. Assuming that *scroll* is the DFE, the clause would have to be construed as meaning: *Hilkiah gave* **the scroll** (*and not something else*) *to Shaphan*. This does not fit the context. No other referent competes with the referent *scroll.* It follows that the DFE must be the referent which expresses the recipient of the action, *Shaphan*. We have two equally presuppositional referents, with the second as the DFE. A recourse to word-order change (V-S-IO-DO instead of V-S-DO-IO) is not chosen to establish the NP *to Shaphan* as the DFE. So, one may advance the hypothesis that there exists a principle of end-focality which says that in a clause with unmarked word order, the default position of the DFE is the clause-final position. Such a principle would explain why the normal word order is maintained in (5.41).

One of the two presuppositional referents of the predicate may be expressed pronominally, as in:

(5.42) 1 Samuel 18.27

ויתן־לו שאול את־מיכל בתו לאשה

And Saul gave him his daughter Michal as a wife.

The pronoun IO, whose referent is *David,* is presuppositional and occurs in the immediate postverbal position. The referent *Michal* is presuppositional too. Both referents are mentioned in the preceding context. As for the clause final NP, it belongs to the VP, נתן לאשה, *to give as a wife*, and appears in its expected position. The pragmatic role of word order is not clear in this instance and is better assessed in the light of another comparable example:

(5.43) Genesis 16.3

ותתן אתה לאברם אישה לו לאשה

She gave her to Abram her husband as wife.

In this clause the order of the presuppositional objects is reversed as compared to (5.42). This time it is the direct object which is a PRO and is immediately postverbal, as required by the grammar. The full indirect object NP *to Abraham* follows it. The context shows that it is the referent *Abraham* which is the DFE here. Sarai, Abram's wife, gives her slave-girl to Abram in order to have a child by her. The identity of the recipient is the important point of the utterance. This is confirmed by the further highlighting of the indirect object NP through the apposition *her husband* and the repetition of the NP through a PRO, *to him.* (5.41) and (5.43) make use of the principle of end-focality. In (5.43) the DFE is placed as far towards the end of the clause as the grammar allows. On this basis, it is possible to conclude that in (5.42), it is the referent *Michal* which is the DFE.

These examples show that when both object NPs in a clause are presuppositional, the speaker uses word order to indicate which one is the DFE. The speaker's choice is guided by a principle stating that the referent which is the DFE is placed as far towards the end of the clause as the grammar allows. (5.41) exemplifies this principle in a clause where the word order is not shifted. The clause-final NP is the DFE. In (5.42) and (5.43) the NP is not in absolute final position, because of the particular idiomatic VP used.

This principle explains the obligatory fronting and immediate postverbal position of an object PRO. A referent encoded as PRO is always presuppositional. If it is not chosen as the DFE it must come before the other presuppositional referent and so is immediately postverbal.

iii. *Transitive Clauses with Adverbials*

In transitive clauses with adverbial phrases, the ADVP may be an obligatory argument of the V or a non-obligatory one. This feature must be taken into account when determining which NP in the predicate is the DFE. Locational and temporal ADVPs will be considered. Consider the clause with an ADVP of location:

(5.44) Genesis 41.42

ויסר פרעה את־טבעתו מעל ידו

Pharaoh removed his signet-ring from his hand.

The topical participant is encoded as a full NP subject. The predicate includes a direct object NP, obligatory argument of the V, followed by an ADVP which is not obligatory. The question is whether this ADVP is the DFE or not. The referent of the NP *hand* is presuppositional. It is, in fact, inferable from the meaning of the VP (*removed his signet-ring*): the hearer can infer that the ring was removed from Pharaoh's hand on the sole basis of the meaning of the V + DO. The presuppositional ADVP competes with a non-presuppositional NP direct object and it is the latter which is the DFE. The deletion of the ADVP would in no way change the informational point of the clause.

Consider another example:

(5.45) Genesis 30.14

(1) In the days of the wheat-harvest Reuben went,
(2) וימצא דודאים בשׂדה
and he found mandrakes in the field.

The ADVP is a non-obligatory argument of the V and it is also non-presuppositional. The NP direct object is also non-presuppositional. It is the latter phrase which is the DFE as the context shows. The discovery of mandrakes constitutes the main burden of the utterance, not the place where they were found. The ADVP adds a circumstancial detail which could be omitted without changing the point of the utterance. The peripheral role of the ADVP is also evident in:

(5.46) 2 Samuel 18.14

ויקח שׁלשׁה שׁבטים בכפו
And he took two javelins in his hand.

The ADVP *in his hand* is non-obligatory and also presuppositional through its semantic relation to the V. In fact, its evocation by the VP makes it semantically redundant. It could be dropped, with the VP standing on its own, without any change to the meaning of the utterance. The non-presuppositional referent *three javelins* is the DFE.

In the three examples the referents of the NPs encoded as DOs are non-presuppositional and they are the DFEs. It is to be noted that they are also obligatory arguments of the V. As for the non-obligatory ADVPs expressing details which are not central to the meaning of the propositions, they are not in focus. This is the case even when, as in (5.45), the ADVP is non-presuppositional. There, it competes with a referent which is non-presuppositional too, but which is encoded as an obligatory DO. The obligatory nature of the DO is the criterion which determines that it is the DFE.

It is now necessary to have a look at clauses in which the ADVP is an obligatory element of the VP.[22] Consider:

(5.47) 1 Samuel 17.54

(1) ויקח דוד את־ראש הפלשתי
(2) ויבאהו ירושלם
(1) David took the Philistine's head (2) and brought it to Jerusalem.

The referent *David* is the topic of the two clauses. In (2) the V requires two core arguments, a DO and a locational which is the ADVP *Jerusalem.*[23] Within the focus domain the two referents compete for the status of DFE. The PRO direct object is presuppositional and the ADVP is non-presuppositional. It is the latter which is the DFE. If the focus were on the direct object PRO, the sentence would be interpreted as meaning *He brought* ***him****—and not another one*; this cannot be the case given the context.

In the next example the ADVP of location occurs in a clause in which the NP direct object (1) is topicalized:

(5.48) 2 Kings 24.16

(1) All the men of valour, seven thousand, the artisan and the smiths, one thousand, all of them strong and fit for war,
(2) ויביאם מלך־בבל גולה בבלה
the king of Babylon brought them captive to Babylon.

The ADVP, גולה בבלה, is an obligatory argument of the V. Without it the clause would not be well formed. The suffixed pronoun DO is presuppositional. The locational NP is non-presuppositional. The ADVP encodes the referent which added to the proposition *the king of Babylon took them* makes the utterance a piece of new information, and so it is the DFE.

22. Deciding between obligatory and non-obligatory constituents is not an exercise which is easily carried out in Old Hebrew, as Muraoka acknowledges (1979). It is linked to verb valency and the semantics of the verb. This is an area of the language poorly explored. Decisions have been made here using the well-formedness of the clauses as a criteria.

23. The destination of the object must be specified. The V could be used without an explicit ADVP, but then the destination would have to be inferable from the context.

Another example of a transitive verb with an obligatory locative is found in:

(5.49) Jonah 1.15

(1) וישׂאו את־יונה
(2) ויטלהו אל־הים
(1) They took up Jonah (2) and threw him into the sea.

In (2) the V has two obligatory arguments, the DO and the ADVP of place. The latter is an obligatory argument, given that the entity thrown is a human being.[24] The NP direct object is presuppositional as well as the ADVP: the preceding context has made clear that Jonah had to be thrown into the sea in order for the storm to be stopped. The PRO direct object is not the DFE as the interpretation would be that the sailors threw Jonah overboard, and not another person. The presuppositional ADVP is the DFE. It is to be noted that it is maintained in clause-final position, following the normal word order.

The examples with an ADVP as obligatory argument show that when the ADVP in question is non-presuppositional, it is also the dominant focal element. When the ADVP is presuppositional and competes with a presuppositional direct object NP, it is the ADVP which is the DFE. This can be explained semantically in terms of the relations between arguments within the VP. With a verb of motion, for example, which requires a locative, the locative will represent the significant information in the sentence and so will be the DFE.

It is necessary now to consider more in detail clauses with temporal ADVPs. An ADVP of time is a non-obligatory argument of the V. It may be either presuppositional or non-presuppositional. An ADVP such as ביום ההוא, *on that day*, is always presuppositional because of its deictic element. A shared knowledge of the temporal denotation between speaker and hearer is implied in the expression, otherwise the hearer would be in a position legitimately to respond to the mention of the denotatum with an interjection such as: ‘Wait a minute, which day are you talking about?’ Consider:

24. Because the referent of the NP direct object is a human being, the locational adverbial is required here. It is not usual for a human being to be ‘thrown’. Had the verb been used with an inanimate DO, referring for example to a javelin, the ADVP would not have been a necessary argument.

(5.50) 1 Samuel 12.18

ויתן יהוה קלת ומטר ביום ההוא

And Yahweh sent thunder and rain on that day.

The predicate is (*sent thunder and rain on that day*). *That day* is presuppositional and competes with the other presuppositional denotata *thunder and rain* which have been mentioned previously by Samuel (v. 17). An examination of the context indicates that the point of the incident is not so much that Yahweh thunders at the people as that he shows his willingness to respond to Samuel very promptly. The context shows that it is the temporal ADVP which is the DFE.

This example is comparable to (5.49), where the referents are both presuppositional. The word order is not changed and the last referent mentioned is the DFE. Examples (5.49) and (5.50) seem to point to a principle of end-dominant focus. It is confirmed by the following example in which both the DO and the ADVP are presuppositional:

(5.51) 1 Samuel 14.23

ויושע יהוה ביום ההוא את־ישׂראל

So Yahweh gave Israel the victory that day.

The direct object NP is the DFE. The point of the assertion is not the reference to a particular day, but to the people saved. The DO is moved to clause-final position, preceded by the ADVP. When the speaker wants the DFE to be the NP direct object in a clause in which the DO and the ADVP are presuppositional, a switch in word order is required. The DO occurs in clause-final position.

The assignment of the DFE to the clausal end position in a presuppositional environment is confirmed by other examples. Consider another clause with a temporal ADVP:

(5.52) Genesis 29.20

ויעבד יעקב ברחל שׁבע שׁנים

And Jacob served seven years for Rachel.

Both the prepositional object and the ADVP are presuppositional through the context. That the clause final temporal NP is the DFE is confirmed by a consideration of the ensuing clause. The denotatum *seven years* becomes the topic of the next sentence: *and they* (i.e. the seven years) *seemed but a few days* .

All these examples point to the existence in the Old Hebrew narrative clause of a principle of end-dominant focal element. The final NP in a vayyiqtol clause is the DFE. To conclude, an example with an ADVP of manner will be considered:

(5.53) Exodus 1.13

ויעבדו מצרים את־בני ישׂראל בפרך

The Egyptians made the people of Israel work ruthlessly.

The focus domain has a NP direct object which is presuppositional and an ADVP which is non-presuppositional. The ADVP is a non-obligatory argument of the V. The context of the story helps us to decide that it is the expression *ruthlessly* which is the DFE. The ensuing clauses provide details of the harsh treatment dealt on the Israelites. Here too it is the clause final NP which is the DFE.[25]

iv. *Conclusion*

The following points have been identified:

(1) In a transitive clause with a full NP as object, the DFE is the NP, independently of its presuppositional or non-presuppositional character. This is exemplified in (5.32), (5.33) and (5.34).

(2) In a ditransitive clause, it is the non-presuppositional nature of a NP which is the primary determining factor in the establishment of the DFE, as (5.38), (5.39) and (5.40) show. If one object NP is non-presuppositional and the other one is, the DFE does not need to be indicated through word order. However, when both object NPs are presuppositional, the speaker indicates the DFE through word order, as in (5.41), (5.42) and (5.43). A principle of end-dominance of the focal element controls the choice of word order.

(3) In transitive clauses with ADVPs, the interplay of factors is best summarized with the help of diagrams examining all the clauses in which the ADVP comes last. The examples may be classified in two groups. The first group comprises clauses with a non-obligatory ADVP, (1) to (6). The second group, (7), (8), (9), comprises clauses with an obligatory ADVP. In the Table, the box contains the V and its obligatory argument(s); the star signals the DFE; and n-p and p stand for *non-presuppositional* and *presuppositional,* respectively.

25. The fronting of the ADVP is not, theoretically, an impossibility. בפרך could precede the DO, but as it is non-presuppositional and also the DFE, it is clause-final. The generally non-presuppositional character of ADVPs of manner explains why they are rarely found in a fronted position.

Table 5.1. *Transitive clauses with ADVPs*

(1) Genesis 41.42 (5.44): Pharaoh removed his signet ring from his finger.

Vayyiqtol	DO *	ADVP
	n-p	p

(2) Genesis 30.14 (5.45): He found mandrakes in the fields.

Vayyiqtol	DO *	ADVP
	n-p	n-p

(3) 2 Samuel 18.14 (5.46): He took two javelins in his hand.

Vayyiqtol	DO *	ADVP
	n-p	p

(4) 1 Samuel 12.18 (5.50): Yahweh sent thunder and rain on that day.

Vayyiqtol	DO	ADVP *
	p	p

(5) Genesis 29.20 (5.52): Jacob served seven years for Rachel.

Vayyiqtol	IO	ADVP *
	p	p

(6) Exodus 1.13 (5.53): The Egyptians made the people of Israel work ruthlessly.

Vayyiqtol	DO	ADVP *
	p	n-p

(7) 1 Samuel 17.54 (5.47): He brought it to Jerusalem.

Vayyiqtol	DO	ADVP *
	p	n-p

(8) 2 Kings 24.16 (5.48): The King of Babylon brought them captive to Babylon.

Vayyiqtol	DO	ADVP *
	p	n-p

(9) Jonah 1.15b (5.49): They threw him into the sea.

Vayyiqtol	DO	ADVP *
	p	p

The following observations can be made on the basis of a comparison of the clauses:

(3.1) The criterion of non-presuppositionality is decisive and overrides the obligatory/non-obligatory argument criterion. When one referent is n-p and the other is p, the referent which is n-p is invariably the DFE, whether it is an obligatory argument of the V as in (1), (3), (7) and (8) or a non-obligatory one as in (6). In such cases word order does not need to be modified to indicate the DFE.

(3.2) The criterion of obligatory verbal argument comes into play when a n-p referent competes with another n-p referent as in (2). Then it is the referent whose NP is encoded as a core argument, that is as the object, which is the DFE. No change in word order is needed to specifiy the DFE.

(3.3) Word-order change might be used to signal the DFE when both NPs are presuppositional. The reason is that in such cases the criterion obligatory/non-obligatory argument does not play a role, as is shown by comparing (4) and (5) with (9). Only the principle of end-DFE applies. The NP which is the dominant focal element is clause-final (or as far towards the end of the clause as grammar allows) by default, or through word order change as in (5.51).

(3.4) The criterion of the nature of the argument given in 3.2 can be interpreted in the light of the word order criterion of 3.3, by saying that the obligatory/non obligatory criterion overlaps, in fact, with an unmarked VSOA order.

(3.5) Finally, a comparison of the factors bearing upon the assignment of the DFE in the ditransitive and the transitive clause + ADVP reveals the following parallels:

DITRANSITIVE CL.		TRANSITIVE CL. WITH ADVP	
Presupposit.	*DFE*	*Presupposit.*	*DFE*
n-p + p	n-p	n-p + p (ADVP)	n-p
n-p + n-p	no examples found	n-p + n-p	Oblig. arg.
p + p	End-DFE word order	p + p	End-DFE word order

On the basis of these analyses, a scale of criteria coming into play in the establishment of the DFE in a vayyiqtol clause may be offered. When the DFE has to be selected from one out of two referents, the non-presuppositional nature of a referent is the first key determining factor. This factor might be cancelled out because both referents share the same presuppositional nature, being either both non-presuppositional or both presuppositional.

In the first case, the argument type (obligatory/non-obligatory) of the NPs becomes the determining factor, as in (2): (5.45). In the second case, a combination of the principle of end-DFE with the possibility of word order shift applies. The default DFE is found as far toward the end of the clause as the grammar permits. If the speaker wants to establish as DFE a referent which normally would not be encoded as clause-final, they have to move the element in question as far to the end of the clause as possible.

Presuppositionality, verbal argument and end-DFE are the notions which play a role in the establishement of the DFE. The first one, as would be expected, is pragmatic. The second one is grammatical and semantic. The third one is grammatical, but driven by pragmatic considerations.

A last point needs to be mentioned. It seems legitimate to predict that when the two NPs direct object and adverbial are both at the same time non-presuppositional and obligatory arguments of the V, it is word order too which will indicate the DFE, according to the principle of end-dominant focality.

c. *The Predicate-Focus Structure in the NP + Qatal Clause*

The NP + qatal clause is closely associated with the functioning of the vayyiqtol clause in narratives and so it is also necessary to examine the question of focality in it. The first task is to determine whether the clause is marked or not. In this regard, Niccacci (1986: 35) makes an erroneous claim: 'at the outset it is important to note that QATAL is always non-initial in narrative. That is to say, it never heads a sentence.'

Although they are rare, examples of a qatal clause with a verb in the initial position can be found:

(5.54) 1 Kings 14.24

עשׂו ככל התועבת הגוים

They adopted all the shameful practices of the nations [that Yahweh drove out before the people of Israel].

This indicates that the unmarked word order VSO applies to a qatal clause as well. As a result, the NP + qatal clause must be considered as having a marked word order. It is a clause which offers a speaker the possibility of moving a NP to initial position (forefronting) for various pragmatic reasons.

It is unfortunate that the diversity of the pragmatic uses of the clause is obliterated through its formal description as a 'NP + qatal' clause.[26] This categorization has the drawback of suggesting that the NP + qatal clause-type has one function only. A careful examination of the clauses of this type shows that this is far from being the case. First, the initial NP may encode a referent as subject, direct object or adverbial, and the pragmatic function of the clause varies according to the types of constituent encoded. Secondly, the traditional designation also hides the fact that not all NP + qatal clauses have a predicate-focus structure. Some have an argument-focus structure and others a sentence-focus structure.

The forefrontings considered in this section occur in a NP + qatal clause with a predicate-focus structure; those occuring in clauses with other kinds of focus structure will be considered later in the chapter. Within the predicate-focus group, one type of forefronting has to do with the focus articulation of the clause, the other with the topic articulation of the clause. Forefronting for focus must be distinguished from the forefronting of a NP encoding a topic to indicate a contrast with another topic.[27]

Although the question of topic has been covered in the preceding chapter, for the sake of clarity it seems appropriate to incorporate the special case of topic forefronting in the section which considers the clause from the angle of its predicate-focus structure. This will result in a more comprehensive analysis of the predicate-focus articulation of the clause. Forefronting for focus will be considered first.

i. *NP + Qatal: Y-Movement of the Direct Object NP*

Under the term Y-movement is understood here a specific type of

26. This formal categorization has become commonplace in Old Hebrew grammatical studies. Niccacci and Longacre, among others, use it constantly. It is useful as long as it is clearly understood that it embraces a variety of clausal constructions.

27. In this regard, Givón's description of the Y-movement as used for 'contrastive topicalization' (1990: 705), that is when a referent is contrasted with another one (1990: 752), is unsatisfactory for Old Hebrew. It is too all-inclusive and introduces some confusion between topic and focus. Y-movement is better reserved for the forefronting of a focal element in a non-contrastive context.

forefronting in which a NP in focus is moved to the clause-initial position. Consider:

(5.55) Genesis 27.15-16

(1) Then Rebekah took the best clothes of her elder son, Esau...
(2) ותלבש את־יעקב בנה הקטן
(3) ואת ערת גדיי העזים הלבישה
על־ידיו ועל חלקת צואריו
(2) and she put them on Jacob, her younger son, (3) and the goatskins she put on his arms and upon the hairless part of his neck.

Rebekah has devised a stratagem to ensure that Isaac, her son, should receive a final blessing from his father, instead of Esau his brother. The clause occurs in a procedural context in which two kids are used to trick the father. The animals are killed, cooked and their skins used as described in (3). The referent *goatskins* is encoded in a NP direct object which is forefronted in a clause with a predicate-focus structure. The referent of the DO is presuppositional, the referent of the ADVP is non-presuppositional. The criterion of non-presuppositionality would designate the ADVP as the DFE. However, the forefronting of the DO cancels the effect of this criterion. It indicates that it is the NP direct object and not the ADVP, in spite of its non-presuppositional nature, which is the DFE. The narrative context provides the explanation for the establishment of the referent *goatskins* as the DFE. Jacob is described as smooth-skinned and fears that his father will 'feel' him during the blessing ceremony, as reported earlier: '*Esau is a hairy man and I, my skin is smooth*' (v. 11). For the ruse to be successful, everything hangs on the goatskins, as the outcome of the story shows: *he did not recognize him because his arms were hairy* (v. 23).

Y-movement is also exemplified in:

(5.56) 1 Samuel 6.14

(1) ויבקעו את־עצי העגלה
(2) ואת־הפרות העלו עלה ליהוה
(1) They chopped up the wood of the cart (2) and sacrificed the cows [as a burnt offering] to Yahweh.

The ark, war palladium of the Israelites, has been captured by the Philistines. Now it is returned to the Israelite territory on a cart pulled by two cows. The first people to see the cart immediately stop it and the two cows are sacrificed. The referent encoded as *they* is the topical participant in (1) and (2). In (1) the NP direct object (*wood*) is the DFE. In (2) out of the three NPs in the predicate, one of only two referents may be singled out as the DFE, *Yahweh* and *the cows*. The cognate object *burnt-offering* repeats the idea of the V and could be dropped. The referents of the nouns DO and IO are both presupposed and, were the proposition encoded in a verb initial clause with an unmarked word order, the DFE would fall on the clause-final IO. The speaker, however, has chosen to encode the referent *cows* as the DFE and to give it saliency. This saliency is best explained by the fact that the speaker wants to bring to attention that the sacrifice of two cows was an unusual offering to Yahweh, insofar as the animals sacrificed were not males.[28]

A last example will highlight the use of Y-movement:

(5.57) Judges 7.25

(1) They continued to pursue[29] Midian,
(2) וראש־ערב וזאב הביאו אל־גדעון מעבר לירדן
and they brought the heads of Oreb and Zeeb to Gideon beyond the Jordan.

(2) concludes the account of Gideon's victory over the Midianites, in which the two enemy kings have been killed. The two obligatory arguments in the predicate, the DO and IO, are both presuppositional; the non-obligatory argument, the ADVP, is non-presuppositional. In a clause without word-order shift, the ADVP would be the DFE. Through forefronting the two NPs direct object become the DFEs, the speaker wanting to bring out the unusual treatment of the defeated kings' corpses, as well as the odd nature of the trophies of war brought to Gideon.

In the three examples considered, the effect of the Y-movement has been to demote the clause-final NP from its DFE status and to promote another NP as DFE. This use of the NP + qatal clause must be seen as complementing the use of the post-verbal word order shift noticed on pp. 197-99. But it is also a more radical means of signalling the DFE, which is used by a speaker who wishes to highlight some surprising or unusual aspect of the situation reported in the clause.

28. Cf. Lev. 1.3; 22.19.
29. Read את (object marker) and not אל ('towards the Midianites').

ii. *NP + Qatal: Y-movement of an Adverbial NP*
An ADVP of time may also be forefronted as marked DFE, as in:

(5.58) Genesis 14.4

(1) שתים עשרה שנה עבדו את־כדרלעמר
(2) ושלש־עשרה שנה מרדו
(1) Twelve years they (had) served Kedorlaomer, (2) but in the thirteenth year they rebelled.

(1) and (2) have a predicate-focus structure, with a topical participant encoded as pronoun, *they*, whose referent is five kings. (1) may be compared to the vayyiqtol clause in (5.52): *he served seven years for Rachel*. In (5.52) the ADVP is left in its clause-final position, here it is forefronted. Forefronting is explained by the chronistic style adopted by the speaker. The chronological order of events is the foremost concern of the speaker in the reporting of events and so the DFE, which is the temporal phrase, is forefronted. This style, characteristic of the historical writings of the Hebrew Bible, is also exemplified in:

(6.59) 1 Kings 14.21

(1) Rehoboam was forty-one years old when he began to reign,
(2) ושבע עשרה שנה מלך בירושלם
and he reigned 17 years in Jerusalem.

(2) has a predicate-focus structure, with continuing topic. (1) and (2) are part of an introductory regnal resumé providing information about kings (Long 1984: 158-60, 250). It includes the name of the king, the date of his accession, the age of the king at accession in (1), and the length of his reign in (2). The ADVP of time is forefronted as marked DFE in a discourse whose main purpose is to keep records of accession dates and lengths of reigns.

The ADVP has often an anaphoric function, indicating continuity of temporal setting:

(5.60) Genesis 15.18

ביום ההוא כרת יהוה את־אברם ברית
That day, Yahweh made a covenant with Abram (saying)

In a vayyiqtol clause, the post-verbal and presuppositional ADVP *on that day* would compete with the non-presuppositional DO, and so could in no way be the DFE. Through forefronting, the phrase is established as the DFE. The speaker confirms the meaning of the ritual which has just taken place, pointing specifically to the uniqueness of this day in the life of Abram. This use of the ADVP must be carefully differentiated from its function as a basis.[30]

An ADVP with the function of basis occurs only with a vayyiqtol clause, as the comparison between (5.61) and (5.62) will show.

(5.61) Joshua 4.14

(1) ביום ההוא גדל יהוה את־יהושע בעיני כל־ישראל
(2) ויראו אתו

(1) On that day, Yahweh made Joshua great in the eyes of all Israel, (2) and they revered him [as they had revered Moses all his life].

In (1) the NP provides a temporal reference point relative to which the event reported by the verb is situated. The temporal reference has a clause internal function; the ADVP does not situate temporally the event reported in the following clause (2). This is not the case with a vayyiqtol clause:

(5.62) Genesis 26.32

(1) ויהי ביום ההוא ויבאו עבדי יצחק
(2) ויגדו לו על־אדות הבאר
(3) ויאמרו לו

(1) Now, on that day Isaac's servants came (2) and told him about the well [they had been digging] (3) and they said to him...

The ADVP preceded by ויהי, a discourse marker which indicates the onset of a new episode, has both a backward-looking and forward-looking function. It looks backward, indicating that the discourse which follows is related to what precedes on the basis of temporal continuity. In this, it is similar to the ADVP forefronted in a qatal clause. But it is also looking forward, setting the temporal domain for the chunk of discourse which follows. Serving as an extended temporal framework, the basis has a discourse function. By contrast, the forefronted temporal ADVP with qatal provides a framework confined to the clause.

In a NP + qatal clause, the ADVP may be preceded by ויהי. The discourse marker indicates the beginning of a new episode. But the following ADVP does not function as a new temporal basis for this new

30. The notion of basis is discussed in Chapter 3.

episode, as the following example shows:

(5.63) Exodus 16.27

ויהי ביום השביעי יצאו מן־העם ללקט

Now on the seventh day, some of the people went out to collect (the manna) [but they found none].

The clause which follows, *Yahweh then said to Moses*, does not belong to the temporal domain set by the ADVP *on the seventh day*, which has only a clause-internal function.

iii. *NP + Qatal Contrastive Topics in a Predicate-Focus Structure Clause*

Definition. As contrastive topics constructions have often been confused with other kinds of contrastive or adversative constructions, a clear definition of what is being talked about here is necessary first.[31] Two adjacent clauses with contrastive topics each have their topic used in a predicate-focus construction as in:

Steve and Emma were at the party.
Steve was cheerful, but *Emma* looked very upset.

Two topical referents are contrasted with one another, but the assertion of the second clause does not go against, deny, or correct the truth value of the previously expressed proposition. This differs from a constrastive foci construction made out of two adjacent clauses, and in which the assertion of the second clause denies, goes against or corrects the first one.

Some languages indicate morphosyntactically that the two notions are different in meaning. Given a discourse context in which two friends are backpacking, (A) illustrates contrastive topic in French:

(A) *Toi*, tu chercheras de l'eau, *moi*, je ferai le feu.
You'll fetch the water and I'll make the fire.

Toi and *moi* are contrastive topics. The referents *l'eau* and *le feu* are DFEs. If the two backpackers argue over which job should be done by whom, (B) would illustrate contrastive focus:

31. For example, Herchenroeder (1987: 18-30) analyses them as adversative constructions.

(B) *Je vais chercher de l'eau.*
Non, **c'est** moi *qui chercherai l'eau et* **c'est** *toi prepareras le feu.*

I'll fetch water.
No, *I* shall fetch the water and *you* will prepare the fire.

Here *moi* and *toi* are contrastive foci. The special construction with *c'est*, in which both constituents appear in postverbal position, marks the two Ns as foci.

Special morphosyntactic devices to differentiate between contrastive topics and contrastive foci do not exist in Old Hebrew. It is through inferring from the context that one can establish which notion is encoded in a NP + *qatal* clause. In the contrastive topics construction, the topical referents may be encoded as NPs subject, direct object or indirect object. Each of these categories will be examined in turn.

Contrastive Topics Encoded as Subject NPs. Consider the example:

(5.64) Ruth 1.14

(1) ותשׁק ערפה לחמותה
(2) ורות דבקה בה

(1) Orpah kissed her mother-in-law, (2) while Ruth clung to her.

Naomi has lost her husband and her two married sons and decides to return to her native country. Naomi's two daughters-in-law have to decide whether to go back with her or not. The contrast is between the two topical participants, *Orpah* and *Ruth,* both encoded as subject NPs. The construction is characterized by the pairing of one vayyiqtol clause to a NP + qatal clause whose NP subject is topicalized. As the two verbs have as objects the same referent *mother-in-law*, the contrastive foci (or DFEs) are the denotata of the two verbs. The attitude of one participant is set over the attitude of the other one. Orpah kissed good-bye, whereas Ruth clung to her mother-in-law. In (2), the verbal DFE cannot be clause-final as it is not possible for the prepositional object to precede the V when the S is clause initial.

Usually, when the DFE denotatum is a NP, it is in clause-final position:

(5.65) 1 Samuel 4.1

(1) ויחנו על־האבן העזר
(2) ופלשׁתים חנו באפק

(1) They made camp at Ebenezer, (2) and the Philistine camped at Apheq.

The attention is fixed on two battlecamps. One topical participant encoded as the PRO *they* is set against the other, *the Philistines*. The two contrastive foci referents are the clause-final ADVP *Ebenezer* and *Apheq*. Consider now the following example:

(5.66) Genesis 37.11

(1) ויקנאו־בו אחיו
(2) ואביו שׁמר את־הדבר

(1) His brothers were jealous of him, (2) but his father kept the matter (in mind).

Longacre analyses the paired clauses in the following way:

> We see clearly how the narrator uses a perfect to put an action off the storyline when it is not an action of the same rank and importance to the story as the action indicated by a preterite ... In the total sweep of the story the brother's jealousy is much more tied into the plot structure than the father's meditating as to what the dream might mean (1989: 70).

This explanation is appealing but has two flaws. First, Longacre's interpretation of *his father kept the matter in mind* is debatable.[32] Secondly and more importantly, for the thesis to be true one would expect all NP + qatal clauses to be used to report secondary events, and all vayyiqtol clauses to be used to report events related to the plot structure. This is clearly not the case. Later in the same story, for example, believing that his son Joseph has been devoured by a wild animal, Jacob mourns the death of his son. The story concludes: *and his father bewailed him* (Gen. 37.35). The clause used is a vayyiqtol clause. That the event of Jacob crying the loss of his son is 'more tied into the plot' cannot be advanced as an argument for justifying the use of a vayyiqtol verbal form here. The event is just as off the storyline as the one reported through a NP + qatal clause in Gen. 37.11. The untenability of Longacre's explanation is further confirmed by considering the clause which immediately follows the report of the father's grief. It is a NP + qatal clause: *The Midianites sold him* [Joseph] *in Egypt to Potiphar*. This event is unquestionably directly tied up to the plot structure of Joseph's story, yet is not encoded in a vayyiqtol clause.

The qatal clause in (5.66) does not indicate the relative importance of

32. Because of the repetition of Joseph's dream, it is more likely that his father reflects upon its authenticity and importance. The meaning of the dream seems quite obvious.

the event which it reports. It has this form because it is the second member of a contrastive topics construction, in which the attitude of Joseph's father is set against the attitude of his brothers.

The description of the construction as a constrastive topics construction must not hide the fact that it may also be used to express similarity rather than contrast:

(5.67) Genesis 19.37-38

(1) ותלד הבכירה בן...
(2) והצעירה גם־היא ילדה בן

(1) and the firstborn bore a son ... (2) and the younger one too bore a son.

(1) is an unmarked VSO vayyiqtol clause. The contrast is between two topical participants, the daughters of Lot: *the firstborn* and *the younger*. The focal elements are not so much contrastive, however, as signalling a similarity. The two predicates are synonymous. They are the focus domains in which the two referents *a son* is the DFE.

Subject Topicalized and Dislocated Parallelism. In the examples considered so far, the first clause has a participant A, agent of a single action, and the second one has a participant B, agent of another single action. However, the participants contrasted, either A or B, may be involved not in a single action, but in a series of actions. When this happens, the series of vayyiqtol Vs reporting the actions of participant A is not interrupted to allow the contrast with participant B to take place immediately. The NP + qatal appears only once the sequence of events involving A is completed, as in:

(5.68) Jonah 1.5b

(1) וייראו המלחים
(2) ויזעקו איש אל־אלהיו
(3) ויטלו את־הכלים...
(4) ויונה ירד אל־ירכתי הספינה

(1) and the sailors were afraid (2) and each cried to his own god (3) and they threw the wares...(4) but Jonah had gone down into the hold of the ship.

The two topical participants are *sailors* and *Jonah*. The first participant is involved in a series of successive actions (1-2-3), which the speaker does not want to interrupt. It is contrasted with the other topical participant, *Jonah*, in (4). The symmetry here is between (1-3) and (4). To indicate topic contrast the construction NP + qatal clause is used, but only when the vayyiqtol sequence is finished.

The important temporal implication is that the qatal V will take on a pluperfect meaning, as the action described by the V is no longer contemporary with the action described by the initial vayyiqtol in the sequence. The pluperfect meaning is derived inferentially.

Contrastive Topics Encoded as Object NPs. In a number of examples, a topicalized NP is encoded as a direct object. The forefronting of the direct object NP creates a clause with two topics. Consider:

(5.69) Judges 7.25

(1) וילכדו שׁני־שׂרי מדין את־ערב ואת־זאב
(2) ויהרגו את־עורב בצור־עורב
(3) ואת־זאב הרגו ביקב־זאב

(1) They captured the two chieftains of Midian, Oreb and Zeeb. (2) They killed Oreb at the rock of Oreb (3) and Zeeb they killed at the wine-press of Zeeb.

This is a contrastive topics construction with two identical lexical verbs in (2) and (3). The contrast bears on the different places in which the two chiefs died. (2) and (3) have one common topical referent encoded as the pronoun subject *they*. *They* refers to *the men of Ephraim*, the whole episode describing the military exploits of these men. In (2) the focus domain comprises a presuppositional referent, *Oreb,* and a non-presuppositional one, *rock*. In (3), the presuppositional referent, *Zeeb*, is removed from its post-verbal position and topicalized through forefronting. The locational ADVPs of (2) and (3), which are non-presuppositional, are the contrastive foci and the DFEs, occurring in clause-final position.

When in the transitive clause the predicate comprises only one DO, the forefronting of the direct object NP for topicalization results in the verb being the DFE:

(5.70) Judges 1.25

(1) ויכו את־העיר לפי־חרב
(2) ואת־האישׁ ואת־כל־משׁפחתו שׁלחו

(1) They put the city to the sword, (2) but they let the man and all his family go free.

The respective referents, *town*, *man* and *family* are presuppositional. They belong to a set of referents which have been mentioned in the course of the story. As a result of the direct object NP *the man* being topicalized and moved to the initial position in (2), only the V, *they let go*, is left in the focus domain. Together with the V of (1), *they put to the sword*, it is in a contrastive focus construction. Another example is found in:

(5.71) Genesis 40.21

(1) וישב את־שׂר המשקים על־משקהו...
(2) ואת שׂר האפים תלה

(1) He restored the chief cupbearer to his cupbearing (post) [and he placed the cup in Pharaoh's hand] (2) but the chief baker he hanged.

In (2) the focus domain is the V + DO. The NP direct object, *the chief baker*, is presupposed and topicalized through forefonting, leaving the V detached in the focus domain. The verb is the DFE.

Contrastive topics construction are commonly used with a negative verb:

(5.72) Genesis 4.4-5

(1) וישׁע יהוה אל־הבל ואל־מנחתו
(2) ואל־קין ואל־מנחתו לא שׁעה

(1) And Yahweh directed his gaze on Abel and his offering, (2) but on Cain and his offering he did not direct his gaze.

In (2) the denotata of *Cain* and *offering* are presupposed. Both are topicalized through the forefronting of the NPs. They stand in a contrastive topics constructions with *Abel and his offering*. Only the negative V remains in the focus domain and is the DFE.

To conclude, a referent encoded as DO can become a topic in a NP + qatal clause only if the clause is the second member of a contrastive construction. If this condition is fulfilled, the NP is forefronted as contrastive topic. The denotatum/referent which is the constrative focus (or DFE) in the NP + qatal clause plays a pivotal role as it determines the contrastive import of the construction. The two foci (DFEs) of the construction are clause-final.

d. *The Predicate-Focus Structure: Conclusion*

The NP + qatal clause which forefronts a NP direct object or adverbial through Y-movement belongs to the pragmatic system of focality of the narrative clause. It is related to the focal system operating in the vayyiqtol clause, and together the two clause-types make up a twofold mechanism for conveying focality. A referent or denotatum which is the DFE in the vayyiqtol clause is in unmarked focus. The presuppositional character of the referent, the type of verbal argument it encodes, and the postverbal word-order shift are criteria and devices a speaker can use to establish as DFE a referent of his choice, given the principle that a constituent occurring at the end of a clause is a dominant focal element. A referent in focus occurs in clause-initial position as a NP encoding a direct object or adverbial when it is a marked DFE. Markedness is required in specific contexts to bring out an aspect of a situation which is surprising, unusual, curious.

Besides focality, a referent may be forefronted as a topic in a NP + qatal clause with a predicate-focus structure. This is a special type of topicalization which requires a contrastive construction with contrastive foci.

5. *The Third Person Narrative Clause with Argument-Focus Structure*

In this construction, the predicate is presuppositional and it is the denotatum/referent which has to be added to it in order to produce an assertion, the argument, which is in focus. This structure was examined above in direct speech clauses (see pp. 176-82). Examples were used in which the presuppositional predicate (open presupposition) was given through a question, the answer providing the argument. In a real-life conversation, the presuppositional predicate is often given by the situational context. It is a different matter in a third person written narrative. The information of the presuppositional predicate must be found in the prior written context. It is often provided in the form of a general description in the clause immediately preceding the argument-focus structure clause, as in:

(5.73) Genesis 34.25-26

(1) ויהרגו כל־זכר
(2) ואת־חמור ואת־שכם בנו הרגו לפי־חרב

(1) And they killed all the males (2) and Hamor and his son Shechem they killed with the blade of the sword.

These two clauses come at the end of a story which tells how Simeon and Levi avenged their sister Dinah who had been raped by Shechem. (1) answers the question *what did they do next?* and has a predicate-focus structure. (2) cannot be construed as answering such a question, coming after the assertion of (1), as (1) logically entails (2). The S, V, and ADVP (*they killed with the blade of the sword)* in (2) are presuppositional. (1) is a general statement, (2) repeats the predication of (1) but also supplies a missing argument. It answers an implicit question *Whom did they kill with the sword in particular?* The two main protagonists of the story are the referents in focus. The argument in focus is expressed in the NPs direct object which are forefronted in a qatal clause. Consider another example:

(5.74) Genesis 14.16

(1) וישב את כל־הרכש
(2) וגם את־לוט אחיו ורכשו השיב

(1) He brought back all the possessions (2) and also his kinsman Lot and his possessions he brought back.

(1) is a general statement which is repeated in (2). The predicate (*brought back all the possessions*) is presuppositional in (2). The speaker adds to it a new relevant argument which supplements the general statement of (1). The referent *Lot* in focus is encoded in a clause initial NP preceded by the expanding particle *gam*, in a *qatal* clause. The argument-focus structure of the clause answers the question *what (whom) did he also bring back?* Consider now:

(5.75) Genesis 1.27

(1) ויברא אלהים את־האדם בצלמו
(2) בצלם אלהים ברא אתו

(1) And God created man in his image. (2) In the image of God he created him.

The referent *image* in (1) is non-presuppositional, whereas *man* is presuppositional. *Image* is the DFE. All the denotata of (2) are presuppositional, as the clause repeats the predication of (1). But for the purpose of re-emphasizing the importance of the DFE *image* of (1), the speaker now uses an argument-focus structure clause. The predicate of (1), *he created him,* is presented as presuppositional, and the argument to be highlighted, *in the image of God*, is encoded in a clause-initial NP. It is not 'new' and non-presuppositional and so it can be said that the argument-focus structure is used rhetorically in this clause. Through it, the speaker underlines a referent which was focally dominant in the preceding clause.

In the next example, the argument NP is genuinely non-presuppositional:

(5.76) Numbers 3.49-50

(1) So Moses took the redemption money from those over and above the ones redeemed by the Levites;

(2) מאת בכור בני ישׂראל לקח את־הכסף

From the first-born of the Israelites, he took the money.

The clause is found in an account of the religious practice of the redemption of the firstborn sons in Israel. They belong to Yahweh by right, but may be freed through replacement by the Levites. When Moses makes a count of the Israelite firstborn sons, he finds that their number exceeds that of the Levites. The solution to the problem is that a redemption price is fixed by Yahweh for the number over and above the number of the Levites, as indicated in (1). The VP [*took the money*] is repeated in (2) and so is presuppositional. In the qatal clause, the fronting of the ADVP is for focus on the argument. The ADVP adds precision to the general description of the referent in (1).

In conclusion, the normal argument-focus structure has a NP + qatal form. It is similar in form to the marked form of the predicate-focus structure, but it has a different pragmatic function. The presuppositionality of its predicate is obtained through a repetition of the predicate of the preceding clause. The 'new' element, the missing argument, is encoded as a forefronted NP.

6. *The Third Person Narrative Clause with Sentence-Focus Structure*

As already noted in Chapter 4, the sentence-focus structure clause also has a NP + qatal form. It is the entire proposition in the clause which is asserted since a presuppositional element is absent. The clause has one of two pragmatic functions: it either introduces a new entity or referent in the narrative discourse, or it asserts the occurrence of an event which necessarily involves a referent, but which is incidental to the event itself. In the first case, it is a presentational clause; in the second, an event-reporting clause.

a. *The Presentational NP + Qatal Clause*

i. *The Simple Clause*

As several examples have been given in Chapter 4 (pp. 146-49), one more example will be sufficient here to illustrate the presentational clause:

(5.77) 2 Kings 6.26

(1) The king of Israel was walking on the city wall,
(2) ואשה צעקה אליו
and a woman cried out to him.

The clause cannot be construed as having a topic about which something is predicated. The referent *woman* has a not-yet-activated status and the entire clause is in focus, including the referent *woman*, as its role is to introduce the brand-new referent in the story. The referent becomes a topical participant in the narrative which follows.

ii. *The Anchored Clause*

The presentational clause may be temporally anchored to the preceding context. In this case, the temporal ADVP is forefronted and the brand-new participant is encoded as a post-verbal NP:

(5.78) 1 Kings 14.25

(1a) ויהי בשנה החמישית למלך רחבעם
(1b) עלה שישק מלך־מצרים על־ירושלם
In the fifth year of King Rehoboam, King Shishaq of Egypt came up against Jerusalem.

Part (b) of the clause is in focus, presenting an event without any presuppositional element. The referent *Shishaq* is not a topic about which something is predicated. Rather, it is introduced into the story as a not-yet-activated referent, who will become the topical participant of the following clauses. Part (a) of the clause serves temporally to localize the event asserted in part (b). The singular feature of the clause is that the forefronted NP no longer encodes the not-yet-activated referent, as in *(5.77)*, but the temporal ADVP. Similarly, consider:

(5.79) 1 Kings 16.34

בימיו בנה חיאל בית האלי את־יריחה
In his days, Hiel of Bethel built Jericho.

The initial ADVP provides a temporal reference point through an anaphoric relation to the referent *Ahab* previously mentioned. It anchors the statement to the preceding context. As for the rest of the clause which follows the NP, it is entirely non-presuppositional and has a sentence-focus structure.

In conclusion, the presentational clause has a NP + qatal form. It introduces a new referent in the story. The NP which encodes the referent is forefronted. However, when a new referent is introduced in a clause which is temporally anchored to the preceding context, then the new referent is not forefronted, but the ADVP is.

b. *The Event-Reporting Clause*

i. *The Simple Clause*

The NP + qatal with a sentence-focus structure may be used with an event-reporting function (see Chapter 4 pp. 157-60). What distinguishes it from the presentational clause is that the referent introduced in the clause is not maintained as a topic in the ensuing discourse:

(5.80) 2 Kings 13.14

ואלישע חלה את־חליו אשר ימות בו

Elisha was suffering from the illness from which he died.

The clause is at the beginning of an episode and is followed by an immediate switch of topic. No more information is given subsequently about Elisha and his circumstances. What matters here pragmatically is not *Elisha,* a topical participant about which more information will be given, but the event of his illness against which the subsequent episode is to be understood.

As event-reporting, the NP + qatal clause may appear in the middle of a story to relate an unforeseen event, or an unexpected twist in the development of the action. In (5.81) the event is the out-of-the-blue arrival of Rachel:

(5.81) Genesis 29.9

(1) עודנו מדבר עמם

(2) ורחל באה עם־הצאן אשר לאביה

While he was still speaking with them, Rachel came with her father's sheep.

The NP + qatal clause is preceded by a dependent participial clause expressing simultaneity and it reports the event of Rachel's arrival at the well. But it does not establish the referent *Rachel* as a topical participant of the chunk of discourse which immediately follows. Rachel's presence at the well having been made known, she fades into the background and the narrator concentrates on Jacob's frenzied activity. Predicates with non-agentive subjects or passive constructions make a non-topical interpretation of the S easier, and so these constructions are often found in event-reporting clauses, as in:

(5.82) 1 Kings 13.5

והמזבח נקרע

And the altar burst apart.

The clause is isolated in the middle of a narrative involving various participants. Its sole purpose is to report a sudden and violent event.

ii. *The Anchored Clause*

As is the case with a presentational clause, the situation related in an event-reporting clause might be temporally linked to another situation mentioned beforehand. The ADVP which anchors the event-reporting clause is the constituent forefronted, as in:

(5.83) 1 Kings 14.1

בעת ההיא חלה אביה בן־ ירבעם

At that time Abijah son of Jeroboam fell sick.

As noted earlier at pp. 215-16, the forefronted element is no longer the NP subject, but the ADVP which locates anaphorically the event-reporting clause. The referent *Abijah* disappears from the story after this isolated occurrence.

iii. *The Event-Reporting Clause as Flashback*

In a narrative, the default ordering of events is chronological order. The hearer or reader assumes that events are chronologically related through inferences based on the linearity of linguistic encoding. The order of clauses corresponds to the order of events in real time. However, the storyteller might choose to interrupt the flow of events involving a given participant A, suddenly to focus on one or a series of events which concern another participant B. The event-reporting clause can be used to report the event in which participant B is involved. Then, when the event introduced is not contemporary with the sequence of events currently dealt with, but goes back to an earlier time in the story, the event-reporting clause introduces a flashback:

(5.84) Genesis 31.19

ולבן הלך לגזז את־צאנו

Now Laban had gone to shear his sheep.

This clause occurs in the middle of the account of Jacob's secret flight from Laban, his uncle. Laban is suddenly mentioned as the main participant in a specific event. The whole clause is in focus and it is also out of sequence temporally. The event took place earlier than the 'present moment' in the story, that is, Jacob's flight. The temporal meaning of the V הלך has to be inferred as being a pluperfect. Pragmatically, however, the clause has the normal form of the event-reporting clause.

7. *General Conclusion*

The following points can be drawn.

(1) The two types of narrative clauses, the vayyiqtol and the NP + qatal clause, can encode three types of focus-structures: predicate-focus, argument-focus and sentence-focus.

(a) The predicate-focus structure uses a system comprising both clause-types.
(b) The argument-focus structure is realized only by the NP + qatal clause.
(c) The sentence-focus structure is also realized by the NP + qatal clause alone.

(2) In a narrative context, these clausal forms also indicate markedness or unmarkedness in the expression of information structure.

(2.1) The predicate-focus articulation in the vayyiqtol clause is unmarked because it answers the question typical of narration *what did A do next?* with A as a topical participant.

Given that the pragmatically unmarked focus position is clause-final or near final in the vayyiqtol clause, it is also possible to conclude that the NP + qatal clause with its forefronted focal element is a marked form of the predicate-focus structure.

(2.2) By contrast with the type of focus in the predicate-focus clause, the argument-focus and sentence-focus articulations answer questions which are atypical of a narrative context (respectively *did A do x?* in which '*A did x*' is presupposed; and *what happened?* in which no topical participant is given). It can be said that they both represent marked forms of information structure in a clause, in a narrative context.

(3) In the light of these conclusions, Longacre's thesis invites the following comments.

(3.1) The NP + qatal clause cannot be explained unilaterally through a backgrounding function. It is often used to indicate, in fact, a change of information structure in the sentence.

(3.2) If the analysis presented here is correct, then all the NP + qatal clauses which indicate markedness for the three types of information structure, may be viewed as standing out against the routine development of the narrative provided by vayyiqtol clauses. Such clauses would seem to indicate foregounded rather than backgrounded material.

(3.3) Methodologically, the present analysis shows that grounding should not be viewed as a global notion which works independently of clause contents. Elements in a clause are salient or non-salient (see pp. 193-97 which summarize how the dominant focal element is signalled in the vayyiqtol clause), and an acceptable account of the notion of grounding must pay due attention to and incorporate these factors in the theory.

(3.4) Properly taking into account the degree of saliency of clausal elements stops the circular reasoning which weakens a definition of foregrounding solely based on clausal forms.

(3.5) The study of foregrounding in a specific language should be based on a number of definable factors, some of which have been described in this chapter. No doubt other features indicating saliency might be identified.

(3.6) If foregrounding consists of a number of various factors which might or might not co-occur in a clause, then one might also legitimately conclude that clauses might be more or less foregrounded in proportion to the number of salient elements found in them.

(4) Finally, the above description of information structures in terms of markedness/unmarkedness may be considered diachronically. In the history of Old Hebrew a distinction is made between Classical Hebrew, essentially the language spoken in Judah before the Babylonian exile in 586 BCE, and late Biblical Hebrew (LBH) (Kutscher 1982: 45). One distinctive feature of LBH is the decreased use of the vayyiqtol form. It

is replaced by the use of the qatal (perfect) with the conjunction of coordination ו ('and').This evolution is explained usually by a radical change in the tense-aspect system of Old Hebrew, independently of discourse consideration. But Givón traces a possible correlation between the tense-aspect change and the pragmatics of discourse (1977: 218-54). He observes that the use of the qatal verb is paralleled by a drift from a VSO to SVO word order. He suggests that this change was generated by a principle of discourse topicality in which the perfect was used to mark topic shifting.

Another pragmatic explanation rooted in the clause information structures of the NP + qatal clause can be offered. It was observed that the NP + qatal clause encodes three information structures, thus serving several discourse functions. It is probable that the NP + qatal clause (and not only the one with a subject NP as proposed by Givón) became more frequently used in the evolution of Old Hebrew because of its greater distributional freedom. Because the NP + qatal clause could serve three discourse functions, it became viewed as the unmarked member of a system in which, in contrast, the vayyiqtol clause became marked, with its structure permitting a sentence-focus reading only.

Chapter 6

ASPECTS OF FOREGROUNDING IN NARRATIVE DISCOURSE

1. *Foregrounding in Narratives*

Human beings communicate for three main purposes: to exchange information, to share emotions and attitudes and to get things done. In the stories examined, it is not only the transfer of information, the factual report, which is the concern of the speaker, but also the expression of feeling and opinion. The aim of the stories is not to change specific situations and so a consideration of the conative import can be left out of the analysis.

The informative import and expressive import are realized in three discourse activities to which correspond three different types of linguistic material. The transfer of information involves two tasks. The first is the recounting of the actual events of the story. The second one is the monitoring of the recounting, that is making sure that the story is getting across clearly and is well understood. This is achieved by providing the necessary background knowledge in the form of various explanations and clarifications. Monitoring, together with event-reporting, belong to the informative import of the message. But storytelling has also an expressive import. While narrating a story, the speaker expresses his feelings and opinions about the content, that is the referential material reported. This aspect of storytelling is well known to literary critics and is discussed under categories such as point of view, perspective and focalization. Labov seems to be the first linguist who has seriously taken into account this dimension of storytelling, calling it 'evaluation'.[1] Labov explains that a narrative which contains only informative material is not a complete narrative. It may perform a referential function, but it lacks significance. Evaluation is the means by which the

1. Two seminal papers by William Labov, in 1967 with Joshua Waletzky and in 1972, form the basis for my study of evaluation in narrative.

significance of the story, its reportability, is indicated. In other words, the narrative has a point, a raison d'être, and the speaker uses certain evaluative devices to establish and sustain the point of the story. Evaluation involves the interference of the speaker in the factual report and as such it belongs to the expressive import of a narrative.

The assumption of this analysis is that the two types of import, informative and evaluative, realized in different kinds of material, should be considered separately in relation to foregrounding. As a result, the analysis of the foregrounding of informative material will be presented first and then followed by an account of foregrounding at the expressive level.

In her review of work on foregrounding, Helen Drÿ (1992: 438-41) observes that some linguists approach the question from an a priori view whereby foregrounding is defined either as 'prominence' or as 'salience'. A survey of these two general categories show that the notion of importance can be further subdivided into thematic, human, causal and formal importance; and the notion of salience can be subdivided into figural,[2] cognitive and expectation-based salience.

On the basis of this classification, one can say that Longacre, Niccacci and Dawson, who consider that the foreground of a story is encoded in vayyiqtol clauses, use the concept of 'formal importance' to define foregrounding. Some of the problems associated with this approach have already been highlighted in the preceding chapters. Foreground understood in terms of formal importance, and viewed as correlated to clausal form, is a very general analytical concept. Explanations based on such an assumption are bound to overlook crucial linguistic features, and to simplify linguistic facts.

The analyses which follow could be categorized as belonging to Dry's second category: foregrounding is defined in terms of salience. An element foregrounded is thrown into relief by the writer or speaker and is perceived as such by the reader or hearer. It is possible to identify how this is achieved in a fairly precise way. Some of the mechanisms identified are described in the next section, but the list of mechanisms should not be taken as exhaustive.

2. For example, Wallace (1982) says that the perceptual distinction between figure and ground has its equivalent in prominent and non-prominent morphosyntactic features.

2. *Foregrounding Mechanisms*

Two main mechanisms available to a speaker in order to deliberately foreground an element of a story have been identified.

The first foregrounding device consists in the use of the norms and standards which people assume will be obeyed in communication. Grice (1975) has explained coherence, continuity and meaning in conversation by suggesting that, in verbal exchanges, speakers obey some general principle which compels them to express themselves in such a way as not to impede understanding and interpretation. This 'cooperative principle' says:

> Make your conversational contribution such as is required, at the stage at which it occurs, by the accepted purpose or direction of the talk exchange in which you are engaged (1975: 43).

The cooperative principle comprises four sets of normative maxims of conversation. They are the maxims of quantity, of quality, of relation and of manner.[3] The conversational principle and the maxims represent commmunicative standards. When speakers adhere to the maxims faithfully, they are speaking in a cooperative, rational and efficient way.[4] S. Levinson (1985: 62-68) has reformulated and extended Grice's ideas in such a way that the maxims have become two guiding principles. For each principle a speaker's maxim and a corresponding recipient corollary are established. The principles and their maxims are:

3. (A) *Maxims of quantity*: 1. Make your contribution as informative as is required (for the current purposes of the exchange); 2. Do not make your contribution more informative than is required. (B) *Maxims of quality*:—Supermaxim: Try to make your contribution one that is true. 1. Do not say what you believe to be false. 2. Do not say that for which you lack adequate evidence. (C) *Maxim of relation*: Be relevant. (D) *Maxims of Manner*:— Supermaxim: Be perspicuous. 1. Avoid obscurity of expression; 2. Avoid ambiguity; 3. Be brief (avoid unnecessary prolixity); 4. Be orderly.

4. For Grice, the important features of these maxims is that they determine how all indirect information can be conveyed in utterances. When a speaker knowingly departs from cooperative efficiency by flouting a maxim, the hearer will seek to construct a sequence of inferences which make the utterance relevant or at least cooperative. Converstional implicatures arise from the flouting of the maxims.

1. Q-PRINCIPLE (Quantity principle):

   Make your contribution as informative as is required for the current purpose of the exchange.

   Speaker's maxim:

   Do not provide a statement that is informationally weaker than your knowledge of the world allows, unless providing a stronger statement would contravene the I- principle.

   Recipient's corollary:

   Take it that the speaker made the strongest statement consistent with what he knows.

2. I-PRINCIPLE (Information principle):

   Do not make your contribution more informative than is required.

   Speaker's maxim (THE MAXIM OF MINIMIZATION):

   Say as little as necessary

   This means: *Produce the minimal linguistic information sufficient to achieve your communicational ends (bearing the Q-principle in mind)*.

   Recipient's corollary (THE ENRICHMENT RULES):

   Amplify the informational content of the speaker's utterance, by FInding the most specific interpetation, up to what you judge to be the speaker's intended point.

What needs to be said is that it is especially the information principle which is exploited by a speaker in order to foreground an element of the discourse. Given the implicit and agreed norm *do not make your contribution more informative than is required*, a deviation from this principle will be felt by the hearer or reader to be significant and a deviating element which creates an overloading of information will be perceived as salient. Foregrounding may thus be obtained through the violation of the norms of normal communication.

In Old Hebrew narratives, the information principle is mainly flouted by repetitions of words, phrases or sentences. All the examples which have been identified belong to the expressive level of narratives, but this does not mean that the mechanism is not used at the informative level.

The second mechanism is based on the unexpectedness or unpredictability of an element in context. Hearers or readers are always building up expectations concerning what is coming next in a discourse. These expectations come from a variety of contextual sources.[5] They

5. The context is envisaged here in broad terms as different types of knowledge which speaker and hearer have at any point in time. These knowledge networks consist of general linguistic knowledge (e.g. knowledge derived from the previous section of the discourse), knowledge about the world, cultural, social, experiential knowledge, knowledge about the communication situation (e.g. deicti-

derive partly from the hearer's general knowledge of life, of the way things normally and regularly are. They are also created by the preceding discourse: what has been mentioned raises expectations of what is to follow. They also derive from the hearer's judgment as to what the purposes of the speaker are, and from the hearer's assessment of the communication situation.

Information which matches the expectations of the hearer will be less prominent than information which is unexpected. This is so much the case that referential material which is strongly expected need not be mentioned at all, if the conventions of the language allow it. If someone says *Ted is in the pub most evenings*, the fact that Ted has drinks does not need to be mentioned. There is a strong expectation that to have drinks follows on from being in a pub.

Information which is unexpected or totally contrary to the hearer's expectations has a high degree of prominence. Thus the speaker, being aware of the hearer's expectations, can choose accordingly to make some material prominent by exploiting its unexpected nature. The way these mechanisms are used will be illustrated in the following sections, starting with informative material.

3. *Foregrounding of the Informative Material*

Expectation-based foregrounding of the informative material can be divided into two types, depending on whether the speaker/writer exploits some broad expectations of the hearer, or expectations created by specific knowledge structures.

a. *Foregrounding and Broad Expectations*

Clark and Clark (1977: 238) say that in the planning and encoding of a discourse the speaker first divides experience into chunks. In this process, a given experience is never perceived as a smooth happening. Rather it comprises joints, that is, sudden changes from one state to another, and intervals which are static situations as well as states which continue with no change at all. Joints and intervals are conceptually salient situations which are turned into propositions. Joints, intervals and states[6] may be illustrated in the following way. A sentence in which

cally given information), and, insofar as the speaker can anticipate it, the planned development of the discourse.

6. This classification must not be confused with the classification of situation

the event represents a joint is:

(1) *Sir Ewain sent the tall knight clattering to the ground.*

In the next sentence, the event is an interval (static situation):

(2) *He looked at the tall knight's armour.*

Finally, a state which continues with no change at all is exemplified in:

(3) *The tall knight was the king's half-brother.*

Given a short Old Hebrew narrative made out of clauses (1), (2) and (3) in that order, Longacre would analyse clause (3) as belonging to the backgounded material of the story.[7] The claim made here is that it is not the situation types (reflected in clause/verbal forms) which play a role in grounding, but rather the degree of unexpectedness of a situation, whatever its type. As a result, a static situation such as (3) would be foregrounded in an episode made out of clauses (1), (2) and (3), in that order.

How the unexpectedness of a situation foregrounds a clause in stories can be illustrated by means of a short episode of the story of Samson:

(6.1) Judges 15.19

(1) And he (Samson) was very thirsty (vayyiqtol*)*
(2) and he called on (vayyiqtol) Yahweh and said (vayyiqtol) ...
(3) ויבקע אלהים את־המכתש אשר־בלחי
(4) ויצאו ממנו מים
(3) God split open the hollow place which is at Lehi, (4) and water gushed out of it. [He drank, his strength returned and he revived].

In this terse story all the seven clauses are vayyiqtol clauses. They record the steps from a situation of want to a solution. If we go by Longacre's theory, all the events of the story are foregrounded because they are encoded in vayyiqtol verbal forms. The expectedness/ unexpectedness criterion gives a different perspective. (1) reports a static

types (state, activity, accomplishment, achievement, semelfactive) which are used in discussions of verbal aspect. They are cognitive categories and not semantic ones.

7. In Old Hebrew, the preterite of היה (to be) would be used in (3). According to Longacre's verbal scheme (1989: 81), it would belong to the 'setting'. An alternative clausal form for (3) would be the particle והנה ('and behold') followed by a verbless clause. The verbless clause also belongs to the setting band in Longacre's verb rank scheme (1989: 81).

situation and is a background event. (2) is the plot-initiating event: in a situation of need Samson prays to God. This action has nothing unexpected about it. But (3) reports a totally unexpected intervention of God as a participant. It stands out against the other clauses as foregrounded.

Even in the descriptive section of a story with stative sentences, the situations reported may be foregrounded because of the uncommon and surprising nature of the states reported. Consider the description of the giant Goliath against whom David will fight:

(6.2) 1 Samuel 17.5-6

(1) And a champion named Goliath, of Gath, came out of the Philistine camp. (2) He was six cubits and one span tall.

(3)	וכובע נחשת על־ראשו
(4)	ושריון קשקשים הוא לבוש...
(5)	ומצחת נחשת על־רגליו
(6)	וכידון נחשת בין כתפיו

(3) He had a helmet of bronze on his head, (4) and he was dressed in a plated cuirass...(5) He had greaves of bronze upon his shins (6) and a bronze scimitar was slung between his shoulder.

Goliath is a new participant but the narrator gives minimal information on Goliath's identity. Instead, all the attention is given to the collection of unusual offensive and defensive weapons he carries. The detailed description highlights the terrifying character of Goliath's armour and weapons. It is designed to call attention to the power and invulnerability of David's opponent. As such it is very much unlike any other descriptive section in a story. All the clauses are foregrounded because they report facts out of the ordinary and unexpected.

b. *Foregrounding and Broad Knowledge Structures*

Cognitive psychologists have shown that the experience a person has about what usually happens in a given situation is represented, packaged and stored in the mind as stereotypical knowledge structures. A knowledge structure or knowledge schema can be broadly defined as a mental representation of a typical situation, which includes sets of expectations, and inferences. These schemata play an important role in language understanding which is a memory-based process.[8]

8. During communication, speaker and hearer activate a portion of their stored knowledge in order to understand what the message means and how propositions in

The fact that a knowledge structure presents material according to expectation can be exploited by a speaker. For example, the speaker may modify slightly the structure, or mention an item which is completely foreign to the information the structure normally contains. The unpredictable character of the element modified or added makes it salient.

i. *Types of Knowledge Structures*

Knowledge schemata are of different kinds. Descriptions and labels have been provided by linguists and Artificial Intelligence researchers.[9] A basic classification which is inspired by the work of a number of researchers in this field follows. Four different types of knowledge structures can be distinguished.

1. A *frame* is a data structure triggered by a conceptual centre and representing stereotyped elements. The concept causes an array of semantic information to be elicited and arranged so that access to the relevant information is provided. For example, an airport frame generates the entries: control tower—passenger terminal—parking area—runway. Each one of these entries, in its turn, constitute a frame with slots. The entry passenger terminal generates the entries: check-in area—security check—customs control—passport control—departure lounge and so on. So, a frame functions as a node which is related by a series of links to an encyclopedia of world knowledge. Frames are not used in Old Hebrew for the purpose of grounding. But as noticed in Chapter 4, they play a role in the question of definiteness of nouns.

2. A *schema* has also a node, but the ordered entries the node elicits involve some progression or development. In the airport example, flight arrival constitutes a schema which access information about the various stages the arriving passengers go through: leaving the airplane;—walking back from the terminal—collecting luggage—going through the customs.

a discourse cohere. Stored knowledge has a predicitive power so that, for example, if information is missing or flawed in the output, the hearer will use this stored knowledge in order to fill in or patch up what is necessary.

9. Deborah Tannen provides a survey of the various knowledge structures (1979: 137-81). Some of the terms employed are: frame (Minsky 1980), scripts (Schank and Abelson 1977), schemas (Winograd 1977). Lehnert (1980) explains the role knowledge structures play in language understanding.

3. A *script* is a predetermined, stereotyped sequence of actions, with a specific goal.[10] Also, a script includes participants who have precise roles and who are guided by instructions as to what they should say or do. For example, in the script shopping at the supermarket the roles are played by the customer, the shop assistants and the person at the check-out counter. A script may include a series of props. The props of a supermarket script would be a shopping-basket or shopping-trolley, the groceries on display, the check-out counter, a chequebook, the bags, etc. A script may contain scenes; for example, a restaurant script may contain an entering scene, and ordering scene, an eating scene, and a paying scene.

In a schema or script correctly understood, all the phases or events which they contain are viewed as having taken place. For instance, if John says that he has been to the restaurant, the statement is interpreted as meaning that the whole restaurant script was executed. John went into the restaurant, sat down at a table, asked for the menu, looked at it, made his choice of food and drink, told the waiter. The waiter told the chef what the order was; the chef made up the order, gave it to the waiter who came over to John's table and gave it to John. John ate the food, drank his wine. John asked for the bill, paid it and left the restaurant. All these inferred informations are conveyed by John's statement.

4. A *plan* describes a series of actions projected by an individual who wants to achieve a goal (Schank and Abelson 1977: 71). It differs from a script in that, whereas a script is linked to what is socially or culturally known, a plan is more personal. There is no script as to how a person might buy a car. A car-buying plan will look very different depending on the strategy selected. A person's plan might be to buy a new car, a second-hand car; the person might scan through the car advertising pages of a newspaper, or go straight to a second-hand cars dealer. As a plan is individual, it raises expectations only if it is announced beforehand by the person who summons it up.

As a clear summary of the four knowledge schemata, de Beaugrande's account may be cited:

10. Schank and Abelson (1977) say that a script includes a standard sequence of actions organized in temporal sequence and serving to meet a goal.

> Frames and schemas are more oriented toward the internal arrangement of knowledge, while plans and scripts reflect human needs to get things done in every day interaction. One could argue that schemas are frames put in serial order, that plans are goal-directed schemas, and scripts socially stabilized plans (de Beaugrande 1980: 164).

ii. *Types of Foregounding through Knowledge Structures*

Schema, script and plan may be used to foreground an event in Old Hebrew narratives. These knowledge structures are a blueprint for action development, without the details filled in. They are structures of expectation: the hearer/reader expects that the events in a knowledge structure have taken place. A speaker/writer may choose to exploit this dimension of the structures in order to throw into relief a specific event. The structure corresponds to what the hearer takes for granted. By inserting an element foreign to the structure, the speaker indicates that the hearer should change their expectations. How this is done through the use of specific schemas, scripts or plans will be illustrated in the next sections.

Schema. A recurring schema in stories is the battle schema. It normally includes four progressive stages:

(1) the movement of the armies described with verbs such as יצא, 'to go out', הלך, 'to march', 'to advance', בוא, 'to go';

(2) the military activity described with אסף, 'to gather', חנה, 'to encamp', נלחם, 'to join battle';

(3) the outcome of the battle or of the siege, with the enemy wiped out (נכה, 'to defeat', 'to slaughter', נגף, 'to be struck', 'beaten'), or the city taken (לכד, 'to plunder', לקח, 'to take'), or the routed army fleeing (נוס, 'to flee', רדף, 'to pursue');

(4) the extent of the war (the battle spread from *a* to *b)* or a description of the defeat: *the slaughter was great, there was a great massacre.*

In the first example, an event which is not part of the battle schema is added:

(6.3) 1 Samuel 4.10-11

(1) The Philistines fought (vayyiqtol)
(2) and the Israelites were routed (vayyiqtol),
(3) and they fled, every man to his own tent (vayyiqtol).
(4) There was a very great slaughter,
(5) ויפל מישׂראל שׁלשׁים אלף רגלי
(6) וארון אלהים נלקח

(7) ושני בני־עלי מתו חפני ופינחס

(5) There fell from Israel 30, 000 foot soldiers, (6) *and the ark of God was captured* (7) and Eli's two sons, Hophni and Phinehas, died.

The schema is used to report the defeat of Israel. It provides the background against which an event stands out: the capture of the ark, Israel's military palladium. (6) reports an event which is foreign to the phases of the schema and as such is unexpected. That the clause is foregrounded is confirmed by the following context which reports the tragic consequences of this loss. It is worthy of notice that the salient clause uses a qatal verb and so would be, according to Longacre's scheme, a backgrounded event. Consider now another example of the use of the battle schema:

(6.4) 1 Samuel 31.2

(1) ופלשתים נלחמים בישראל
(2) וינסו אנשי ישראל מפני פלשתים
(3) ויפלו חללים בהר הגלבע
(4) וידבקו פלשתים את־שאול ואת־בניו
(5) ויכו פלשתים את־יהונתן ואת־אבינדב

(1) As the Philistines were fighting with Israel, (2) the men of Israel fled before them, (3) and many fell slain on Mount Gilboa. (4) *The Philistines pressed hard after Saul and his sons*. (5) They killed his sons Jonathan, Abinadab and Malki-Shua.

(4) is inserted into the battle schema. The narrator adds a description of the fate of King Saul, in the middle of the massacre phase of the battle reported in (3) and (5). This phase provides a panoramic view of the disorderly retreat of the Israelite troops. Against this backdrop, attention is focused on one isolated incident in which the king occupies central stage. This incident which is added to the development of the schema and cannot be foreseen by the hearer, is foregrounded. It also provides a link between this episode and the next one which reports how the king died.

In some cases, the normal unfolding of the schema might be interrupted as in:

(6.5) 1 Kings 12.21-24

(1) Rehoboam ... assembled all the house of Judah and the tribe of Benjamin to fight against the house of Israel ... (2) The word of God came to Shemaiah the man of God: '... thus says Yahweh':

(3) ולא־תעלו
(4) ולא־תלחמון עם־אחיכם בני־ישׂראל
(5) שׁובו אישׁ לביתו

(3) 'You shall not go up (4) and you shall not fight against your brothers the people of Israel. (5) Go home every one of you.'

(1) creates the expectation of the unfolding of a battle schema through the lexical item *to fight*. But the frame is prevented from developing through an interference presented in quoted direct speech. The interference contradicts the expectation of the hearer and so becomes pragmatically salient. The two negative clauses which encode the interference and go against the schema are foregrounded. In this example, the foregrounded clauses are in the direct discourse section. This shows the importance of taking into account the direct speeches too in the analysis of foregrounding.

Another much used schema is the 'marriage and birth' schema. Its entries are spelt out (underlined expressions) in the following passage:

(6.6) Genesis 38.2

Judah met the daughter of a Canaanite man named Shua, he *married her* and *lay with her*, she *became pregnant* and *gave birth* to a son who *was named* Er.

In the first example, only the first phase of the schema has taken place: Jacob is married to Rebekah (cf. Gen. 25.20a: *Isaac was 40 years old when he married Rebekah*); then the schema unfolds in the following way:

(6.7) Genesis 25.21

(1) ויעתר יצחק ליהוה לנכח אשׁתו
(2) כי עקרה הוא
(3) ויעתר לו יהוה
(4) ותהר רבקה אשׁתו

(1) *Isaac prayed to Yahweh on behalf of his wife* (2) *because she was barren.* (3) *Yahweh answered his prayer* (4) and his wife Rebekah became pregnant.

The expected unfolding of the schema is interrupted by an interference reported in (2). (1) reports a prescription, that is, a corrective action to rectify the presence of an interference (Schank and Abelson 1977: 52). The interference in the schema is reported in the subordinate clause and follows the prescription. Both interference and prescription present a high degree of unexpectedness as they constitute a departure from the marriage and birth schema which was triggered by the preceding context. Clauses (1) and (2) are foregrounded against the background of the schema. The prescription has a double aspect: the prayer of Jacob and the answer given by Yahweh in (3). Both events serve to overcome the interruption of the schema. The schema resumes normally in (4). It is important to note that according to this analysis, the foregrounded interference is encoded in a verbless subordinate clause, which those who adhere to the formal view of grounding would classify as background or setting

The phases of a schema may articulate a whole story with several episodes. In the story of the birth of Samuel (1 Sam. 1.1-28), the marriage phase has taken place (Hannah is married to Elkanah) but an interference in the schema (v. 5: *Yahweh had closed her womb)* gives rise to several episodes whose goals are to provide a prescription for the removal of the obstacle so that the schema can be allowed to unfold.

It is when a promise is finally made to Hannah that her sterility will end, that the schema can resume:

(6.8) 1 Samuel 1.19

(1) וידע אלקנה את־חנה אשתו
(2) ויזכרה יהוה

(1) Elqannah knew his wife Hanna (2) and Yahweh remembered her.

(2) is a prescription for the removal of the interference. The clause which has a vayyiqtol V, stands out against the backgound of the schema which the hearer takes for granted. The schema resumes immediately after: *in the course of time she conceived and gave birth to a son* (v. 20).

Script. The script presents a predetermined sequence of actions which have a specific goal. A typical script is the summoning of the tribes by a hero to wage war. It occurs in:

(6.9) Judges 6.34-35

(1) ורוח יהוה לבשה את־גדעון
(2) ויתקע בשופר
(3) ויזעק אביעזר אחריו
(4) ומלאכים שלח בכל־מנשה

(1) The spirit of Yahweh came upon Gideon (2) and he blew the trumpet. (3) He summoned the Abiezerites to follow him.(4) He sent messengers throughout Manasseh [calling them to arms].

First the hero is empowered by the divine spirit to perfom wondrous feats of arms. Full of this surge of strength, the leader blows the shofar and also sends messengers to call the tribes together. Compare now with the same script in:

(6.10) 1 Samuel 11.6-7

(1)	ותצלח רוח־אלהים על־שׁאול...
(2)	ויחר אפו מאד
(3)	ויקח צמד בקר
(4)	וינתחהו
(5)	וישׁלח בכל־גבול ישׂראל ביד המלאכים

(1) The spirit of God came upon Saul in power...(2) *and he became enraged.* (3) *He took a yoke of oxen*, (4) *he cut them in pieces* (5) and sent them throughout all the territory of Israel by messengers.

In this script, between the first phase (empowering by the spirit) and the last one (the sending of messengers) the anger of Saul and the dismembering of oxen are mentioned. These two elements do not pertain to the script and the two clauses reporting Saul's anger and his bizarre method of summoning help are set in relief against the background of the normal unfolding of the script. (2), (3) and (4), with their vayyiqtol verbs, report events which are more salient than the ones reported in the vayyiqtol clauses (1) and (5).

The treatment of a script may be more complicated as the next example from the story of Jonah shows. Yahweh's objective is to send an emissary-courier to the Assyrian town of Nineveh, in order to warn its people of their impending destruction. The story starts with a 'messenger activity' script which is directed by Yahweh:

(6.11) Jonah 1.1-2

(1) And the word of Yahweh came to Jonah, the son of Amittai, saying:
(2a) 'Get up,
(2b) go to Nineveh, the great city,
(2c) and proclaim Judgment upon it
(2d) for its wickedness has come up before me.'

The opening uses a lexical frame of divine oracle with the idiom *and the word of Yahweh came to. The word of Yahweh* is a technical term used in the opening of a prophetic message. The semantic information activated by the idiom is unpacked in a command expressed by three imperatives: *get up*, *go* and *proclaim judgment*. This command creates the script of messenger activity: the emissary is sent by a superior on a mission which involves the delivery of a message. Jonah has the role of the emissary.

The expected stereotyped execution of the orders by Jonah is reported in a truncated form: only the first verb of the command sequence is repeated in the execution sequence in v. 3. Then an interference occurs which prevents the normal continuation of the script.[11]

(6.12) Jonah 1.3

(1) ויקם יונה
(2) לברח תרשישה מלפני יהוה

(1) And Jonah arose (2) to flee towards Tarshish away from the presence of Yahweh.

The interference is encoded not as a main vayyiqtol clause, but as a subordinate infinitive clause of purpose. The ensuing narrative reports how Jonah carries out his intention. He goes to Jaffa and boards a ship going to Tarshish. Because of Jonah's contrary response, a condition which would enable the script to run smoothly is now missing. This particular type of interference can be categorized as *obstacle*. In an obstacle, an 'enabling condition is missing' (Schank and Abelson 1977: 52). The clause of purpose signals the obstacle unit and stands out as an obstacle marker against the routine vayyiqtol clauses background. The obstacle is clearly highlighted by a variety of devices, particularly the grammatical and lexical repetition of the infinitive clause which creates an envelope figure. The sentences of v. 3 are organized as follow:

(3a) and Jonah arose
(3b) TO FLEE to Tarshish away from the presence of Yahweh
(3c) and he went down to Joppa
(3d) and he found a ship going to Tarshish
(3e) and he paid the fare
(3f) and he went down in it
(3g) TO GO to Tarshish away from the presence of Yahweh.

Two infinitival clauses of purpose with verbs of movement (v. 3b: לברח, 'to flee', and v. 3g: לבוא, 'to go') and the repetition of the prepositional phrases *away from the presence of Yahweh* frame this unit which gives a

11. What the normal script looks like can be found by looking at Jon. 3.1-3 where the execution of the command is reported by: 'and Jonah got up and went to Nineveh according to the word of Yahweh.'

detailed account of the obstacle. The goal originally enjoined in the script, Nineveh, is contrasted three times with the goal of Jonah's flight, Tarshish.

An obstacle is rectified by a *prescription*. The corrective action has the objective of getting Jonah to follow the script and so first to stop the ship on which he flees. This is done through a great gale churning the sea (4a and 4b):

(6.13) Jonah 1.4

(4a) ויהוה הטיל רוח־גדולה אל־הים
(4b) ויהי סער־גדול בים
(4c) והאניה חשבה להשבר
(4a) and Yahweh threw a great wind upon the sea (NP + qatal clause),
(4b) and there was a great storm on the sea (vayyiqtol of verb 'to be').
(4c) The ship expected itself to crack up (NP + qatal clause).[12]

The prescription is linked to the obstacle by anadiplosis or the repetition of the last part of a unit (v. 3: *from the presence of* <u>*Yahweh*</u>) at the beginning of the next (v. 4: *but* <u>*Yawheh*</u>). The use of this rhetorical figure results in the occurrence of a NP + qatal clause in (4a). The NP + qatal clause signals not so much a change of participant, but the formal marking of the beginning of the prescription. Clause (4c) which is the last one of the prescription is linked formally to (4a) by a similar NP + qatal clause. So an envelope figure is created through the repetition of two NP + qatal clause. Other rhetorical devices are used to underline some elements of the prescription, such as the repetition of the end of (4a) in (4b). With the Hebrew word order these endings read:

a wind great upon the sea (4a).
a tempest great on the sea (4b).

The amount of material foregrounded and the number of devices used for foregrounding the material is quite remarkable. Repetitions, envelope figures, use of NP + qatal clauses contribute to make the whole section salient. No active vayyiqtol clause is used at all.

Plans. A plan describes a sequence of actions decided by an individual to reach a goal. It is not predictable through social or cultural knowledge. As a result, in order to identify the situation foregrounded, a plan

12. The translation is arranged so as to bring out the patterning of the text.

must be first spelled out and then compared to the account of its implementation.

In the first example, the Israelites are in the desert and have complained about lack of food and water. The deity punishes them with a plague of seraph snakes. Moses intercedes on their behalf and the deity proposes a plan to remedy the situation. The plan is offered in direct speech:

(6.14) Numbers 21.8-9

(1) עשׂה לך שׂרף
(2) ושׂים אתו על־נס
(3) והיה כל־הנשׁוך
(3) וראה אתו
(4) וחי

(1) 'Make a seraph figure (2) and mount it on a standard. (3) If anyone who is bitten looks at it, (4) he shall recover.'

The execution of the plan is reported immediately afterwards:

(5) ויעשׂ משׁה נחשׁ נחשׁת
(6) וישׂמהו על־הנס
(7) והיה אם־נשׁך הנחשׁ את־אישׁ
(8) והביט אל־נחשׁ הנחשׁת
(9) וחי

(5) So Moses made a bronze snake (6) and mounted it on a standard. (7) When anyone was bitten by a snake (8) and would look at the bronze snake, (9) he would recover.

Taking the form of a command and its execution, the plan is realized to the letter. No particular event is foregrounded in the execution as the sequence of happenings is expected by the hearer.

But the account of the implementation of the plan might not parallel so neatly the initial proposal. An example is found in the story of Abram in Egypt. Abram is going to Egypt to find food there. He fears that the locals will kill him on account of his beautiful wife Sarah:

> I know what a beautiful woman you are. When the Egyptians see you, they will say: 'This is his wife.' Then they will kill me but they will let you live (Gen. 12.11-12).

To ensure his survival, Abram proposes the following plan (Gen. 12.13):

(1) 'Say you are my sister
(2) so that it may go well with me for your sake
(3) and that my life may be spared because of you.'

The account of how the plan is implemented is the following:

(6.15) Genesis 12.15

(1) ויראו אתה שׂרי פרעה
(2) ויהללו אתה אל־פרעה
(3) ותקח האשׁה בית פרעה
(4) ולאברם היטיב בעבורה

(1) The officials of Pharaoh saw her (2) and they praised her to Pharaoh. (3) *The woman was taken into Pharaoh's house* (4) and he treated Abram well for her sake.

Phase 1 of the plan ('Say you are my sister') is not reported; it is assumed to have taken place between clauses (2) and (3) of the execution. The unforeseen consequence of this false identity is reported in clause (3): Sarah is taken into Pharaoh's harem. It is followed by the expected phase of the original plan reported in (4). Clause (3) is thus thrown into relief as an unexpected event, against the background of the expected unravelling of the plan. That Sarah becomes one of Pharaoh's wives creates a problem which will be resolved in the end part of the story.

A last example is found in the story of the escape of the Israelites out of Egypt. The Israelites are trapped between Pharaoh's chariot troops and the sea. They complain and protest to Moses. The deity offers him a plan of escape: Moses must stretch out his hand and the sea will part before the Israelites. This part of the plan is realized but the Israelites are chased by the Egyptians. Yahweh interrupts their chase by clogging their chariot wheels. Then Yahweh proposes a new plan reported in (1) and (2). Speaking to Moses, he says:

(6.16) Exodus 14.26-27

(1) נטה את־ידך על־הים
(2) וישבו המים על־מצרים על־רכבו ועל־פרשׁיו
(3) ויט משׁה את־ידו על־הים
(4) וישב הים לפנות בקר לאיתנו
(5) ומצרים נסים לקראתו
(6) וינער יהוה את־מצרים בתוך הים
(7) וישבו המים
(8) ויכסו את־הרכב ואת־הפרשׁים

(1) Stretch out your hand over the sea (2) and the waters will flow back over the Egyptians and their chariots and horsemen. (3) Moses stretched out his hand over the sea, (4) and at daybreak the sea went back to its

> bed. (5) As the Egyptians were fleeing they met it head-on. (6) *Yahweh tossed them into the sea.* (7) The waters flowed back (8) and covered the chariots and the horsemen.

The plan comprises two simple phases: Moses must stretch out his hand and the divided waters will flow back on the Egyptians. The accomplishment of the first phase is reported in (3). The accomplishment of the second phase (*and the waters will flow back over the Egyptians and their chariots and horsemen)* is not reported as a single block but is split into two accounts in (4) and (7)–(8). That the two accounts belong to the same phase is indicated by the resumptive repetition of the verb שׁוב, to return. Sentences (5) and (6) are inserted in the middle of the report of the second phase. Clause (5), with its verb in the participle, connects the phase temporally to the preceding episodes (Exod. 14.25: 'let's get away from the Israelites'). But (6) introduces an element which is completely new. The unexpected action of Yahweh himself is foregrounded against the mention of the anticipated happenings of the plan.

iii. *Conclusion*

The foregrounding of informative material occurs principally through the inherently unexpected or disruptive nature of an event reported. An event which is unexpected is salient against the background of more predicable happenings.

Such an event may be encoded in a variety of clausal forms: in the vayyiqtol clause, in a NP + qatal clause, even in a verbless clause. The clauses may be main clauses or subordinate ones. Foregrounding does not rely on distinctive clausal forms.

Foregrounding based on the notions of predictability and unpredictability may be reinforced by the repetition of phrases or clauses. Interestingly, the two complementary devices are both based on the concept of deviation: they are either 'frame-breaking' or 'principles-flouting'.

The mechanisms identified point to the necessity of adopting a contextual approach to foregrounding rather than to postulate the existence of a grammatical correlate vayyiqtol-foregounding. When they consider that foreground information is information which is central to the development of the plot, Longacre and Niccacci, in fact, point to material which could be called 'naturally' salient. This is the sort of saliency to which hearers react when they recognize that something is inherently interesting. Human beings are interested in anything which creates tension or resolves it, for example, or which poses a problem and solves it. But this cannot mean that, because such material is encoded as sequential material in vayyiqtol clauses, the vayyiqtol tense is a foregrounding tense. To give a correct account of the use of vayyiqtol clauses, it is important to say that, very often, events reported through vayyiqtol verbs are not unexpected and so the vayyiqtol form cannot be understood as having a foregrounding function.

Foregrounding in Old Hebrew narratives could be described as special salience. In the development of a story, there are specific events which are more arresting than others, because they happen 'out-of-the-blue'. These do not require morphosyntactic foregrounding. In a similar way, the supporting material may be salient because of its unexpected nature. Frame-breaking salience (and information-principle-flouting salience) shows that the view which equates foreground with a sequence of temporally ordered main clauses is flawed. Not all temporally ordered clauses are equally important in a story. Vayyiqtol clauses may report pivotal events but may also report familiar and routine sequences of action.

A contextual view of foregrounding leads to the conclusion that the organization of the informative material (factual report) in Old Hebrew stories does not fit into an a priori categorization of experience as Longacre's thesis would like us to believe, but rather, that the experience is filtered by the subjectivity of an individual, the narrator. Through the ascription of saliency to elements of the story, the narrator aims at some kind of influence on the hearer or reader. These foregrounding devices are marks in the discourse which guide the reader towards a specific interpretation.

That foregrounding has to do with the configuration of experience by an individual is even more obvious in the next foregrounding device to be considered: evaluation.

4. *Foregrounding and Evaluation*

The evaluative import of communication has not been studied a great deal in linguistics.[13] One explanation is certainly that it is often felt that this dimension of storytelling is the concerns of poetics, stylistics and

13. Mention must be made of Schiffrin (1994: 306-14), Linde (1993: 71-84) and Polanyi (1989: 21-26).

literary studies rather than linguistics. This is confirmed by the number of extensive literary studies dedicated to the subject.[14] Evaluation exhibits a variety of surface structures which are not always easily captured through grammatical categories. Moreover, until very recently, a heavy concentration on written data has naturally inclined towards a study of the 'objective' referential content of narrative discourses and not their affective dimension: not too many written stories contain an outpouring of a writer's inner attitudes and emotions.

Because the focus of many narrative studies has been the event-line structure, foregrounding has also been thought to apply to the referential material exclusively. However, foregrounding must be considered in its connection with evaluative material as well, and the claim made here is that evaluative material is in fact foregrounded material. Within the constraints of this analysis, it is not possible to investigate in great detail the connection between foregrounding and evaluation, but the following points are worthy of consideration:

(1) Evaluation marks the interference of the speaker in the factual report.

(2) Through evaluative devices, speakers present what they see as important in accordance with their appraisal of a situation or a participant. Labov explains that the devices indicate to the hearer or reader that an event just mentioned is, for example, weird, crazy, terrifying or dangerous (1972: 361).

(3) Evaluative material, which by definition expresses the relationship of speakers to the story they are telling, pertains to the 'point' of the story. Labov says that it discloses the raison d'être of the story, why it was told and what the storyteller is getting at.[15]

(4) Through evaluation, speakers lead hearers to draw the conclusions favoured by them. Evaluation determines the response of the hearer to the story. From this perspective, evaluation and foregrounding may be seen as the two sides of the same coin. Hopper and Thompson describe the interface between discourse point and foregrounding in the following way:

> In any communicative situation, narrative or non-narrative, some parts of what is stated are more relevant or central than others. That part of a discourse that does not immediately contribute to a speaker's goal, but

14. Studies by Uspensky (1973) and Lanser (1981), for example.
15. See point 1 above.

> which merely assists, amplifies, or comments on it, is referred to as background. By contrast, that material which supplies the main points of the discourse is known as foreground (1980: 280).

Given that evaluative material, precisely, communicates the point of the story, providing evidence of its tellability, it must be categorized as foreground material. Before giving specific examples of evaluation, one more definitional detail must be spelt out.

Labov's description of evaluation emphasizes the psychological attitude of the storyteller towards a given story content. But a speaker's involvement in the telling of a story is not only emotional; it has also an ideological dimension. The ideological dimension of evaluation involves the conveying of appraisal, approval, disapproval based on a system of ideas, values or prejudices, whether social, political or cultural, held by the speaker.[16] Stories are not told merely to pass on information, but to make a point, to persuade the hearer or reader to adopt a particular point of view or ideology.

a. *Evaluation Devices in Old Hebrew*

Evaluation has two main characteristic features. First, it may be global or local, as opinion or emotion may be expressed about one particular section of the story or the whole of the story. Secondly, evaluation may be external or internal. In external evaluation, the narrator-speaker leaves the story world to address the comment directly to the hearer. In internal evaluation, the narrator's reflection is integrated in the story world.[17]

In the following survey of evaluation in Old Hebrew narrative, the devices will be examined according to the two main categories of internal and external evaluation.

16. A distinction is made here for the sake of clarity, but the two aspects of evaluation are very often intertwined and not easy to separate in practice.

17. This last distinction differs slightly from the one offered by Labov. Labov distinguishes evaluation occurring outside the narrative clauses and that occurring inside them. His criterion for determining external and internal evaluation is the narrative clause. As a result, for him, evaluation occurring in dialogues between participants is external. This is rather confusing and explains why I have sought another more satisfactory criterion for identifying externality and internality. Evaluation occurring in the comment of a participant in a story is considered as internal in my analysis, whereas Labov would consider it as external. My criterion is the world of the story, incuding dialogues between participants.

i. *Labov's Internal Evaluation Categories*

Focusing on clause-internal evaluation, Labov identifies four types of devices: intensifiers, comparators, correlatives, explicatives.

Intensifiers include the following devices. *Gestures* in oral storytelling are usually accompanied by a deictic 'this' or 'that': 'He swung and hit me like *that*.' *Expressive phonology*: a speaker may pronounce a word in a distinctive or distorted way, often lengthening vowels, or may use verbalized noises such as *Phth!* Exaggerating *quantifiers* such as *all* are the most common way of intensifying a clause: 'He was *all* bruised.' *Ritual utterances* (for example, an oath formula in Old Hebrew stories) mark and evaluate a situation, although they do not contain any overt markers of emphasis. *Repetition* serves also to intensify the action: 'He went to see a third time, and *he didn't come back*, and *he didn't come back*.' In Old Hebrew stories, repetition is a prevalent evaluative device which is often used in combination with other devices. It is closely linked with the information principle which has been described in sect. 2 above.

Comparators provide evaluation by referring to events that occurred and comparing them with events which might have happened but did not. The contrast between what happened and what did not happen serves to evaluate the happening. One important type of comparator is *negation*. Negations express the defeat of an expectation that something would happen. A negative sentence draws on a cognitive background that is richer than the event which is obseved. Two other types of comparators are *modality* and *futurity,* expressed in auxiliary verbal elements in English. Other comparators are *questions*, since all requests are to be understood against an unrealized possibility of negative consequences if they are not answered; and *imperatives*, since the force of the command is 'you must do this or else'. More complex comparators are *comparatives* and *superlatives*, *metaphors* and *similes*.

Correlatives bring together two events which did occur in a single independent clause. In English, Labov notes the use of the following devices: *progressive* ('and we were sitting, waiting for this thing to start'); *appended participles* ('I was sitting there, smoking my cigarette'); *double appositives* which heighten the effect of a description ('the knife, a long one, a dagger'); *double attributives* ('the old red car'); and *left-hand participles* ('an unsavoury-looking character') often used to characterize tha antagonist, are also correlatives.

Explicatives are subordinate clauses appended to the narrative clause or to an explicit evaluative clause. They specify the reason, the motivation, the extent of the event reported ('we realized that we were really out of danger'). Explicatives may be *qualifications* introduced by 'while' or 'though' or *causal* introduced by 'since' or 'because'.

As the examples will show, not all of these devices are found in Old Hebrew narratives. Moreover, for global evaluation, devices not listed by Labov have been identified.

ii. *Repetition*

The phenomenon of repetition is a predominant technique in Old Hebrew texts. It takes a number of forms: words, phrases, sentences, paragraphs. It also serves a variety of goals: intelligibility, cohesion, resumption, overlay or backlooping, patterning of texts, dramatic effect, change of point of view, etc. But we are concerned here only with the kind of repetition which has evaluation as its purpose.

A common type of repetition is repetition expressing emotions:

(6.17) Lamentations 1.16

My eye, my eye flows down water.

(6.18) Judges 5.12

Arise, arise, Deborah! arise, arise, utter a song!

(6.19) 2 Samuel 18.33

O my son, Absalom, my son, my son Absalom!
Would I have died instead of you,
O Absalom, my son, my son.

The emotion, whether grief as in (6.17) and (6.19) or enthusiasm as in (6.18), is too extreme to be articulated only in a few words. Evaluative comments are very often closely related to aspects of a story which stir up feelings or with which the speaker feels emotionally involved. Consider the utterances:

The children crying all night long. Crying, crying, crying.
And no one to hear them. That is what I remember.

And he hit me, and hit me, and hit me!

Through the repetition of the verb, the speakers make a statement about the extreme suffering and despair of the children or the violence of the beating. Repetition is an intensifier; the over-profusion in the expression is evaluative: it hammers home the content of the utterance to the hearer. At the same time, it reflects how deeply the matter affects the speaker.

b. *External Evaluation*

In external evaluation, the author steps outside the story to speak more directly to the reader. The comment comes from outside the framework of the world of the story. The author takes on the voice of the narrator in the third person to give a personal opinion, and presents an aside with a shift of attention away from the development of the action. External evaluation is generally global in Old Hebrew narratives, indicating the point of the story, giving the justification for the telling of the story (e.g. unusual or embarrassing situation, apologetic or didactic purpose).

The story of Jacob stealing his brother's birthright finishes in the following way:

(6.20) Genesis 25.34

ויבז עשׂו את־הבכרה

Thus Esau despised his birthright.

The writer passes judgment on the events just described. The evaluative comment is expressed through a vayyiqtol clause which follows a purely informational sequence of such clauses. There is no grammatical indication of a switch from the domain of the story-world to expressive import. On the contrary, the use of the vayyiqtol has the effect of concealing the expressive value of the verb. In (6.20), the opinion is given on a story which has just been told and is known by the reader. Sometimes, the opinion expressed may precede the situation which, it is assumed, will give rise to the evaluative comment. Consider:

(6.21) 2 Kings 22.2

(1) ויעשׂ הישׁר בעיני יהוה
(2) וילך בכל־דרך דוד אביו
(3) ולא־סר ימין ושׂמאול

(1) He did what was right in the sight of Yahweh (2) and walked in all the way of his father David; (3) he did not turn aside to the right or to the left.

This evaluative comment uses two vayyiqtol clauses and a comparator, a negative qatal clause. It occurs at the beginning of King Josiah's story and it has a counterpart at the end of the story, in clauses in which another comparator is used too: *Before him, there was no king like him, who turned to Yahweh with all his heart with all his soul and with all his might, nor did any like him arise after him* (vv. 25-27). Together, the two elements are foregrounded and form a framework to the story. The narrator thus signals that the purpose of reporting the events which follow, is to illustrate the righteousness and obedience of King Josiah. Although the opinion expressed is not a narrative event, the speaker encodes the comment through the narrative vayyiqtol form

External evaluation is comparatively rare in Old Hebrew narratives. It occurs mainly in the historical narratives where the ideological view of the author or narrator requires a straightforward comment or explanation. But the preference, in general, is for internal evaluation which is more persuasive, as the following examples will show.

c. *Internal Evaluation*

In internal evaluation, the evaluative devices belong to the story-world proper. They may be found in the actual verbal representation of the story in the surface structure, or at the level of story content, characters or events.

One strategy may be used to complement the other, with devices related to the story-world being strengthened by surface structure devices. Internal evaluation may be global or local.

i. *Internal Evaluation with a Global Scope*

Repetition of a Key Word. Martin Buber was the first to identify an Old Hebrew narrative technique which he called *Leitwortstil* ('leading word style'), the use of key words in Old Hebrew texts (1936: 211).[18] *Leitwortstil* consists in the repetition of a characteristic word or root throughout a text and is used by the narrator to indicate the intended thrust or purpose of a story or an episode. The repetition of a word hammers home the intended message of the story to the hearer. Through it, the speaker ensures that the message of the story is correctly perceived. By tracing the repeated key word of a text, the hearer opens the central meaning of the story. As such, the use of key words belongs

18. The text is quoted in translation by Alter (1981: 93).

to the collection of evaluative devices. Buber believes that the repetition of key words is the most effective way of making a point without disrupting the flow of the story. An example of the use of a key word is found in the story of King Jeroboam (1 Kgs 11.26–14.20), which is structured in the following way:

A. 11.26-28 Exposition: Jeroboam and Solomon

B. 11.29–12.24 Prophecy of Ahijah and its fulfilment

C. 12.25-33 Jeroboam's disobedience

D. 13.1-32 The story of the man of God

C'. 13.33-34 Jeroboam's disobedience

B'. 14.1-18 Prophecy of Ahijah and its fulfilment

A'. 14.19.20 Conclusion. Death of Jeroboam

The story has a concentric structure which gives prominence to an embedded story (D) about a man of God who announces the desecration of a new altar set up by King Jeroboam. Having delivered his oracle, the man of God leaves, but is met by an old prophet who, through deception, induces him to return with him and eat and drink, thus making him disobey part of his commission. Subsequently, the man of God is punished by being killed by a lion. In this story the verb שׁוב ('to turn back', 'to return', 'to go back') is used as a key word, being repeated eleven times. The repetition highlights the fact that the physical change of direction of the man of God was the cause of his death. But this key word also links the man of God story to the Jeroboam story: the verb שׁוב can also refer to a change of direction at the religious level, either a move towards God (i.e. 'to return', 'to repent') or away from God, indicating apostasy and disobedience. The narrator's comment which follows the man of God story plays on the first meaning of the verb:

(6.22) 1 Kings 13.33

(1) אחר הדבר הזה לא־שב ירבעם מדרכו הרעה
(2) וישב

(1) After this event Jeroboam did not turn (*šûḇ*) from his evil way, (2) but he went back (*šûḇ*) [and made priests for the high places.]

Through the placement of the man of God story at the centre of the Jeroboam story and through the use of a key word as a link, the author makes the meaning of the man of God story to bear directly on the Jeroboam story. As the man of God went back with the prophet (the V שׁוב is repeated in vv. 18, 19, 20, 22, 23) to eat and drink and so disobeyed Yahweh, the life of Jeroboam is characterized by a turning away from God. The key word שׁוב stands out through repetition in the story of the man of God's disobedience, and it can be said that all the sentences in which it appears are foregrounded. Coming after the disobedience episode in which it was so often mentioned, the key word שׁוב, repeated twice in (6.22), serves to underline the narrator's opinion of King Jeroboam: the life of the king is characterized by disobedience. This example illustrates well the functioning of key words. They are bonds which create a net of highlighted sentences communicating the evaluation of the narrator.

Participants' View. The narrator may decide not to let his voice be heard at all by bringing in the discourse an opinion voiced by a participant. This is done through the use of direct speech or through the use of cognitive verbs.

Direct speech is the most concealed strategy as the author disguises his voice as the voice of one of the characters:

(6.23) 1 Samuel 24.17-18

(1) Saul lifted up his voice and wept. He said to David:
(2) צדיק אתה ממני
(3) כי אתה גמלתני הטובה
(4) ואני גמלתיך הרעה
(2) 'you are more righteous than I, (3) for you have repaid me good, (4) whereas I have repaid you evil.'

This utterance is spoken by Saul after David had spared his life when he had fallen at his mercy. It shows clearly that the purpose of storytelling may not simply be the reporting of events but may be to influence the view which the hearer/reader holds about one of the participants in the story. The story is apologetic, defending David's legitimacy as a king.[19] The threats to his legitimacy came from circumstances in his

19. Another apologetic story, parallel to this one, is found in 1 Sam. 26, with evaluation by Saul in 26.21, 25 ('*You will do many things and will succeed in them*'). Most of the stories found in the first book of Samuel (chs. 17 to 31) are apologetic in nature.

rise to power. He had especially a conflict with king Saul, his predecessor on the throne, which turned into virtual rebellion. It is shown in many stories that David played no part in the disaster which ruined Saul's dynasty and was not responsible for any blood-guilt in relation to Saul. The narrator here creates a dialogue between David and Saul in which the self-confessing Saul testifies himself to the innocence of David. The lesson of the story drawn by Saul himself is a more powerful way to exculpate David than if it were done by the narrator. Later in the same speech, Saul even acknowledges David's high destiny: *I know that you shall surely be king and the kingdom of Israel shall be established in your hand* (v. 20). Sentence (2), in particular, gives the reason why the plot has been told and is foregrounded as an evaluative comment. (3) and (4) may be classifed in the same way. Foregrounding here is no longer done through linguistic means but is rather a device which belongs to the domain of poetics.

The second device is the use of cognitive verbs. The narrator's opinion may be attributed to a participant through verbs of cognition such as 'to know, to understand'. Consider:

(6.24) 2 Samuel 3.37

(1) וידעו כל־העם וכל־ישׂראל ביום ההוא
(2) כי לא היתה מהמלך להמית את־אבנר בן־נר

(1) So all the people and all Israel understood that day (2) that the king had no part in the killing of Abner, son of Ner.

The purpose of the story in which this comment occurs is to show King David's innocence in the assassination of Abner, the commander of the troops of Saul, the former king. The assassination of Abner was very fortunate for David's cause as it removed a large obstacle from his path to the throne of Israel. The narrator shows that David was not implicated in the murder, by first describing him as grieving over the death of Abner. Then he testifies that those who witnessed these events were convinced of the king's innocence.[20] The salient clause is not the vayyiqtol clause with its verb of cognition, but the subordinate object clause which states the opinion of the people. The evaluation is rein-

20. It could be argued that this is an internal evaluation. The argument which can be advanced to support an external evaluation is that the description has nothing to do with the main action, and so reads as a comment.

forced by the comparator which describes an event which did not happen.[21] Consider another similar example:

(6.25) 1 Samuel 18.28

(1) וירא שׁאול
(2) וידע כי יהוה עם־דוד
(1) Saul saw (2) and he knew that Yahweh was with David.

Two verbs of cognition are used, indicating that Saul knew it to be true that Yahweh was with David. The evaluation is done through the eyes of a participant, Saul, and here also the foregrounded information is expressed in the object clause describing the cognitive content of the two main verbs.

ii. *Internal Evaluation with Local Scope*

In local evaluation, the element evaluated is some particular action or happening in the story, or a particular attitude, trait or disposition of a participant.

Events. All the main devices described above can be found in clauses used to foregound events through evaluation. Additionally, examples of evaluative vocabulary, sometimes reinforced by repetition, are found as well.

Evaluative vocabulary. In every culture there are words which evoke positive feelings and other which create negative ones. Consider the example:

(6.26) 1 Kings 1.5

(1) ואדניה בן־חגית מתנשׂא לאמר
(2) אני אמלך
(1) Adonijah, son of Haggith, was growing pretentious, saying: (2) I shall be king!

This comment is found at the beginning of the intrigue to elevate the heir-apparent, Adonijah, to the regency. By using the verb מתנשׂא, the speaker shows his attitude towards Adonijah. In other words, the pretentiousness and vanity of the heir-apparent is brought out by using a

21. The comparator functions as a global evaluative device and not merely as a local one.

verb which has a negative connotation. Even though the V is in the participle, the clause is foregrounded because it is evaluative. Its effect upon the reader is to cast Adonijah in a bad light and to evoke disapproval of his behaviour right at the start of the story. Consider now:

(6.27) 2 Samuel 15.6

ויגנב אבשלום את־לב אנשי ישראל

Absalom stole the heart of the men of Israel

The sentence comes at the end of a section in which the narrator explains how Absalom prepares a coup d'état against David by building a base of support among the population. After a long section where the habitual actions of Absalom are described, the narrator gives a dramatic evaluative comment on these actions. The verb phrase (*stole the heart*) refers to the success of Absalom's devious scheme which is met with complete disapproval on the part of the narrator. At the same time, the comment brings out the gravity and seriousness of the situation. It stands out against the apparently inconsequential actions of Absalom reported before. The reader could not have anticipated that Absalom's patient strategy of exploiting people's grievances could results in such a dramatic change of side. The clause has a vayyiqtol V.

Evaluative vocabulary with repetition

(6.28) 2 Samuel 13.15

(1) וישׂנאה אמנון שׂנאה גדולה מאד
(2a) כי גדולה השׂנאה
(3) אשׁר שׂנאה
(4) מאהבה (2b) אשׁר אהבה

(1) Amnon hated her with a very great hatred, (2a) indeed the hatred (3) he felt towards her (2a-b) was greater than the love (4) he had felt for her.

This psychological observation is also evaluative in character. It occurs at the point when suddenly things are turned upside down in the story of the rape of Tamar by Amnon.The passion of Amnon for his half-sister Tamar had provided the impetus for the story. But after the rape of Tamar, hatred takes over and this reversal is highlighted as emphatically as possible by the narrator who leaves the reader in no doubt as to how significant, as well as odious and repugnant, this change of feeling is. The two verbs 'to love' and 'to hate' are used with a cognate object (*love* and *hatred*) and in the case of 'to hate with hatred' the expression is repeated twice. Moreover, the adjective *great* which is an intensifier is used twice, once in an attributive function, once in a predicate function. In its attributive use, it is reinforced by another intensifier, *very*. In its predicative use, it occurs in a clause which is explicative and also comparative. (6.28) is characterized by a piling up of evaluative devices through which the three clauses are made to stand out.

Intensifiers. Among intensifiers, *quantifiers* are the most common devices used to establish evaluation:

(6.29) 1 Samuel 16.21

(1) ויבא דוד אל־שאול
(2) ויעמד לפניו
(3) ויאהבהו מאד

(1) And David came to Saul (2) and entered his service (3) and Saul loved him greatly.

The very positive nature of Saul's feelings for David is indicated in (3) first by a lexical choice. The verb 'to love' is a loaded lexis departing from the routine verbal expressions used in the surrounding clauses (1) and (2). Moreover, the verb is also used with an intensifier, מאד, which establishes the whole statement as evaluative. Clause (3) is foregrounded because of its evaluative nature. In the context of the whole story, Saul's feelings for David are important later in the development of their relationship. Saul's rejection of David and attempts to kill him appear all the more disloyal in light of his earlier feelings underlined here.

Quantifiers are also exemplified in:

(6.30) 1 Samuel 22.1-2

David left there and he escaped to the cave of Adullam,

(1) וישמעו אחיו וכל־בית אביו
(2) וירדו אליו שמה
(3) ויתקבצו אליו כל־איש מצוק וכל־איש אשר־לו נשא וכל־איש מר־נפש
(4) ויהי עליהם לשר

(1) His brothers and *all* his father's house heard (of it) (2) and they went down there to him. (3) *Every* man who was distressed gathered round him and *every* man who was in debt and *every* man who was discontended (4) and he became their leader.

The evaluative intensifier כל is used four times in this passage whose clauses are foregrounded. The key point made in clause (3) is that David becomes the leader of all those men who have suffered some kind of deprivation which has left them embittered. David becomes the champion of the discontented, the mistreated and oppressed. The use of intensifiers here shows how complete is the support that David now enjoys. A new and unique situation has now arisen.

Within the category of intensifiers, evaluation is also achieved by the *repetition* of the report of a single event. In the following example the narrator describes a single event, the inundation of the earth, by selecting two typical phases of the event: the mounting water and the submersion of the land. These two phases are reported through repeated verbs:

(6.31) Genesis 7.17-19

(1) v.17	וירבו המים...
(2) v.18	ויגברו המים
(3)	וירבו מאד על־הארץ...
(4) v.19	והמים גברו מאד מאד על־הארץ...
(5) v.20	חמש עשרה אמה מלמעלה גברו המים
(6)	ויכסו ההרים

(1) The waters increased (רבה)...(2) and the waters prevailed (גבר) (3) and they increased (רבה) greatly (מאד) over the earth...(4) The waters prevailed (גבר) exceedingly greatly (מאד מאד) over the earth...(5) fifteen cubits deep they prevailed (גבר), (6) and they covered the mountains.

Clauses (1) to (5) are heavily foregrounded by a variety of devices. The relentless increase and the predominance of the water are depicted through two verbs *to increase* and *to prevail*, denoting surge and struggle. Not only is the verb גבר evaluative in itself, but it is also repeated in (2) and (4). This suggests the image of the water as a force subduing the dry land. The repetition of רבה ('to increase') in (1) and (3) evokes the idea of the unremitting swell of the flood. Both verbs are successively reinforced by the intensifier מאד ('much') used once in (3) and twice in (4).

Finally event evaluation may be established through another type of intensifier: *ritual utterance*, as in:

(6.32) 2 Kings 2.6

(1) ויאמר לו אליהו
(2) שב־נא פה
(3) כי יהוה שלחני הירדנה
(4) ויאמר חי־יהוה וחי־נפשך אם־אעזבך
(5) וילכו שניהם

(1) Then Elijah said to him: (2) 'Please, stay here, (3) for Yahweh is sending me to the Jordan.' (4) But he replied: 'As Yahweh lives, and as you yourself live, I will not leave you.' (5) And they went on together.

The ritual utterance in (4) is has the form of an oath. In normal circumstances, an oath is a means of impressing on someone the obligation to speak the truth or to keep a promise. An oath must be kept. Here, the oath is evaluative: it underlines that a certain course of action described in (1) is unthinkable and that it is another one that is required. Similarly:

(6.33) 2 Kings 4.30

(1) ותאמר אם הנער
(2) חי־יהוה וחי־נפשך אם־אעזבך
(3) ויקם וילך אחריה

(1) Then the mother of the child said: (2) 'As Yahweh lives, and as you yourself live, I will not leave you.' (3) So he arose and followed her.

The son of the wealthy woman of Shunem has just died. She goes to Elisha to ask for help. Elisha is content to deal with the crisis by dispatching his servant Gehazi with his staff, no doubt intended as a pledge of his personal engagement and a guarantee of his power. But Elisha's means of allaying the mother's impatience is insufficient. Action by proxy and from a distance will not do. The oath evaluates negatively Elisha's plan and makes clear that the mother requires Elisha's attendance at the scence.

Comparators. A comparator contrasts a realized event with an event which is feasible but not realized. Negatives are exemplified in:

(6.34) 2 Samuel 11.9, 10

(9a) וישכב אוריה פתח בית המלך את כל־עבדי אדניו
(9b) ולא ירד אל־ביתו
(10a) ויגדו לדוד לאמר
(10b) לא־ירד אוריה אל־ביתו
(10c) David said to Uriah

(10d) הלוא מדרך אתה בא

(10d) מדוע לא־ירדת אל־ביתך

(9a) But Uriah slept at the door of the king's house with all the servants of his lord, (9b) and did not go down to his house. (10a) They told David: (10b) 'Uriah did not go down to his house. [(10c) David said to Uriah] (10d) 'You have just come come from a journey. (10e) Why didn't you go down to your house?'

King David has just received word from Bathsheba that she is pregnant by him. David summons Bathsheba's husband, Uriah, with the intention of getting him to have intercourse with his wife in order to conceal that he himself is the real father of the child. David commands Uriah, who has come from the battlefield, to go home (v. 8: *go down to your house*) and to lie with his wife.[22] But Uriah does not go to his house (9b) and he lies (שׁכב) at the door of the palace with his servants (9a), instead of lying with his wife. The negative clause is evaluative, using a comparator to refer to what did not happen.

David does not give up. He invites Uriah to stay in Jerusalem another day, and makes him drunk, again with the intent of getting him to have sexual intercourse with his wife. The narrator uses the same negative comparator: *he did not go down to his house* (v. 13).

Grimes (1975: 64-70) classifies negative comparators in the category of collateral information.[23] He believes that the role of collateral information is to throw into relief the real event. This seems a correct analysis of the example he proposes:

> The canoe overturned. The father did not die. The mother did not die. The children did not die. Instead they all escaped to land (1975: 64).

The negative collateral clauses are used rhetorically to delay the affirmative statement and create a sense of progression towards it. The list of non-events strengthens the significance of the real event. But in (6.34) the order is different. The negative clause comes after the affirmative statement. Its first aim is not so much to highlight the realized event, to throw it into relief, as to provide evaluation. Clause (9b) is evaluative and, as a result, is foregrounded. Its saliency is corroborated by its repetition in direct speech in (10b) and (10d). The fact that

22. The expression used is *wash your feet*; it is a euphemism for sexual intercourse; the normal term is שׁכב as Uriah's answer (v. 13) to David's question shows: *'My lord Joab and the servants of my lord are camping in the open field. Shall I go down to my house to eat, drink and lie* (שׁכב) *with my wife?'*

23. Grimes deals separately with evaluative and collateral information.

Uriah has not gone home is the crucial point of the episode.

Explicatives. The use of a *causal* is exemplified in:

(6.35) 1 Samuel 18.3

(1) ויכרת יהונתן ודוד ברית
(2) באהבתו אתו כנפשו

(1) Jonathan made a covenant with David (2) because he loved him as himself.

In 1 Sam. 18.1-5 the feelings and actions of Jonathan are highly evaluated. He becomes one with David in spirit, and he is said to love David as himself (v. 1). This information is repeated in the infinitive evaluative clause (2), in connection with a pledge of loyalty made to David. The event reported in a vayyiqtol clause is a covenant made by the crown prince with his friend David. Such a covenant has political implications: through it and through the giving of his clothes and armour, sword and bow to David Jonathan is described as transferring his privilege of succession to his friend. The point of the evaluative information is to make clear to the hearer or reader that it was willingly and spontaneously that Jonathan, the rightful heir, made such a covenant. The information foregrounded is evaluative in character but is encoded grammatically in a subordinate clause.

Participant. Hebrew narratives are rather sparse in their descriptions of character. The narrators prefer to guide the reader into a discovery of what kind of a person a particular character is by describing the character in action. As a result, we often find sequences of events which are evaluative in character. But great use is also made of intensifiers, such as quantifiers, repetition and ritual utterances. Through explicatives such as causals or verbs of perception, the speaker is also able to introduce evaluative information in the story. Illustrations of the use of these devices will be provided in the following sections.

Evaluative sequence of events. Evaluation of a participant may done by reporting some specific actions performed by a character. These reports function as evaluative comments. Consider:

(6.36) 2 Kings 9.33-34

(1) They threw her down,
(2) ויז מדמה אל־הקיר ואל־הסוסים
(3) וירמסנה
(4) ויבא ויאכל וישת
(2) and some of her blood splattered on the wall and on the horses. (3) He trampled her, (3) then he went in and ate and drank.

From the perspective of the plot, the events reported are marginal. They do not belong to the main events of the story. Jehu has achieved his goal, that is to kill Queen Jezebel. But the author's interest is to describe Jehu negatively, as a ruthless soldier driven by his hatred of Jezebel. This moves him to report the happenings which immediately follow Queen Jezebel's death. Thrown out of the window, Jezebel hits the ground and her blood splatters on the wall of the palace and on the horses. This informs the hearer that Jezebel's body lies near Jehu's chariot. Then follows a description of Jehu's actions which reflects his brutality and callousness. He behaves as though nothing had happened. This short sequence of actions provides an evaluation of the character by the author, and as such, they stand out as foregrounded. The events are in the foreground not because they are encoded as vayyiqtol verbs, but because they belong to an evaluative sequence.

Intensifiers. We have come across intensifiers used to evaluate events, but intensifiers such as quantifiers, repetition and ritual utterances may also be used to provide evaluation of a participant.

Evaluation is established by a quantifier in the next example:

(6.37) 1 Samuel 18.5

(1) ויצא דוד
(2) בכל אשׁר ישׁלחנו שׁאול ישׂכיל
(3) וישׂמהו שׁאול על אנשׁי המלחמה
(4) וייטב בעיני כל־העם וגם בעיני עבדי שׁאול
(1) David went out (2) and was successful wherever Saul sent him (3) so that Saul set him over the men of war. (4) And this was good in the sight of all the people and also in the sight of Saul's servants.

Quantifiers are used to evaluate David's character: first, in clause (2), where David is described as succeeding in everything (בכל) Saul sends him to do. Moreover, (4) is a vayyiqtol clause which reports how David's deserved high rank in the army pleases all the troops and also

Saul's officials. It is evaluative, not only because of the semantics of the verb used but also because of the use of the quantifier (כל).

Evaluation of participants through *repetition* is found in:

(6.38) 1 Samuel 8.3, 5

(3a) ולא־הלכו בניו בדרכיו...
(5a) הנה אתה זקנת
(5b) ובניך לא הלכו בדרכיך

(3a) His sons did not walk in his ways, [but turned aside after gain. They took bribes and perverted justice. So all the elders of Israel gathered together and came to Samuel at Ramah and said to him.] (5a) 'you are old (5b) and your sons do not follow in your ways.'

The narrator first gives an external evaluation of Samuel's sons which calls attention to their corruption (3a) It uses a comparator (negative clause). The elders' complaint in (5b) repeats the evaluative statement of the narrator. The repetition has a double effect. The conformity of the complaint with the narrator's comment validates the elder's grievance. But the repetition of the evaluation also highlights the special importance of this situation in Israel's history, as it will lead to the eventual change of the political system. Clauses (3a) and (5b), although negative, are foregrounded.

Explicatives. In the following example, the evaluative information is encoded in a subordinate clause of cause introduced by כי:

(6.39) 1 Samuel 18.12

(1) וירא שאול מלפני דוד
(2) כי־היה יהוה עמו
(3) ומעם שאול סר

(1) Saul was afraid of David (2) because Yahweh was with David (3) but had left Saul.

The narrator provides evaluation of David through a description of Saul's attitude and by spelling out the cause for the state reported. The explicative clause of causality (2) is all the more potent in that it is a positive evaluation which is given by the character who fears and is jealous of David.

In the following example, evaluation is established through a verb of perception followed by an object clause:

(6.40) 1 Samuel 18.13-15

v. 13 So Saul removed him from his presence, and made him a commander of a thousand and he went out and came in before the people,

(1) v. 15 וירא שׁאול
(2) אשׁר־הוא משׂכיל מאד
(1) and Saul saw (2) that he had great success.

David's military success is highlighted through an evaluation of David through the eyes of Saul, using a verb of perception ('Saul saw'). Again, it is a subordinate clause which presents the foregrounded information. The explicative is itself strengthened by the intensifier מאד.

Conclusion

Foregrounding of material through evaluation throws seriously back into question the thesis of grammatical foregrounding through vayyiqtol. Reported evaluated events stand out against 'objectively' reported events. Moreover, all vayyiqtol clauses are not necessarily central to the plot, as Longacre claims. Vayyiqtol clauses may have the specific function of evaluating a participant or an event and are foregrounded for this reason, not because they are part of the main narrative line.

Evaluative material also shows that foregrounding is not necessarily bound to the verbal form vayyiqtol . Evaluative foregrounding may take place at any level of the narrative discourse: direct speech, vayyiqtol main clause, subordinate clause. It may apply to a word, a phrase, a clause or a sequence of clauses. In the case of clauses, it may apply to a participial clause, a vayyiqtol clause or a qatal clause.

The examples discussed point to the fact that foregrounding in Old Hebrew stories is not one of a monochrome kind. The central weakness of the thesis that foregrounding takes place uniformly through vayyiqtol forms in stories is that it assumes that a story is made up entirely of facts reported (the narrated) and that it ignores totally that there is also a different type of material, one which reflects the voice of the speaker. What happens in a story goes hand in hand with what is said about it. The involvement of the speaker carries as much weight as the events of the story themselves because they indicate what the true meaning of the story is. The examination of evaluation shows above all that foregrounding is the preserve of the storyteller and is constructed by the speaker by a variety of means. It is not dictated by grammatical forms.

5. *General Conclusion*

The analyses of this chapter have taken us into the domains of literary pragmatics and cognitive psychology. We have reached the point at which the study of foregrounding becomes interrelated with the 'poetics' of biblical Hebrew narrative, if we define poetics in the words of Alter, as seeking to find 'the modes of literary communication which were shared by Hebrew storyteller and audience' (1983: 117). The various foregrounding mechanisms represent a type of linguistic performance and, as a result, they fall outside the scope of a rule-based description. This should not surprise us as, in the end, foregrounding consists in a speaker manipulating linguistic structures to achieve a certain effect on the hearer. Its determination is not, as Longacre wants us to believe, a question of linguistic competence.

Chapter 7

General Conclusion

The various pragmatic and cognitive analyses carried out in the preceding chapters have helped to assess the correctness and usefulness of one view of foregrounding in Old Hebrew stories, and at the same time they have allowed me to set up signposts which point towards a definition of the true nature of foregrounding.

The notion of foregrounding deemed inadequate is the one which relies upon a basic distinction between events and non-events. Events, it is claimed, stand out against non-events—for example, backgrounded actions, activities and setting—and so represent foregrounded material against the background of non-events. As the vayyiqtol verb is viewed as having a preterite meaning, a direct correlation of the vayyiqtol clause, called the narrative clause, with the foregrounded or main line events is established. Moreover, as narrative events are assumed not only to be presented in chronological sequence but also to move the action forward, these two notions also become definitional of the foreground.

This view of foregrounding has been found to be defective for two main reasons. First, a number of linguistic facts undermine its correctness. Vayyiqtol clauses are not used exclusively for the reporting of chronological sequences of events; that is the vayyiqtol clause is not always a 'typical' narrative clause. An evaluative comment, a descriptive detail, a summary, an enumeration may be encoded in a vayyiqtol clause, too. In these cases, the clause does not move the action forward. Similarly, explanatory information such as flashbacks may also be encoded in vayyiqtol clauses.

These observations mean that, depending on its function in discourse, the vayyiqtol clause may or may not be foregrounded. In addition, temporally sequenced events need not be encoded in a uniform grammatical class (main clause), nor in a homogeneous formal class (vayyiqtol clauses) as the view assumes.

Secondly, this conception of foregrounding is faulty because, by grammaticalizing the notion of foregrounding it also ends up by grammaticalizing the notion of importance. By maintaining that all events reported through vayyiqtol verbs belong to the backbone of the story, it asserts that vayyiqtol events represent the most important events of a story. As a general comment, it must be stressed that there is no reason to assume that the narrative temporal sequence should automatically be more important than the non-narrative clauses. This has been demonstrated by an examination of some examples. The encoding of an event in a vayyiqtol clause does not mean that the event in question is important for the story. Sequences of relatively secondary events, of routine actions which could be omitted, are often reported through vayyiqtol clauses. Conversely, clauses which, according to the theory, encode secondary actions have been shown to belong, in fact, to the backbone of a story. This means that (a) the vayyiqtol form needs to be sharply distinguished from event importance; and that (b) the criterion of importance needs to be determined by factors other than grammatical form, as both factors inevitably define each other in a circular fashion.

Even if it were possible to accept that the non-main line material is the material against which the foreground is thrown into relief, one would have to query the methodological usefulness and credibility of such a view. A story in which all the events were uniformally foregrounded would be extremely boring and dull and also hard to pay attention to.

The analyses of Chapters 3 to 6 can help also to sketch a view of saliency and foregrounding which takes into account some of the true mechanisms involved in foregounding. Chapter 3 has shown that there exists a type of saliency in Old Hebrew stories which is connected to the question of topicality. In the unfolding of a story, a main topical participant may receive the status of topical peak when the attention of the hearer is made to be centred at the same time on the participant in question and another topical participant.

Chapter 4 has shown that the choice between the vayyiqtol and NP + qatal clause is linked to the assessment made by the speaker of the cognitive states of referents in the mind of the hearer and is not dictated by the distinction foreground/background. The vayyiqtol clause works in tandem with the NP + qatal clause and not in opposition to it.

Chapter 5 studied the types of focus structures used narration. It has established that in a VSO clause there is one constituent, called the dominant focal element, which is salient. The DFE depends upon an array of pragmatic, semantic and grammatical criteria, and is indicated through word order. Moreover, a constituent can be established as a marked DFE in a NP + qatal clause. These factors suggest that clauses may be more or less foregrounded, according to the change in word order, or the forefronting of a referent.

Chapter 6 entered into areas which bordered on literary studies. Different types of foregrounding which exploit either the unexpected character of an event or the flouting of the informational principle (repetititon), or else using evaluative comments, have been identified.

In my view, all these mechanisms and devices should be considered together to account for the notion of foregrounding. Foregrounding is multifaceted and is not a property of any one given linguistic structure. There is not, in Old Hebrew, a unilateral mapping of foreground on to a single grammatical category. Rather, a variety of linguistic items can be put to use for foregrounding. Foregrounding also affects the various planes of a narrative text: the informative component with its event reporting strand and its supporting material, the expressive component and the reported dialogues.

The variety of foregounding devices shows that the determinations of foregrounding do not reside and are not dictated by language. Rather, it is the narrator/speaker who constructs foregrounding by using pragmatic articulations, by playing on the cognitive states of referents or flouting the information principle, for example.

A last point may be made using a 'mining' metaphor. Perhaps Longacre's view of foreground, which he sees as running continuously through the narrative, could be compared to a vein of metal running through the rock. But the reality is that foreground occurs in Old Hebrew narratives like isolated and localized deposits of metal in the rock. These deposits are the result of the speakers' pragmatic activity, as they choose to make salient specific elements of a story for the purpose of ensuring that the message gets across successfully and that the interpretative process goes in the desired direction. The analysis has brought to light some linguistic facts pointing to the inherent weakness of the binary theory of foreground. Once we are acquainted with even more facts, it is likely that the binary distinction will be found to be no longer useful. In order to confirm this probability, additional research on foregrounding would need to be undertaken in the verbless and subordinate clauses in particular.

Appendix

Genesis 22.1-14: Clause Display

1a ויהי אחר הדברים האלה
1b והאלהים נסה את־אברהם

Episode 1 (1c-2f)

1c ויאמר אליו
1d אברהם
1e ויאמר
1f הנני
2a ויאמר
2b קח־נא את־בנך את־יחידך
2c אשר־אהבת
2b את ־יצחק
2d ולך־לך אל־ארץ המריה
2e והעלהו שם לעלה על אחד ההרים
2f אשר אמר אליך

Episode 2 (3a-3g)

3a וישכם אברהם בבקר
3b ויחבש את־ חמרו
3c ויקח את־שני נעריו אתו ואת יצחק בנו
3d ויבקע עצי עלה
3e ויקם
3f וילך אל ־ המקום
3g אשר־אמר ־לו האלהים

Episode 3 (4a-5e)

4a ביום השלישי וישא אברהם את ־ עיניו
4b וירא את־המקום מרחק
5a ויאמר אברהם אל־נעריו
5b שבו־לכם פה עם־החמור
5c ואני והנער נלכה עד־כה
5d ונשתחוה
5e ונשובה אליכם

Episode 4 (6a-6d)

6a ויקח אברהם את־עצי העלה
6b וישם על־יצחק בנו
6c ויקח בידו את־האש ואת־המאכלת
6d וילכו שניהם יחדו

Episode 5 (7a-9d)

7a ויאמר יצחק אל־אברהם אביו
7b ויאמר 7c אבי
7d ויאמר 7e הנני בני
7f ויאמר
7g הנה האש והעצים
7h ואיה השה לעלה
8a ויאמר אברהם
8b אלהים יראה־לו השה לעלה בני
8c וילכו שניהם יחדו
9a ויבאו אל־המקום
9b אשר אמר־לו האלהים

Episode 6 (9c-f)

9c ויבן שם אברהם את־המזבח
9d ויערך את־העצים
9e ויעקד את־יצחק בנו
9f וישם אתו על־המזבח ממעל לעצים

Episode 7 (10a-12f)

10a וישלח אברהם את־ידו
10b ויקח את־המאכלת 10c לשחט את ־ בנו
11a ויקרא אליו מלאך יהוה מן־השמים
11b ויאמר 11c אברהם אברהם
11d ויאמר 11e הנני
12a ויאמר
12b אל־תשלח ידך אל־הנער
12c ואל־תעש לו מאומה
12d כי עתה ידעתי
12e כי־ירא אלהים אתה
12f ולא חשכת את־בנך את ־יחידך ממני

Episode 8 (13a-13f)

13a וישׂא אברהם את־עיניו
13b וירא
13c והנה־איל אחר נאחז כסבך בקרניו
13d וילך אברהם
13e ויקח את־האיל
13f ויעלהו לעלה תחת בנו

Episode 9 (14a-14d)

14a ויקרא אברהם שׁם־המקום ההוא
14b יהוה יראה
14c אשׁר יאמר היום
14d בהר יהוה יראה

BIBLIOGRAPHY

Allan, Keith

1986 *Linguistic Meaning* (2 vols.; London: Routledge and Kegan Paul).

Alter, Robert

1981 *The Art of Biblical Narrative* (New York: Basic Books).

Alter, R., and F. Kermode (eds.)

1987 *The Literary Guide to the Bible* (London: Collins).

Amit, Yairah

1989 'The Story of Ehud (Judges 3.12-30): The Form and the Message', in Cheryl J. Exum (ed.), *Signs and Wonders: Biblical Texts in Literary Focus* (Atlanta: Scholars Press): 97-131.

Andersen, Francis I.

1966 'Moabite Syntax', *Orientalia NS* 35: 81-120.

1970 *The Hebrew Verbless Clause in The Pentateuch* (Nashville: Abingdon Press).

1974 *The Sentence in Biblical Hebrew* (The Hague: Mouton).

Bailey, Nicholas A., and Stephen H. Levinsohn

1992 'The Function of Preverbal Elements in Independent Clauses in the Hebrew Narrative of Genesis', *Journal of Translation and Textlinguistics* 5.3: 179-207.

Bal, Mieke

1985 *Narratology: Introduction to the Theory of Narrative* (Toronto: University of Toronto Press).

Bar-Efrat, Shimon

1986 'Narrator', in A. Preminger and E.L. Greenstein (eds.), *The Hebrew Bible in Literary Criticism* (New York: Ungar).

1989 *Narrative Art in the Bible* (Transl. from 2nd Hebrew Edition, 1984; Sheffield: Sheffield Academic Press).

Barr, James

1973 'Hebrew Lexicography', in P. Fronzaroli (ed.), *Studies on Semitic Lexicography* (Quaderni Di Semitistica, 2; Firenze: Università di Firenze): 102-26.

Barthes, Roland

1966 'Introduction à l'analyse structurale du récit', in R. Barthes, *The Semiotic Challenge* (trans. Richard Howard 1988; Oxford: Basil Blackwell): 95-135.

Beaugrande, Robert de

1980 *Text, Discourse, and Process: Toward a Multidisciplinary Science of Text* (Norwood: Ablex).

Benes, E.
1962 'Die Verbstellung im Deutschen, von der Mitteilungsperspektive her-betrachtet', *Philologia Pragensia* 5: 6-19.

Berlin, Adele
1983 *Poetics and Interpretation of Biblical Narrative* (Sheffield: Almond Press).

Blau, Joshua
1976 *A Grammar of Biblical Hebrew* (Wiesbaden: Otto Harrassowitz).
1977 *An Adverbial Construction in Hebrew and Aramaic: Sentence Adverbials in Frontal Position Separated from the Rest of the Sentence* (Jerusalem: The Academy of Sciences and Humanities).

Bloomfield, Leonard
1935 *Language* (London: Allen & Unwin).

Booth, Wayne, C.
1983 *The Rhetoric of Fiction* (Chicago: University of Chicago Press, 2nd edn).

Brown, Gillian, and George Yule
1983 *Discourse Analysis* (Cambridge: Cambridge University Press).

Buber, Martin
1936 'Leitworstil in der Erzählung des Pentateuchs', in M. Buber and F. Rosenzweig, *Die Schrift und ihre Verdeutschung* (Berlin: Schoken): 211-38.

Buth, Randall
1992 'Topic and Focus in Hebrew Poetry: Psalm 51', in Hwang Shin Ja J. and William R. Merrifield (eds.), *Language in Context: Essays for Robert E. Longacre* (Arlington: SIL and the University of Texas): 83-96.

Chafe, Wallace
1976 'Givenness, Contrastiveness, Definiteness, Subjects, Topics and Point of View', in N.C. Li (ed.), *Subject and Topic* (New York: Academic Press): 25-56.
1987 'Cognitive Constraints on Information Flow', in Tomlin (ed.) 1987: 21-51.

Chatman, Seymour
1978 *Story and Discourse: Narrative Structure in Fiction and Film* (Ithaca: Cornell University Press).

Clark, Herbert H.
1992 *Arenas of Language Use* (Chicago: University of Chicago Press).

Clark, Herbert H., and Eve V. Clark
1977 *Psychology and Language: An Introduction to Psycholinguistics* (New York: Harcourt Brace Jovanovitch).

Coats, George W.
1973 'Abraham's Sacrifice of Faith', *Interpretation* 27: 389-400.
1983 *Genesis, with an Introduction to Narrative Literature* (The Forms of Old Testament Literature, 1; Grand Rapids: Eerdmans).
1985 *Saga, Legend, Tale, Novella, Fable: Narrative Forms in Old Testament Literature* (Sheffield: Sheffield Academic Press).

Cohen, David
1970 'Les formes du prédicat en Arabe et la théorie de la phrase chez les anciens grammairiens', in *Mélanges Marcel Cohen* (réunis par D. Cohen; The Hague: Mouton): 224-28.

Cohn, Robert L.
1985 'Literary Techniques in the Jeroboam Narrative', *Zeitschrift für altestamentliche Wissenschaft* 97: 23-35.
Comrie, Bernard
1981 *Language Universals and Linguistic Typology: Syntax and Morphology* (Oxford: Basil Blackwell).
Conroy, Charles
1978 *Absalom! Absalom!* (Rome: Biblical Institute Press).
Cooper, C.R., and S. Greenbaum (eds.)
1986 *Studying Writing: Linguistic Approaches* (Beverly Hills: Sage Publications).
Culley, Robert C.
1990 'Five Tales of Punishment in the Book of Numbers', in Susan Niditch (ed.), *Text and Tradition: The Hebrew Bible and Folklore* (Atlanta: Scholars Press): 25-34.
1992 *Themes and Variations: A Study of Action in Biblical Narrative* (Atlanta: Scholars Press).
1993 'Psalm 102: A Complaint with a Difference', *Semeia* 62: 19-35.
Davies, Graham I.
1991 *Ancient Hebrew Inscriptions: Corpus and Concordance* (Cambridge: Cambridge University Press).
Dawson, David Allan
1994 *Text-Linguistics and Biblical Hebrew* (JSOT Supplement Series; Sheffield: Sheffield Academic Press).
De Vries, Simon J.
1989 *1 and 2 Chronicles* (The Forms of Old Testament Literature, 11; Grand Rapids: Eerdmans).
Dijk, Teun A. van
1977 *Text and Context: Explorations in the Semantics and Pragmatics of Discourse* (London: Longman).
Dijk, Teun A. van, and Walter Kintsch
1983 *Strategies of Discourse Comprehension* (New York: Academic Press).
Dik, Simon C.
1981 *Functional Grammar* (Dordrecht: Floris).
1987 'Some Principles of Functional Grammar', in R. Dirven and G. Radden (eds.), *Concepts of Case* (Tübingen: Gunter Narr): 37-53.
1989 *The Theory of Functional Grammar* (Dordrecht: Foris Publications).
Dirven, R., and V. Fried (eds.)
1987 *Functionalism in Linguistics* (Amsterdam: John Benjamins).
Driver, Geoffrey Rolles
1936 *Problems of the Hebrew Verbal System* (Edinburgh: T. & T. Clark).
Dry, Helen Aristar
1992 'Foregrounding: An Assessment', in Hwang Shin Ja J. and William R. Merrifield (eds.), *Language in Context: Essays for Robert E. Longacre* (Arlington: SIL and University of Texas): 435-50.
Eco, Umberto
1979 *The Role of the Reader: Explorations in the Semiotics of Texts* (Bloomington: Indiana University Press).

Exum, J. Cheryl
1981 'Aspects of Symmetry and Balance in the Samson Saga', *Journal for the Study of the Old Testament* 19: 3-29.

Fillmore, Charles J.
1968 'The Case for Case', in E. Bach and R. Harms (eds.), *Universals in Linguistic Theory* (New York: Holt, Rinehart & Winston): 1-88.
1981 'Pragmatics and the Description of Discourse', in P. Cole (ed.), *Radical Pragmatics* (New York: Academic): 143-66.
1982 'Frame Semantics' in Linguistic Society of Korea (eds.), *Linguistic in the Morning Calm* (Hanshin Pub. Co.): 111-38.

Firbas, Jan
1979 'A Functional View of "Ordo Naturalis"', *Brno Studies in English* 13: 29-59.
1986a 'A Case-Study in the Dynamics of Written Communication', in D. Kastovsky and A. Szwedek (eds.), *Linguistics across Historical and Geographical Boundaries*. II. *Descriptive, Contrastive and Applied Linguistics* (Berlin: W. de Gruyter): 859-76.
1986b 'On the Dynamics of Written Communication in the Light of the Theory of Functional Sentence Perspective', in Cooper and Greenbaum (eds.) 1986: 40-71.
1987a 'On the Delimitation of the Theme in Functional Sentence Perspective', in Dirven and Fried (eds.) 1987: 137-56.
1987b 'On Two Starting-Points of Communication' in R. Steele and T. Threadgold (eds.), *Language Topics: Essays in Honour of Michael Halliday*, I (2 vols; Amsterdam: Benjamins): 23-46.
1992 *Functional Sentence Perspective in Written and Spoken Communication* (Cambridge: Cambridge University Press).

Fishbane, Michael A.
1979 *Text and Texture: Close Readings of Selected Biblical Texts* (New York: Schocken Books).

Fokkelman, Jan P.
1975 *Narrative Art in Genesis: Specimen of Stylistic and Structural Analysis* (Assen: Van Gorcum).

Foley, William A., and Robert E. Van Valin
1984 *Functional Syntax and Universal Grammar* (Cambridge: Cambridge University Press).

Fox, Andrew
1983 'Topic Continuity in Biblical Hebrew Narrative', in T. Givón (ed.), *Topic Continuity in Discourse* (Amsterdam: John Benjamins): 215-54.

Freitag, Gustav
1894 *Technique of the Drama* (trans. Elias J. MacEwan; Chicago: Scott).

Frisch, Amos
1991 'Structure and its Significance: The Narrative of Solomon's Reign (1 Kings 1–12.24)', *Journal for the Study of the Old Testament* 51: 3-14.

Gammie, John G.
1979 'Theological Interpretation by Way of Literary and Tradition Analysis: Genesis 25–36', in Martin J. Buss (ed.), *Encounter with the Text: Form*

and History in the Hebrew Bible (Philadelphia: Fortress Press; Missoula, MT: Scholars Press): 117-34.

Geller, Stephen A.

1991 'Cleft Sentences with Pleonastic Pronoun: A Syntactic Construction of Biblical Hebrew and Some of its Literary Uses', *Journal of Ancient Near Eastern Studies* 20: 15-33.

Genette, Gérard

1972 *Figures III* (Paris: Le Seuil).

Gibson, John C.

1994 *Davidson's Introductory Grammar: Syntax* (Edinburgh: T. & T. Clark, 4th edn).

Givón, Talmy

1977 'The Drift from VSO to SVO in Biblical Hebrew: The Pragmatics of Tense-Aspect', in C.N. Li (ed.), *Mechanisms of Syntactic Change* (Austin: University of Texas Press): 181-254.

1988 'The Pragmatics of Word-Order: Predictability, Importance and Attention', in Hammond, Moravcsik and Wirth (eds.) 1988: 243-84.

1989 *Mind, Code and Context: Essays in Pragmatics* (Hillsdale: Erlbaum).

1990 *Syntax: A Functional-Typological Introduction*, II (2 vols.; Amsterdam: John Benjamins).

Gooding, David W.

1982 'The Composition of the Book of Judges', *Eretz-Israel, Archeological Historical and Geographical Society. XVI. H.M. Orlinsky Volume* (Jerusalem: Israel Exploration Society): 70-79.

Green, Barbara

1982 'The Plot of the Biblical Story of Ruth', *Journal for the Study of the Old Testament* 23: 55-68.

Green, Georgia M.

1989 *Pragmatics and Natural Language Understanding* (Hillsdale: Erlbaum).

Grice, H. Paul

1975 'Logic and Conversation' in P. Cole and J.L. Morgan (eds.), *Syntax and Semantics*. III. *Speech Acts* (New York: Academic Press): 41-58.

Grimes, Joseph E.

1975 *The Thread of Discourse* (The Hague: Mouton).

Gross, Walter

1987 *Die Pendenskonstruktion im biblischen Hebräisch* (St Ottilien: EOS Verlag).

Gundel, Jeanette K.

1977 *Role of Topic and Comment in Linguistic Theory* (Bloomington: Indiana University Club).

1985 '"Shared Knowledge" and Topicality', *Journal of Pragmatics* 9: 83-107.

1988 'Universals of Topic-Comment Structure', in Hammond, Moravcsik and Wirth (eds.) 1988: 285-301.

Gundel, Jeanette K., Nancy Hedberg and Ron Zacharsky

1993 'Cognitive Status and the Form of Referring Expressions in Discourse', *Language* 69: 274-307.

Gunn, David M.

1974 'Narrative Patterns and Oral Traditions in Judges and Samuel', *Vetus Testamentum* 24: 286-317.

1976 'Traditional Narrative Composition in the "Succession Narrative" ', *Vetus Testamentum* 26: 214-29.

1987 'Joshua and Judges', in Alter and Kermode (eds.) 1987: 102-21.

Gunn, David, M., and Danna Nolan Fewell

1993 *Narrative in the Hebrew Bible* (Oxford: Oxford University Press).

Hadas-Lebel, Mireille

1977 *Histoire de la langue Hébraïque* (Paris: Publications Orientaliste de France).

Haiman, John

1985 *Natural Syntax: Iconicity and Erosion* (Cambridge: Cambridge University Press).

1988 'Incorporation, Parallelism and Focus' in Hammond, Moravcsik and Wirth (eds.) 1988: 303-20.

Halliday, Michael A.K.

1967 'Notes on Transitivity and Theme in English: Part II', *Journal of Linguistics* 3.2: 199-244.

1985 *An Introduction to Functional Grammar* (London: Arnold).

Hammond, M., E. Moravcsik and J. Wirth (eds)

1988 *Studies in Syntactic Typology* (Amsterdam: John Benjamins).

Hendel, Ronald S.

1987 *The Epic of the Patriarch: The Jacob Cycle and the Narrative Traditions of Canaan and Israel* (Atlanta: Scholars Press).

Herchenroeder, Michael B.

1987 'Adversative Couplets in Hebrew Narrative', *OPTAT* 1: 18-30.

Hopper, Paul J., and Sandra Thompson

1980 'Transitivity in Grammar and Discourse', *Language* 56: 251-99.

Hoey, Michael

1991 *Patterns of Lexis in Text* (Oxford: Oxford University Press).

Horn, Laurence R.

1986 'Presupposition, Theme and Variations', *Chicago Linguistic Society* 22: 168-92.

Humphreys, W. Lee

1988 *Joseph and his Family: A Literary Study* (Columbia: University of South Carolina Press).

Iser, Wolfgang

1974 *The Implied Reader* (Baltimore: The John Hopkins University Press).

Jackson, J.J., and M. Kessler (eds.)

1974 *Rhetorical Criticism: Essays in Honor of James Muilenburg* (Pittsburgh: Pickwick Press).

Jongeling, K.

1991 'On the VSO Character of Hebrew', in K. Jongeling *et al.* (eds.), *Studies in Hebrew and Aramaic Presented to Professor J. Hoftijzer* (Leiden: E.J. Brill): 103-11.

Joüon, Paul

1965 *Grammaire de l'hébreu biblique* (Rééditée et corrigée; Rome: Pontifical Biblical Institut).

Joüon, Paul, and Muraoka Takamitsu

1991 *A Grammar of Biblical Hebrew* (2 vols.; Rome: Biblical Institute).

Khan, Geoffrey

1988 *Studies in Semitic Syntax* (Oxford: Oxford University Press).

Kikawada, Isaac M.

1974 'The Shape of Genesis 11.1-9', in Jackson and Kessler (eds.) 1974: 18-32.

Kogut, Simcha

1986 'On the Meaning and Syntactic Status of *hinneh* in Biblical Hebrew' in Sarah Japhet (ed.), *Studies in the Bible: 1986* (Jerusalem: Magnes Press): 133-54.

Kustár , Péter

1972 *Aspekt im Hebräischen* (Basel: Reinhardt).

Kutscher, E. Yechezkel

1982 *A History of the Hebrew Language* (edited by R. Kutscher; Jerusalem: Magnes Press; Leiden: E.J. Brill).

Labov, William

1972 'Language in the Inner City: Studies in the Black English Vernacular', *Conduct and Communication* 3: 354-96.

1987 'The Overestimation of Functionalism', in Dirven and Fried (eds.) 1987: 311-32.

1994 *Principles of Linguistic Changes.* I. *Internal Factors* (Oxford: Basil Blackwell).

Labov, William, and Joshua Waletzky

1967 'Narrative Analysis: Oral Versions of Personal Experience', in Helms June (ed.), *Essays on the Verbal and Visual Arts* (Seattle: University of Washington Press): 12-44.

Lambdin, Thomas O.

1973 *Introduction to Biblical Hebrew* (London: Darton, Longman & Todd).

Lambrecht, Knud

1986 'Pragmatically Motivated Syntax: Presentational Cleft Constructions in Spoken French', *Chicago Linguistic Society* 22: 115-26.

1987 'On the Status of SVO Sentences in French Discourse', in Tomlin (ed.) 1987: 217-61.

1988 'Presentational Cleft Constructions in Spoken French', in J. Haiman and S. Thompson (eds.), *Clause Combining in Grammar and Discourse* (Amsterdam: Benjamins): 135-79.

1994 *Information Structure and Sentence Form* (Cambridge: Cambridge University Press).

Landes, George M.

1967 'The Kerygma of the Book of Jonah', *Interpretation* 21: 3-31.

Landy, Francis

1989 'Narrative Techniques and Symbolic Transactions in the Akedah', in J.C. Exum (ed.), *Signs and Wonders* (Atlanta: Scholars Press): 1-57.

Lanser, Susan Snaider
1981 *The Narrative Act: Point of View in Prose Fiction* (Princeton: Princeton University Press).
Lategan, Bernard C.
1989 'Coming to Grips with the Reader in Biblical Literature', *Semeia* 48: 3-17.
Lategan, Bernard C., and Willem S. Vorster,
1985 *Text and Reality: Aspects of Reference in Biblical Texts* (Philadelphia: Fortress Press).
Leech, Geoffrey N.
1983 *Principles of Pragmatics* (London: Longman).
Leech, Geoffrey N., and Michael H. Short
1981 *Style in Fiction: A Linguistic Introduction to English Fictional Prose* (London: Longman).
Leech, Geoffrey N., and Jan Svartvik
1975 *A Communicative Grammar of English* (Harlow: Longman).
Lehnert, W.G.
1980 'The Role of Scripts in Understanding', in Metzing (ed.) 1980: 79-95.
Lemaire, André
1977 *Inscriptions hébraïques*. I. *Les ostraca* (Paris: Cerf).
Levinson, Steven
1983 *Pragmatics* (Cambridge: Cambridge University Press).
1985 'Minimization and Conversational Inference', in J. Verschueren and M. Bertucelli-Papi (eds.), *The Pragmatic Perspective: Selected Papers from 1985 International Pragmatic Conference* (Amsterdam: Benjamins): 61-129.
Licht, Jacob
1978 *Storytelling in the Bible* (Jerusalem: Magnes Press).
Linde, Charlotte
1979 'Focus of Attention and the Choice of Pronouns in Discourse', in T. Givón (ed.), *Syntax and Semantics*. XII. *Discourse and Syntax* (New York: Academic Press): 337-54.
1993 *Life Stories: The Creation of Coherence* (Oxford: Oxford University Press).
Lode, Lars
1984 'Postverbal Word Order in Biblical Hebrew: Structure and Function', *Semitica* 9: 113-64.
Long, Burke O.
1984 *1 Kings with an Introduction to Historical Literature* (Grand Rapids: Eerdmans).
1985 'Historical Narrative and the Fictionalizing Imagination', *Vetus Testamentum* 35: 405-416.
Longacre, Robert E.
1976 'The Discourse Structure of the Flood Narrative', in G. MacRae (ed.), *Society of Biblical Literature Seminar Papers 1976* (Missoula, MT: Scholars Press): 235-62.
1983 *The Grammar of Discourse: Notional and Surface Structures* (New York: Plenum).

1985 'Interpreting Biblical Stories', in Teun A. van Dijk (ed.), *Discourse and Literature: New Approaches to the Analysis of Literary Genres* (Philadelphia: John Benjamins): 169-85.

1986 'Who Sold Joseph into Egypt ?', in R. Laird Harris, Swee-Hwa Quek and J.R. Vannoy (eds.), *Interpretation and History* (Singapore: Christian Life Publishers): 75-91.

1989 *Joseph: A Story of Divine Providence. A Text Theoretical and Textlinguistic Analysis of Genesis 37 and 39–48* (Winona Lake, IN: Eisenbrauns).

1990 *Story Line Concerns and Word Order Typology in East and West Africa* (Los Angeles: University of California Press).

1992a 'Discourse Perspective on the Hebrew Verb: Affirmation and Restatement', in Walter R. Bodine (ed.), *Linguistics and Biblical Hebrew* (Winona Lake, IN: Eisenbrauns): 177-89.

1992b 'The Analysis of Preverbal Nouns in Biblical Hebrew Narratives: Some Overriding Concerns', *Journal of Translation and Textlinguistics* 5: 208-24.

Lord, Albert B.

1960 *The Singer of Tales* (Cambridge, MA: Harvard University Press).

Mayer, Lambert

1972 *Traité de grammaire hébraïque* (corrected and completed by G.E. Weil; Hildesheim: Gerstenberg, 2nd edn).

McFall, Leslie

1982 *The Enigma of the Hebrew Verbal System: Solutions from Ewald to the Present* (Sheffield: Almond Press).

Merwe, Christo H.J. van der

1990 *The Old Particle Gam: A Syntactic-Semantic Description of Gam in Gn–2 Kg* (St. Ottilien: Eos Verlag).

1991 'The Function of Word Order in Old Hebrew: With Special Reference to Cases where a Syntagmeme Precedes a Verb in Joshua', *Journal of Northwest Semitic Languages* 17: 129-44.

1993 'Old Hebrew Particles and the Interpretation of Old Testament Texts', *Journal for the Study of the Old Testament* 60: 27-44.

Mettinger, Tryggve N.D.

1973 'The Hebrew Verb System', *Annual of the Swedish Theological Institute* 9: 64-84.

Metzing, D. (ed.)

1980 *Frame Conception and Text Understanding* (Berlin: W. de Gruyter).

Mey, Jacob L.

1993 *Pragmatics: An Introduction* (Oxford: Basil Blackwell).

Miner, Earl

1990 *Comparative Poetics: An Intercultural Essay on Theories of Literature* (Princeton: Princeton University Press).

Minsky, Marvin

1980 'A Framework for Representing Knowledge', in Metzing (ed.) 1980: 1-25.

Muraoka, Takamitsu
1979 'On Verb Complementation in Biblical Hebrew', *Vetus Testamentum* 29: 425-35.
1985 *Emphatic Words and Structures in Biblical Hebrew* (Jerusalem: Magnes Press).

Niccacci, Alviero
1990 *The Syntax of the Verb in Classical Hebrew Prose* (trans. W.G.E. Watson; Sheffield: JSOT Press).

Niditch, Susan
1987 *Underdogs and Tricksters: A Prelude to Biblical Folklore* (San Francisco: Harper & Row).

Norton, David
1993 *A History of the Bible as Literature*. II. *From 1700 to the Present Day* (Cambridge: Cambridge University Press).

Ong, Walter, J.
1981 'The Psychodynamics of Oral Memory and Narrative. Some Implications for Biblical Studies', in Robert Masson (ed.), *The Pedagogy of God's Image* (Chico, CA: Scholars Press): 55-73.
1982 *Orality and Literacy: The Technologizing of the Word* (London: Methuen).

Paprotté, Wolf, and Chris Sinha
1987 'Functional Sentence Perspective in Discourse and Language Acquisition', in Dirven and Fried (eds.) 1987: 265-96.

Payne, Geoffrey,
1991 'Functional Sentence Perspective: Theme in Biblical Hebrew', *Scandinavian Journal of the Old Testament* 1: 62-82.

Polanyi, Livia
1989 *Telling the American Story: A Structural and Cultural Analysis of Conversational Storytelling* (Cambridge, MA: MIT Press).

Prince, Gerald
1982 *Narratology: The Form and Functioning of Narrative* (New York: Mouton).

Radday, Yehuda T.
1981 'Chiasmus in Hebrew Biblical Narrative', in John W. Welch (ed.), *Chiasmus in Antiquity* (Hildesheim: Gerstenberg Verlag): 50-115.

Reinhart, Tanya
1982 *Pragmatics and Linguistics: An Analysis of Sentence Topic* (Bloomington, IN: Indiana University Linguistics Club).

Revell, E. J.
1989a 'The System of the Verb in Standard Biblical Prose', *Hebrew Union College Annual* 60: 1-37.
1989b 'The Conditioning of Word Order in Verbless Clauses in Biblical Hebrew', *Journal of Semitic Studies* 34: 1-24.

Richter, Wolfgang
1980 *Grundlagen einer althebräischen Grammatik*. B. *Die Beschreibungsebenen*. III. *Der Satz* (St. Ottilien: Eos Verlag).

Ridout, George
1974 'The Rape of Tamar', in Jackson (ed.) 1974: 75-84.

Rimmon-Kenan, Shlomit
1983 *Narrative Fiction: Contemporary Poetics* (London: Methuen).

Rosenberg, Joel
1986 *King and Kin: Political Allegory in the Hebrew Bible* (Bloomington: Indiana University Press).

Ross, Alan P.
1988 *Creation and Blessing: A Guide to the Study and Exposition of Genesis* (Grand Rapids, MI: Baker Book House).

Sáens-Badillos, Angel
1993 *A History of the Hebrew Language* (Cambridge: Cambridge University Press).

Sasson, Jack M.
1990 *Jonah* (New York: Doubleday).

Savran, George
1987 '1 and 2 Kings', in Alter and Kermode (eds.) 1987: 146-64.

Schank, Roger C., and Robert P. Abelson
1977 *Scripts, Plans, Goals and Understanding* (Hillsdale: Erlbaum).

Schiffrin, Deborah
1994 *Approaches to Discourse* (Oxford: Basil Blackwell).

Schneider, Wolfgang
1985 *Grammatik des biblischen Hebräisch* (Munich: Claudius, 6th edn).

Seters, John van
1975 *Abraham in History and Tradition* (New Haven: Yale University Press).

Siedl, S.H.
1971 *Gedanken zum Tempussystem im Hebräischen und Akkadischen* (Wiesbaden: Otto Harrassowitz).

Siewierska, Anna
1991 *Functional Grammar* (London: Routledge).

Sinclair, John McH.
1985 'On the Integration of Linguistic Description', in T.A. van Dijk (ed.), *Handbook of Discourse Analysis*. II. *Dimensions of Discourse* (London: Academic Press): 13-28.

Sperber, Dan, and Deidre Wilson
1991 'Pragmatics and Modularity', in Steven Davis (ed.), *Pragmatics: A Reader* (Oxford: Oxford University Press): 583-95.

Sternberg, Meir
1985 *The Poetics of Biblical Narrative: Ideological Literature and the Drama of Reading* (Bloomington: Indiana University Press).

Talstra, Epp
1983 *II Kön.* III. *Etüden zur Textgrammatik* (Amsterdam: Free University Press).

Tannen, Deborah
1979 'What's in a Frame', in R. Freedle (ed.), *New Directions in Discourse Processing* (Norwood: Ablex): 137-81.
1982 'Oral and Literate Strategies in Spoken and Written Narratives', *Language* 58: 1-21.
1989 *Talking Voices: Repetition, Dialogue and Imagery in Conversational Discourse* (Cambridge: Cambridge University Press).

Thompson, Thomas L.
1987 *The Origin Tradition of Ancient Israel.* I. *The Literary Formation of Genesis and Exodus 1–23* (Sheffield: Sheffield Academic Press).

Tomlin, Russell S.
1983 'On the Interaction of Syntactic Subject, Thematic Information and Agent in English', *Journal of Pragmatics* 7: 411-32.
1985 'Interaction of Subject, Theme and Agent', in Jessica R. Wirth (ed.), *Beyond the Sentence: Discourse and Sentential Form* (Ann Arbor: Karoma Publishers): 61-80.
1986 *Basic Word Order: Functional Principles* (London: Croom Helm).

Tomlin, Russell S. (ed.)
1987 *Coherence and Grounding in Discourse* (Amsterdam: John Benjamins).

Toolan, Michael J.
1988 *Narrative: A Critical Linguistic Introduction* (London: Routledge).

Ullendorf, Edward
1977 'Is Biblical Hebrew a Language?', in *idem*, *Is Biblical Hebrew a Language: Studies in Semitic Languages and Civilizations* (Wiesbaden: Otto Harrassowitz): 3-17.

Uspensky, Boris
1973 *A Poetics of Composition: The Structure of the Artistic Text and Typology of a Compositional Form* (Berkeley: University of California Press).

Vande Kopple, William J.
1986 'Given and New Information and Some Aspects of the Structures, Semantics, and Pragmatics of Written Texts', in Cooper and Greenbaum (eds.) 1986: 72-111.

Walkte, Bruce, K., and M.P. O'Connor
1990 *An Introduction to Biblical Hebrew Syntax* (Winona Lake, IN: Eisenbrauns).

Wallace, N. Howard
1985 *The Eden Narrative* (Atlanta: Scholars Press).

Wallace, Stephen
1982 'Figure and Ground: The Interrelationships of Linguistic Categories', in P. Hopper (ed.), *Tense-Aspect: Between Semantics and Pragmatics* (Amsterdam: Benjamins): 201-23.

Warren, Martin
1987 'Communicative Activities and Discourse Activities', in M. Coulthard (ed.), *Discussing Discourse: Studies Presented to David Brazil on his Retirement* (Discourse Analysis Monograph, 14; University of Birmingham): 196-202.

Watters, John Roberts
1979 'Focus in Aghem', in Larry M. Hyman (ed.), *Aghem Grammatical Structure* (Southern California Occasional papers in Linguistics, No 7; Los Angeles: University of Southern California Linguistic Department): 137-97.

Weinreich, Harald
1977 *Tempus: Besprochene und erzählte Welt* (Stuttgart: Kohlhammer).

Westermann, Claus

1985 *Genesis 12–36: A Commentary* (English translation of the 1981 German edition; London: SPCK).

Widdowson, Henry G.

1975 *Stylistics and the Teaching of Literature* (London: Longman).

Williams, Ronald J.

1976 *Hebrew Syntax* (Toronto: University of Toronto).

Wilson, Deidre, and Dan Sperber

1986 *Relevance: Communication and Cognition* (Oxford: Basil Blackwell).

Winograd, Terry

1977 'A Framework for Understanding Discourse', in M.A. Just and P.A. Carpenter (eds.), *Cognitive Processes in Comprehension* (Hillsdale: Erlbaum): 63-88.

Wolff, Hans Walter

1987 *Jonah* (London: SPCK).

Zevit, Ziony

1988 'Talking Funny in Biblical Henlish and Solving a Problem of the *YAQTUL* Past Tense', *Hebrew Studies* 29: 25-33.

INDEXES

INDEX OF REFERENCES

INDEX OF AUTHORS

JOURNAL FOR THE STUDY OF THE OLD TESTAMENT
SUPPLEMENT SERIES

243 Henning Graf Reventlow (ed.), *Eschatology in the Bible and in Jewish and Christian Tradition*
244 Walter E. Aufrecht, Neil A. Mirau and Steven W. Gauley (eds.), *Urbanism in Antiquity: From Mesopotamia to Crete*
245 Lester L. Grabbe (ed.), *Can a 'History of Israel' Be Written?*
246 Gillian M. Bediako, *Primal Religion and the Bible: William Robertson Smith and his Heritage*
247 Nathan Klaus, *Pivot Patterns in the Former Prophets*
248 Etienne Nodet, *A Search for the Origins of Judaism: From Joshua to the Mishnah*
249 William Paul Griffin, *The God of the Prophets: An Analysis of Divine Action*
250 Josette Elayi and Jean Sapin, *Beyond the River: New Perspectives on Trans-euphratene*
251 Flemming A.J. Nielsen, *The Tragedy in History: Herodotus and the Deuteronomistic History*
252 David C. Mitchell, *The Message of the Psalter: An Eschatological Programme in the Book of Psalms*
253 William Johnstone, *1 and 2 Chronicles, Volume 1: 1 Chronicles 1–2 Chronicles 9: Israel's Place among the Nations*
254 William Johnstone, *1 and 2 Chronicles, Volume 2: 2 Chronicles 10–36: Guilt and Atonement*
255 Larry L. Lyke, *King David with the Wise Woman of Tekoa: The Resonance of Tradition in Parabolic Narrative*
256 Roland Meynet, *Rhetorical Analysis: An Introduction to Biblical Rhetoric*
257 Philip R. Davies and David J.A. Clines (eds.), *The World of Genesis: Persons, Places, Perspectives*
258 Michael D. Goulder, *The Psalms of the Return (Book V, Psalms 107–150): Studies in the Psalter, IV*
259 Allen Rosengren Petersen, *The Royal God: Enthronement Festivals in Ancient Israel and Ugarit?*
260 A.R. Pete Diamond, Kathleen M. O'Connor and Louis Stulman (eds.), *Troubling Jeremiah*
261 Othmar Keel, *Goddesses and Trees, New Moon and Yahweh: Ancient Near Eastern Art and the Hebrew Bible*
262 Victor H. Matthews, Bernard M. Levinson and Tikva Frymer-Kensky (eds.), *Gender and Law in the Hebrew Bible and the Ancient Near East*
264 Donald F. Murray, *Divine Prerogative and Royal Pretension: Pragmatics, Poetics, and Polemics in a Narrative Sequence about David (2 Samuel 5.17–7.29)*
266 J. Cheryl Exum and Stephen D. Moore (eds.), *Biblical Studies/Cultural Studies: The Third Sheffield Colloquium*

268 Linda S. Schearing and Steven L. McKenzie (eds.), *Those Elusive Deuteronomists: 'Pandeuteronomism' and Scholarship in the Nineties*
269 David J.A. Clines and Stephen D. Moore (eds.), *Auguries: The Jubilee Volume of the Sheffield Department of Biblical Studies*
270 John Day (ed.), *King and Messiah in Israel and the Ancient Near East: Proceedings of the Oxford Old Testament Seminar*
271 Wonsuk Ma, *Until the Spirit Comes: The Spirit of God in the Book of Isaiah*
272 James Richard Linville, *Israel in the Book of Kings: The Past as a Project of Social Identity*
273 Meir Lubetski, Claire Gottlieb and Sharon Keller (eds.), *Boundaries of the Ancient Near Eastern World: A Tribute to Cyrus H. Gordon*
274 Martin J. Buss, *Biblical Form Criticism in its Context*
275 William Johnstone, *Chronicles and Exodus: An Analogy and its Application*
276 Raz Kletter, *Economic Keystones: The Weight System of the Kingdom of Judah*
277 Augustine Pagolu, *The Religion of the Patriarchs*
278 Lester L. Grabbe (ed.), *Leading Captivity Captive: 'The Exile' as History and Ideology*
279 Kari Latvus, *God, Anger and Ideology: The Anger of God in Joshua and Judges in Relation to Deuteronomy and the Priestly Writings*
280 Eric S. Christianson, *A Time to Tell: Narrative Strategies in Ecclesiastes*
281 Peter D. Miscall, *Isaiah 34–35: A Nightmare/A Dream*
282 Joan E. Cook, *Hannah's Desire, God's Design: Early Interpretations in the Story of Hannah*
283 Kelvin Friebel, *Jeremiah's and Ezekiel's Sign-Acts: Rhetorical Nonverbal Communication*
284 M. Patrick Graham, Rick R. Marrs and Steven L. MacKenzie (eds.), *Worship and the Hebrew Bible: Essays in Honor of John T. Willis*
286 Wesley J. Bergen, *Elisha and the End of Prophetism*
287 Anne Fitzpatrick-McKinley, *The Transformation of Torah from Scribal Advice to Law*
288 Diana Lipton, *Revisions of the Night: Politics and Promises in the Patriarchal Dreams of Genesis*
289 Jože Krašovec (ed.), *The Interpretation of the Bible: The International Symposium in Slovenia*
290 Frederick H. Cryer and Thomas L. Thompson (eds.), *Qumran Between the Old and New Testaments*
291 Christine Schams, *Jewish Scribes in the Second-Temple Period*
292 David J.A. Clines, *On the Way to the Postmodern: Old Testament Essays, 1967–1998 Volume 1*
293 David J.A. Clines, *On the Way to the Postmodern: Old Testament Essays, 1967–1998 Volume 2*
295 Jean-Marc, Heimerdinger, *Topic, Focus and Foreground in Ancient Hebrew Narratives*